HOW TO BE A DAD:

THE SELFISH MAN'S GUIDE TO ADEQUATE PARENTING

Ali Gray

For Victoria.
Cheers for the kids.

CHAPTERS

#1

So, You've Impregnated a Woman

First things first: congratulations on the successful completion of sexual intercourse! I'm going to go ahead and assume you've already taken care of the famously difficult 'sex' part of impregnation at this point. I'm not sure how much help I could have been in that department anyway. For everyone's sake, let's just assume that, from this paragraph onwards, you've already done the sex part. If you haven't already done the sex part yet, please stop reading now. This is not a sex manual. If anything, it's the opposite of a sex manual.

Just the sex-havers left? Excellent! Given that you own this book, or at the very least you're flicking through it absentmindedly in a book shop, it's safe enough to assume you're already on the baby-making timeline. I would estimate you're somewhere between: 1) The ecstatic moments immediately after correctly identifying a positive icon on a wee-covered piece of life-changing plastic; and 2) That mad, clawing panic that you feel deep in the pit of your stomach when you realise that, oh my god, you - YOU – are going to be responsible for the inception and upkeep of an actual real life human being.

That's right: you are now bound to the inescapable contract of creation that you signed with the tip of your penis the moment you dipped your wick in your good lady's ink pot. I won't second guess how you're feeling at this point but I can probably guarantee that at least one awful person in the outer orbit of your friends has said to you, upon hearing the news, something like "You've done your bit now!" or "The hard part's over!" and then they hit you slightly too hard on the arm in that way that only people you hate seem to do. This person is incorrect. There is much to do. You have much to learn. For starters, you're going to have to start picking up the slack on the tea-making rota for the foreseeable future. The ratio of cups of tea you make against cups of tea made for you is going to be seriously out of whack. That's the least of your problems, but that's where I hope to come in. Not literally, I can't redress the tea-making balance for you. You're just going to have to lump it.

Who am I? Good question. I don't have a big newspaper column, or an award-winning parenting blog, or a popular Twitter account that gets loads of RTs from people like Caitlin Moran and Robert Webb, or rich parents who work in the publishing industry, or 'talent'. I don't even have a way with words. My friend Big Sam once told me "Do you know what I like about you, Ali? You can kill a conversation stone dead just by contributing to it." When I took offence to this, he backtracked and tried to pretend like he was paying me a compliment, but by virtue of the fact I had responded to the conversation, I'd inadvertently made it awkward and killed it stone dead, thus proving his point.

What I do have is two kids of my own - let's call them Kid A, aged 9, and Kid H, aged 6 - plus a very patient wife named Vicky, a laptop, and a desire to write the kind of book about fatherhood that I wished was around after I myself had done the sex part. By the way, if the kids' ages seem to bounce around from one chapter to the next in this book, that's because it took me almost three years to write it. That's how patient my wife is.

A few years ago, I was attending some after-work drinks in London with some office colleagues, when one of our systems engineers, Jarrett, ran out of systems-based conversation topics and asked me what it was like being a parent. It was probably asked out of desperation or kindness, but as we'd both had several drinks, I gave him an honest answer and ran the full gamut: the pros, the cons, the straight truth. Yes, it's exhausting and frustrating and scary and challenging in all sorts of ways, but there's also a considerable upside: the unconditional love, the joy of having a little person form before your eyes, the way it gives your life renewed purpose and focus.

Jarrett told me he'd never really heard anyone extol those virtues before, which surprised me somewhat, because I figured it was commonplace to have dads sounding off about how great their kids were. Apparently not. "That's really great, and I'd love to hear more," he said, patiently, "but I really need to go and throw up in the toilet." Which he then proceeded to do. Clearly I had overwhelmed him with my inspiring mission statement.

I'm not uniquely qualified to discuss parenting at all - my observations and insights are not earth-shattering revelations, but hopefully they come across as relatable and helpful. Think of me not as a wise old oracle, but as a sort of ever-present barfly, ready with a sympathetic ear and a few relevant anecdotes that'll hopefully make you feel less terrified about your situation. I want you to feel better about your impending responsibilities, but mainly I just want you to like me. See? I'm just like you! I'm the anxious everyman! The sotto voice of the proletariat! Saying that, an RT from the odd celebrity wouldn't go amiss. Claudia Winkleman, expect a DM slide.

Everyone you'll meet in the days and weeks following your pregnancy announcement will be an instant expert in at least one facet of parenthood, and you're expected to nod sagely as you soak in all this bewildering and extremely esoteric information, like you're one of the professional poindexters from TV quiz show The Chase. Really I'm no different from the bullshitters on the street, the nosey old biddies who lean into the pram, the family friend and father of three who sits smugly across the kitchen table from you like he's Chris Tarrant on an episode of 'Who Wants To Be A Brilliant Dad?' with all the answers on a bit of card.

You don't know me. Why should you trust me? I can't answer that: ultimately only you and your partner will know what constitutes the right or wrong approach to bringing a new life into the world. I will say this, though: Supernanny doesn't even have any kids of her own, so at the very least I've got to be more qualified than Supernanny. Oh, everyone look at me, I haven't ever actually *discovered* any ancient antiquities myself, but I do have loads of *theories* on ancient antiquities, so I guess that makes me *Indiana fucking Jones*.

Because I decided to pursue a career in the exciting world of local videogame mail order catalogue design when I left school, I went to university late and quickly settled into the role of 'Guy who looks too old to be here but not quite old enough to be a mature student'. That meant that most of the friends in my adult life were around five years younger than me. Now, this is great if you love spending time explaining who Steve Guttenberg is or pronouncing the word 'meme' wrong for years, but it's not so great if you're looking for frame of reference for the expected achievement of life goals.

The consequence of the age difference between me, Vicky and our friends was that we were technically the most 'grown-up' couple in our social circles ('grown-up' being very much a relative term). We were the first couple to get married and didn't have a clue how you were supposed to do it, so instead of buying a nice fitted three-piece I rented a tux from Moss Bros like a dick and had to wear a ten-tonne, size-too-big, padded-shoulder morning suit like I was Lord Snooty at Ascot.

Once we'd finally saved up to buy a house, we were so confused by the jargon and the forms and the gigantic sums of money flying around that we paid for two separate solicitor firms at great expense - one to handle the sale of our existing flat, another to handle the purchase of the new place - because no one told us that you're only supposed to get one to do both.

When we decided to have a baby, there was no one our age that we could turn to for calming words or timely advice or cheap hand-me-downs. I don't want to sound like the classic 'beleaguered dad' stock photo archetype, head in my hands with scrunched hair and bemused expression, but this life stuff is complicated. Without someone you know who has trodden that path first, it's all on the line.

To continue the inaccurate and hugely flattering analogy, I was Indiana Jones stepping out into the chasm in The Last Crusade, praying my foot landed on the invisible ledge. Frankly, life is scary enough without having to jump headfirst into the abyss of adulthood without so much as the crumpled bones of a brave Sherpa to break your fall.

'Read the baby book if you're worried', said Vicky. Ah yes, the baby book: the jaunty colourful font on the cover belying the thickness and general appeal of a scientific textbook. The baby book: parenthood is easy if you just read and remember the information within these 800 pages of dense, dry prose! The baby book: the one single object in your household that could shape the man you'll one day become, if only it weren't the one single object in your household you'd least like to interact with. Baby books are all well and good, but... well, they're not exactly page-turners, are they? Would it kill the baby-having experts to chuck a couple of gags in there amongst all the patronising platitudes? Any baby books that proclaim to make parenthood easy or offer all the answers are by definition either so prescriptive they feel like boring university coursework or so broad as to be meaningless shelf-wasters.

My book is not a baby book that will make being a dad a breeze. My book is not really going to make you a better father. My book is not the book you turn to when your little Jolyon starts choking on a cherry tomato, Jesus, for god's sake call an ambulance or go on the internet or yell for help over a fence or something.

Put simply, my book is a book that wants you to know that it's been through what you're going through, and recognises that yes, you're correct: it *is* all completely mad as a box of tits. Oh, and that there's loads of fun to be had along the way. Even the scary bits that make your pubes go grey.

I found no solace in reading about fatherhood from books that were written like they were providing correct answers to impossible questions. I reckon it's always better to hear advice from a real life person than it is to scour the pages of a book like you're cramming for a test. In essence, this is my only real qualification: I, like you, am a real life person.

So, you won't find any wordy dissertations here, no stern lectures, no smug 'I told you so's, no homework or reading lists - just honest commentary and observations from your man on the inside. A bit like a nod from a fellow jogger. I'd say it was "real talk" if I wasn't at least five years too old to use that kind of language credibly.

Not to pull back the curtains on the author's process or anything, but I'd say I'm aiming for a ratio of around 75% humour to 25% profundity - like, maybe I'll reel you in with an hilarious analogy about Game of Thrones or something, then out of nowhere I'll hit you with a pearler of an anecdote about scraped knees that'll make you so overwhelmingly emotional, you'll have no choice but to go online and give me a five-star review on Amazon.

My real angle though, if you can call it that, is that I am secretly hugely and inescapably selfish, like most men. On the surface, I appear to be a helpful and considerate husband and father. I've gotten quite good at projecting that over the years. Yeah, I look like I'm effortlessly balancing work, family and creative endeavours, but beneath the facade I am never not wondering to myself how long it'll be before I get to stop doing things for other people and sit down. Maybe eat a sandwich by myself in silence. Play some video games for a bit. Doomscroll on the old bird app on my phone. Just, you know... *exist*.

In short, my USP is that I'm a wanker. If I may be so bold, I feel like there are lots of you out there who might also be wankers to a certain extent. You can be a wanker and a dad at the same time, it's not illegal, there's no way anyone else ever needs to know. So that's me. I am reporting from the front line of fatherhood and broadcasting only hot steaming truth, even when the truth stinks. Of course I want you to raise smart and wonderful children while being a devoted husband, but I'm also looking out for you and the things that really matter for modern men. There's no facade here: we're all equally selfish in our own little ways. This isn't a Men's Rights thing, by the way. Fuck those losers. We don't deserve rights, because we're awful.

Mostly though, you should expect childish jokes and slightly outdated pop culture references that try to make you feel better about the smoking crater that's appeared in your sleep routine. Just a taster of what's to come, there. I won't mention the fact you can expect to develop the dress sense of someone who's been rehoused after a hurricane, and that your new permanent expression will be of a man who's been recently stabbed. You've got to laugh, even though laughing hurts now.

As part of my exhaustive and not at all last minute research process for writing this book, I decided to ask Kid A some questions before bedtime. "Am I a good daddy?" I said, trying not to coerce the witness. "Yes," he said, without duress, not even looking at me or even seemingly paying attention, probably because of all the feelings he was feeling. That's a good start, I thought, but I need to push the process, get some real insight from my own kin, because surely part of being a good father is being aware of your weaknesses.

"What could I do better?" I asked, hoping for some more positive feedback. It's a big question. He thought for a minute, leaving me hanging on his reply. "Hmm," he mused. "... Everything."

There you have it. I can't help you in bed, I have no social skills, my friends would rather puke than listen to my advice, my opinions on parenthood are probably bullshit, I'm a selfish prick and even my own kids rate my performance as mediocre.

Just in case you were wondering, this book is non-refundable.

#2

Getting in a Baby State of Mind

Right then. Deep breath: fatherhood. It has already begun. You may not even realise it, but your initial response to hearing the words "I'm pregnant" has already been noted, logged and internally scrutinised. It's the first real test of fatherhood, and no amount of pulling happy faces in the mirror can prepare you for it. React to the news with too much enthusiasm and it might come off as too practised - woah there, James Franco! Give yourself over to your facial muscles and their natural response and it's pot luck - maybe you nail it, but maybe your face contorts into an alien emotion so unrecognisable you have to pretend you've recently developed a facial tic and have to keep up the masquerade for the rest of your life. Hopefully your instinct upon finding out was to grin, have a cuddle and do a bit of a cry, and not to flip open the pages of this book for inspiration. Is she... is she still standing there holding the pregnancy test, waiting for you to react? Do something, you idiot! No, wait - don't go straight to the crying!

It's clear we've got a lot of work to do. I'll admit, it's a lot to take on board - those words hang heavy with portent. While I have you here, this is a good time to remind yourself that [legal voice] getting pregnant was a voluntary act agreed upon in advance as part of a verbal contract between yourself and the woman you love, hereafter referred to as your "partner", and you brought this on yourself, forgoing the right to any recognised form of complaints and/or financial recompense. Just a bit of small print there to really get you in the mood.

Fatherhood shouldn't be a word you shy away from, it's a word that should be embraced, nay, exclaimed! *Fatherhood!* Repeat the following words to yourself, calmly and confidently: "I am having a baby! I am having a baby! I am having a baby!" Don't say it out loud, obviously, because if someone hears you then you might end up getting sectioned and that's not a good look for you right now. Say it to yourself, and start believing it, because it's time you got in the headspace of someone who's about to bring a +1 into the world, an unruly little party guest whose unpredictable behaviour you're going to have to vouch for until the end of time.

There are countless unavoidable practical considerations to having a baby, including but not limited to: moving to a bigger house, painting and decorating, learning to drive, saving money to buy baby stuff, researching burping techniques, Googling endlessly, just always Googling something or other, downloading an app to you phone that tells you how to dislodge rusks from an infant's windpipe in an emergency, more Googling, and, of course, learning how to efficiently wipe an arse that is not your own. That's your common or garden baby preparation behaviour. But first things first, before you start browsing the Mothercare website and before you start crying when you see how much cots cost, you need to get yourself mentally prepared for parenthood.

Do not be tempted to skip this crucial first step, because the most foolish thing an impending dad can do is think that spending hundreds of pounds on furniture and clothes and nappies is the same thing as being ready. Don't be the dickhead at school who turns up to P.E. wearing the latest Chelsea kit, including officially branded shin pads and club snood, who twats the football onto the Geography department roof the first time he's clean through on goal. Here's a handy rhyme to make sure you remember the order in which to prepare: 'Once you're up the duff / Make sure you're tough enough / Then buy all the stuff'. I made that up myself. Can you tell?

Luckily, human biology is here to lend a helping hand with an in-built buffer zone. It takes 40 weeks for a baby to gestate, give or take, and you've probably found out with about nine months left on the clock. Nine months is the perfect amount of time to get yourself adequately prepared for a life-changing event like childbirth. If it was any quicker than nine months you'd probably find yourself running around like a blue-arsed fly, screaming bloody murder at anyone who asks if you're okay, at least 41 different Amazon browser tabs open on your phone at all times.

Look to the natural world to see how much worse you could have it. Take the humble opossum, for example: their entire gestation period is completed in full after 12-13 days. That's less than two weeks from "I want to start a family" to "Where the *hell* is the goddamn sippy cup, *Janet?*" There are young opossums out there getting wrecked, shagging around and smashing out babies all before you'll get your next paycheque - we should count ourselves lucky that our species gets the duration of an entire Premier League football season to mull over the full ramifications of baby-making.

Conversely, if it took longer than nine months to cook the buns in one's oven, you'd get complacent, or over-confident, and you'd inevitably take your eye off the prize. I mean, who prepares for something *a year in advance*? That's basically the future - and only a madman would try to predict the future. And in any case, in a year's time there'll probably be an app that does parenthood for you, or it'll all be done with nanobots or Alexa or whatever. Look again to nature for a cautionary tale: female elephants carry their babies for 660 days - that's just under two years - and although they look graceful and stately and majestic, they're almost certainly longing for the sweet release of death by the eighth trimester. Be careful when relaying this information to your pregnant and highly sensitive partner, because "It could be worse, you could be an elephant" is easily misconstrued - maybe try the opossum angle.

No, nine months feels finely balanced - not too soon, not too far away, plenty of time to readjust and make some big life changes, not enough time to lose focus. Juuuuust right. Why, it's almost like time is linear and it's only your *perception* of the passing of time that changes, and in any case you have no say in the matter whatsoever and we're all completely clueless, hurtling through space on a giant rock, clinging on for dear life! It's almost exactly like that!

Nine months might seem like a fair distance away, like it's a thing that's not happening to you but to a future version of yourself. One good way of making the impending birth feel more personal is to think about it in actual terms, and the best way to do that is to get that due date locked into your calendar, where it can start to bed in and really get its roots wrapped around the rest of your life.

Start to see what else is happening in nine months' time to better understand what time-frame you're working with. For example, list cultural events that are relevant to you that happen after the birth for a timeline you can relate to. My wife and I got pregnant with our first baby at the beginning of 2012, and throughout the year I found it quite sobering to think that by the time Peter Jackson's blockbuster adaptation of The Hobbit would be in cinemas, I would be a father. The Hobbit and the baby became inextricably linked - every time I'd see a trailer or a poster or a bus, or even just Martin Freeman, it'd be a stark reminder of my impending responsibilities. (As it happens, sneaking off to see The Hobbit: An Unexpected Journey in the week before Christmas was my first real bit of 'me time' after the birth of our son, so I paid £19.50 to see the much-touted 48FPS version in a Deluxe Screen at the Vue in Westfield, and reader, let me tell you, it was 182 minutes of absolute hog shite).

Find a forthcoming pop culture event that resonates with you. How many new Marvel movies will you have seen by the time your baby is crowning? Which will happen first: the announcement of a new James Bond, or the dilation of your partner's cervix? Who knows what gigantic version of the iPhone you'll be using to film the birth of your first child?

There's more to this technique than just slotting your child into your pop culture calendar - it also forces you to realise that your major interests are about to take a hit. Again, use movies as an example. Right now, going to the cinema is a fun, if expensive, way to spend a lazy Saturday afternoon: you buy your ticket, plop yourself in your oversized chair and graze on £6 popcorn like a big disgusting human cow for a couple of hours. Going to see a movie in nine months' time, however, is a highly risky strategy wherein you voluntarily step into a communications black hole for a few hours despite your extremely pregnant partner bursting at the seams back at home, leaving you completely cut off from civilisation in a dark and distracting environment where checking your phone isn't just discouraged but is actively punished. There's every chance you could enter Transformers 7: Intergalactic Boogaloo a boy, and leave a father.

I still smile thinking about a friend of mine who is the world's biggest Star Wars geek, who managed to conceive his second

13

child at the worst possible time - exactly nine months to the day before the opening weekend of Star Wars: The Last Jedi. It wasn't so much that he'd be unable to see the movie when it first opened, so much as his hilarious inability to be annoyed about it - because to do so would be to admit that Episode VIII of the Skywalker saga holds as much significance to him as the miracle of childbirth, which I'm assured is not true.

Some people time their conception perfectly so they give birth at an optimum time of the year - I've known teachers to time their pregnancy so that they get the August school holidays off as usual, have the baby in the first week of September, then chain together maternity leave and Christmas holidays to combo together one big unstoppable MEGA ULTRA XL MATERNITY LEAVE. With enough practice, one can even impregnate a woman so precisely that they can ensure the birth of their child on the birthday weekend of an unwanted associate, giving them a valid excuse to skip it every year until the end of time. That's the galaxy brain level you need to be thinking at now, chum. These are the opportunities you're already missing.

For now though, start small and slow, and don't bite off more than you can chew. Give yourself a win and ease yourself into parenthood by accomplishing the easiest responsibility first: the simple act of not telling anyone you're having a baby. You need to keep it a secret for 12 weeks, the three month marker being the point in pregnancy where the chance of miscarriage drops to 10%. You don't technically have to do anything - your goal is to *not* do something. You can *not* do a thing, right? You've done pretty well so far in your life by not doing things, so why should this be any different? It's the equivalent of scoring a mark on a school paper for writing your name. All you have to do is keep your pregnancy to yourself for a few months. Easy. Absolute piece of piss. Right? Except, of course it isn't. The mental toll of this simple task is massive and the impact is immediate. Your brain short-circuits and suddenly your mouth is calling the shots, broadcasting unchecked information live to the nation without a time delay. All of your friends and family seem to develop Sherlock Holmes-levels of intuition, needling deeper with each innocuous question, inadvertently getting closer to the truth with every idle chit-chat. Your partner always wears baggy clothes, but does it look like you're trying too hard to cover something up now? Is it hot in here? You insist on engineering social situations that, on paper at least, look friendly and easy-going, but end up feeling like police interrogations.

All it takes is one well-placed question, one harmless remark about belly fat, one unwise jumper, *one single instance where alcohol is shunned*, and the whole house of cards starts to wobble. The walls are closing in, man. The web of lies is too great to maintain. They know. They all know. They've known from the start. It feels... really, really hot in here. Oh, how *are* we, you ask? How *are* we? I bet you'd like to know, wouldn't you, Aunt Carol. I bet you would. How about you mind your own fucking business, you nosey old hag. Jesus, 12 weeks of this? It's only been 15 minutes. This is conclusive evidence that you would make a terrible undercover cop and would definitely have died in the first season of The Wire, a stuttering narc that gets shot up the bum by a Stringer Bell foot soldier.

Try to take your mind off your crumbling dynasty of falsehoods by concentrating on baby stuff for a while. That thing is really growing in there! A good way to chart its progress is to download an app - seriously, most of the first trimester revolves around downloading apps for things - that gives you regular informative updates on your baby's gestation. Honestly, it's super cute.

Weeks 1 and 2: not much to report, it's still basically a bit of jizz with legs. Week 5: now it has a tail. Week 10: oh shit, now it has a face. I may be paraphrasing, I'm not a scientist.

Some apps give you a handy guide as to the size of your kid by comparing it to fruit. This week, your baby is the size of a lemon pip. Aww! This week, your baby is the size of a grape. Squee! It's all extremely adorable and lovely until the small fruits start to mutate into larger vegetables, and you get told your foetus has the girth of a Chinese Cabbage, or that there's a humongous Beef Tomato inside the woman you love. Do not skip ahead to the third trimester fruit and veg comparisons, because you'll never look at a marrow in the same way ever again.

In any case, it's a nice, accessible way of learning about how your cabbage is progressing. In following these regular check-ins, you quickly learn to process time in weeks not months and months not years, sending you down the path where you eventually become that person who says with a straight face that their kid is '32 months old' like some sort of autistic math genius.

Your slow progress can be a mite frustrating, because for all your research (in the app store) and reading (of the apps), it's still preparing for fatherhood at arms' length - at some point, you need to log some man-hours with actual, real-life babies. In the absence of a respectable or legal hire service, a Rent-a-Baby if you will, your experience will vary wildly depending on the size of your family, and the availability therein of actual children you can take for a test drive.

My family, for example, is fairly small, and until we had our kids, was resolutely baby free: with no cousins and no younger siblings, at age 32 I was the baby in the family, which made it extremely difficult for me to locate any other babies to have a go on. Vicky's family, however, pumps out nieces and nephews like they're on a bloody production line - you can't move in her family home for babies, toddlers, infants and teenagers, the full spectrum of youth.

This was obviously amazing, because I got to practice on every model in the shop before putting my deposit down. Yeah, liking the feel of the baby, got a good weight to it, probably about... what, 2 or 3 wee- yeah, that's what I thought, three months old, nice. Yeah, look at this little guy, walking all by himself at age tw- yeah, 13 months, I knew that, classic. I'll just have a conversation with this little angel and ask her all about school- yep, the school she won't go to for another 18 months, cool, cool cool cool. I'll just humour the 7-year-old lad here by playing him at FIFA, and... bloody hell, are you using cheat codes, this... I didn't even know you could do... wait, that was offside, that was clearly offside... in any case these aren't even my controls, I usually do a custom set-up so it was never going to be fair. Yeah, good game, good game, now if you'll excuse me I have to go and age 100 years in two seconds flat and crumble into dust. Call me when you get pubes, you little shits.

Family is a great way to observe and report on kids, but you must be careful you don't run before you can walk. My friend Jay, who doesn't yet have any children of his own, gave his sister an incredible wedding present: not only did he pay for her and her partner to go away on holiday, but he offered to look after their 1-year-old daughter, his niece, for the entire duration. That's five full days of child-minding. A WORKING WEEK.

Incredibly generous, I'm sure you'll agree. Also, absolutely insane. I cannot imagine how quickly that offer was accepted. If someone offered to take care of my kids for five days while jetting me off to sunnier climes I'd probably write them into my will. I daresay that over the course of those five endless days, Jay learned a new appreciation for how gruelling full-time childcare can be, giving him a healthy dose of reality and putting him in good stead for when he decides to drop sprog of his own. I promise I'm not exaggerating when I say on the sixth day, he did a triathlon to relax.

You don't learn to drive in a brand new car, so it figures that the first baby you ever hold probably shouldn't be your own newborn; you don't want to dent the bodywork, as it were. There exists a photo of me on Facebook in which a random baby has been thrust upon me unexpectedly and I'm wearing the expression that henchmen usually have in action movies where they realise the hero pulled the pin on their grenade just before it explodes. Therefore, I would recommend that - in the least creepy way possible - you hold a baby, anyone's baby, literally just *a* baby, before you get your hands on your own merch.

Women are never not holding babies. Knowing how to hold a baby is not a thing that worries women. It's something they are genetically programmed to know how to do from an early age, kind of like how men instinctively know the difference between HDMI and SCART cables. But babies? We fear them at first. We hear tales of their soft little heads. We worry that one unexpected squirm will catch us unaware and they will fall and thud and accidentally perish by our hand and we'll never get over it and we'll be shunned by society, the murderous idiot klutz who lives in a cave who can't even hold a baby. So yeah, it's important to know the fundamentals.

Let's officially break it down: how to hold a baby, lesson 1 of 1, school is in session. The old joke is that a man will hold a baby like he's holding a football, even though that joke doesn't work in the UK because British people don't hold footballs, it's an Americanisation, the clue's in the name of the sport you guys. Here's where you're really going to go wrong: if you're holding the baby and for whatever reason your arms are fully extended, you're holding the baby wrong; if you're holding the baby and your hands are anywhere other than clasped underneath their armpits, you're holding the baby wrong; if you're holding the baby and the head-end is anything less than absolute north, you're holding the baby wrong. The silent but horrified looks of nearby women will clue you in if you're not certain.

All you need to do is make sure that a) whatever position the baby is in when you pick it up, make sure you're giving it some neck and head support, and b) when you have achieved pick-up, you're going to want to bring that bad boy in close to your chest as soon as possible so you don't look like you're disposing of roadkill. Eventually, with a bit of shuffling, you want to aim to have the baby's head nestled in the crook of one arm, with your forearm underneath it and one hand holding its bum, leaving the other hand free for additional support and/or booping. Follow these simple rules and you'll avoid being flagged as a rank amateur likely to futz a baby right into a bin or nearby shredder.

Suddenly, office babies take on a whole new dimension. You know office babies, right? You hear them before you see them: the unexpected squeak of a pram wheel in the lobby, the chatter of doting colleagues, the squawk of a baby getting its first taste of the world of work. *There's a baby where a baby normally isn't!* Office babies! Before now, you probably rolled your eyes, gave a cursory nod and a raise of the eyebrows from a distance but remained rooted to your chair and invested in your spreadsheet. Tsk, bringing babies to work, honestly. What do they want, a medal?

Now, newly enlightened and woke to parenthood, you understand that it's not a medal they crave at all, but any meaningful interaction with another human being that is not poo-based. For god's sake, the least you can do is toss the bones of some small talk in their direction, because this will 100% be you one day, desperate to show your colleagues and desk-adjacent stapler thieves how you've become a responsible adult, a man that at least one woman decided was capable of raising a child. Put *that* in your binder and smoke it, Sandra from HR - how's that "inappropriate behaviour for the workplace" looking right about now, huh?

Your time for gloating will come, but for now, you should use every office baby visit to your advantage, and log some valuable parenthood practice minutes in the field. When baby is in play, this is how you're going to want to play it:

- Squat down in front of the pram and introduce yourself formally to the baby, including your job title, because that shit is hilarious

- Have a boop on any of the following socially acceptable boop zones: nose, chin, belly, hand or foot. Never boop near eyes, mouth, genitals or the ass, for reasons pertaining to each area that should be obvious

- Engage the parent in the smallest small talk possible, in the knowledge that conversation this basic will be gratefully received and hungrily devoured

- Enquiry as to the baby's age and impress onlookers by effortlessly converting months into weeks

- Ask "How are you sleeping?" because this is a topic that new parents love talking about and the length of the answer means you won't need to worry about asking too many follow-up questions

- Tell the parent the baby really looks like them, even if it doesn't; this is a universally accepted white lie that has been scientifically proven to have no negative consequences, so fill your boots

- Play dumb and say something like, 'We don't have any toys for you to play with here, but...' and then pretend to offer them a staple remover or a hole punch or something else highly inappropriate; again, even your most basic comedy material will kill in this environment

- Compliment the pram, and relax in the knowledge that you have given the parent the highest praise they could possibly receive

That's right: you're expected to have opinions on prams now. Opinions on prams that aren't just about pram prices. Maybe you enjoy analysing the benefits of wheeled machinery and you'll take to this like a natural, but if you're like me, and your understanding of cars extends to 'how to drive them' and 'what colour they are', then you might struggle with this.

Prams, you'll quickly discover, come in all sorts of shapes and sizes (the prices, I'm sorry to say, are all largely the same, which is to say they all cost 'More than you thought'). You've got prams, carrycots, buggies, strollers, pushchairs and travel systems, some of which are the same thing. They come in standard, lightweight, umbrella fold-up, combi and all-terrain versions, sometimes with three wheels, sometimes with four, and they all come with buttons that seemingly perform no function.

Once baby is six months old and can support his or her own head instead of lolling around like a drunk, you might need to upgrade the pram to a more upright version. And that's before you even get into car seats, the forward-facing and backwards-facing varieties therein, ISOFIX compatibility and more. If you thought you could get away with carrying the baby everywhere in a sturdy Bag For Life until it learns to walk, then I'm afraid to say you are mistaken.

I took my kids to the park recently, and another dad sidled up next to me as I watched them play. I could tell straight away he had opinions about pushchairs that he was not willing to keep to himself.

"Nice model," he said.
"Sorry?" I replied.
"Nice pushchair. What is it, a Chicco?"
I glanced at the logo on the side, possibly for the first time ever.
"Yes."
"Nice little goers, aren't they?"
"I, er... yeah, it gets the job done."
"I've got one of those Egg ones," he said, pointing at his own pushchair. I could instantly tell from the design that it was at least £500 more expensive than my own.
"Yeah, it's a nice ride, smooth. Pricey but worth it. They take corners really well."
I lost myself in thought for a moment, imagining the man running down a Formula 1 track as fast as he could, taking the racing line into and out of corners, the terrified child within holding on for dear life.
"Looks like a good' un," I said, politely.
"Oh, you know. They're all pretty much the same underneath," he lied, richer than me.
"I suppose."
"Chrome," he said, apropos of nothing.

I tried to change the topic of conversation. "Which ones are yours?" I said, pointing at the kids on the playground. I can definitely do more small talk about kids if necessary: their names, and ages, for example. I'll think of more if it comes to that. "Yeah, we thought about going with a Chicco," he said, ignoring me. "But you just can't beat the Scandinavians at this sort of thing." I still don't really understand what he was getting at to this day, but it was clear he wasn't interested in making dad friends, he was just comparing pushchairs. I smiled, then invented an escalating crisis with the kids that urgently needed my full attention; a playground false flag that allowed me to escape the conversation. For all I know he still stalks that playground, cornering other dads with his posh egg on wheels, making them feel inferior by talking at them nicely and being social. The monster.

Like my new friend the playground pushchair bragger, fatherhood affects different people in different ways: some men might find themselves in their element, and some, not to put too fine a point on it, might not. The most important thing you need to consider at this early stage is how parenthood will fundamentally change your life in ways you might not predict. Not just in terms of your relationship with your partner, your mental and physical health, your time and your finances, but *everything else in your life too.*

On the face of it, having a baby doesn't necessarily stop you from continuing to do the things you love that you've done all your life: socialising with friends, drinking, travelling, spontaneous nights out, writing off entire days to hangovers and lying in a crumpled heap watching E4 while considering a takeaway, and so on. What might surprise you is that your desire to do all of these things might naturally fade over time, due to the overwhelming and overriding life changes that are part and parcel being a dad. That is to say, your very personality, the things that make you you, will never feel more malleable than they do over the next few years. One of the best pieces of parenting wisdom I received was from a work friend, a new dad himself, who was congratulating me on our pregnancy announcement. We were waiting by the lift, idly watching football highlights playing on a nearby TV. He sighed, the young players now unrecognisable to him, and said: "Having kids just turns the volume down on everything else. I used to think I gave a shit about a lot of stuff."

He might have been talking about football, but in a way, he was also talking about everything. This is probably the most succinct way of summing up parenthood: you'll find that everything in your life, from your likes and dislikes, your pastimes and hobbies and even your friends, will all have to be dialled back to make room for baby. Maybe only slightly. Maybe significantly. And maybe, probably, eventually, you'll get to a point where you can start scaling these things back up again, in order to feel a bit more like yourself. But be prepared for them to take a hit in the short term, because you might find that what you consider to be 'yourself' changes somewhat in the interim.

It's only natural, really. With mouths to feed and nappies to change and sleep to be slept back home, chances are you won't be able to socialise at the pace you might be used to, nor will you want to. Even speaking as someone whose baby-days are largely behind him, few things pre-exhaust me as much as the concept of doing two nights out in a row. I'm knackered just writing about thinking about it. There is absolutely no shame in switching allegiance and becoming a 'night in' person. Join us. We are so comfy. We have booze too, but also, blankets.

You might find that friendship groups thin out as a result of you having less time and energy to - as the kids presumably still say - 'have it large' on a semi-regular basis. And maybe that's okay. Perhaps your friends are coupling up, getting married and having babies of their own. Or perhaps not. Either way, it doesn't have to mean anything. I've found that as I've grown older and matured (no laughing at the back), I've developed a new category of friend: the kind that you don't see all that often but also the kind that doesn't mind. The friend who you maybe see once a year, but when you catch up it's like no time has passed at all. Usually, not coincidentally, these friends also have kids.

There's no intentional distance or reason for the gaps between friends, just paths that ended up going different ways, like the final scene of that classic movie about friendship, Fast & Furious 7. Parenthood is the seismic event that shifts the tectonic plates of your friendships - a bit of continental drift is to be expected.

As I read this chapter back, I realise this all seems frightfully negative. Panic attacks! Lies and schemes! Constant disruption! Expensive things! Accidental cranial damage! Men in public places talking to you! Absent friends! It's! All! A! Bit! Much!

And exhale. You've just had a glimpse into what the next nine months might have in store. *Might*. It's impossible to say for sure. There's every chance that, given this opportunity to show what you're really made of, you'll flourish in this chaotic environment; if you're blessed with time, money, friends, family and patience, maybe baby will be a breeze, a walkover, a laugh, just a bit of #banter to share with the #lads at the next #saturdaysesh. Forget drifting apart from friends, you'll more than likely make new ones - that Dave and Joanne at NCT seem like a nice couple; funny, cool, not too clingy, not weird like John and Amber the close-talkers in the matching denim, not pretentious like the Sussex couple with the matching haircuts.

And anyway, having a baby together is the most loving, wonderful, life-affirming thing a couple can do. Pregnancy will bring you closer than ever, the experience of childbirth will harden you like steel, the responsibility of raising a child will be the making of you. You'll be the first ever actual Cool Dad. Your kids will have mad respect for you, and won't make fun of the way you use 'mad' as a quantitative adjective. Your neighbours will praise you for your calm and collected parenting style. Your hair will go grey, but in the cool way, like you did it on purpose, for fashion. And then, one day, one perfect sunny Saturday afternoon, you'll gaze at your whole family, splashing and playing in the paddling pool, like something out of a picture book, or at least an advert for a paddling pool, and you'll think to yourself: I can't believe I ever thought this would be tough.

I sincerely hope that's the case. But... y'know... just in case it doesn't happen like that, then... well. That's what the rest of the book is for. And if the worst comes to the worst, and you struggle to adapt, and you wrestle with the weight of the responsibility, and you feel like you're going to fold under the financial demands of pregnancy, and it's all getting too much... just remember, it could always be worse: at least you're not the one who has to give birth at the end of it, ha ha ha.

(To any women who are reading this, know that I am very, very sorry, the bigger boys led me on, I apologise for my behaviour and I thank you for your service).

#3

The 50 Worst Bits of Being a Dad

S o this is it, this is 'the talk', in book form. This is me sitting you down, turning off the telly and telling you straight how it is and how it's going to be. You might not like some of the things I'm about to say. You might find me callous or pretentious or just think me a bit of a twat. But that's fine, because we are having this talk for one reason and one reason only: because I am a dad, and I've lived through fatherhood, and you, as of right now, have not. In this situation, you are the cocky, wet-behind-the-ears Army cadet and I am the grizzled old shit-talking Sergeant, whose abrasive nature may initially seem unnecessary but is later revealed to be essential in hardening you for the coming horrors of war. So relax!

One of the best things to remember about the months and years ahead is that the universe tends to balance things out over time. So, while you are undoubtedly going to enjoy some good times - the most rewarding times of your life, no less - you're also going to have to eat a mountain of shit in the process. That, sadly, is the nature of the beast. There's no Easy Mode to fatherhood, no cheat codes, no YouTube tutorial worth your time. Just a mountain of shit, and a fork.

Fatherhood is nothing less than a test of your mettle. Are you Private Joker in this analogy, where your sarcastic veneer slowly gives way to the dawning realisation that life is hard and the world is fucked? Or are you Private Pyle, liable to metaphorically blow your brains out the back of your head because life keeps smashing you in the ribs with a big bag of soap? You have to be prepared. You deserve to know what's coming. It is essential that you are fully briefed on the 50 most difficult, least inspiring and just plain fucking exhausting facets of parenthood - both in the short term and long term - in convenient list form.

There is good news, though. The good news is that if you can chow down on that mountain of shit and learn how to stomach it, you're basically golden - it's all upside from here on in. If you can read the following testaments to tiredness without wanting to walk slowly and fully-clothed into the sea, then there's a good chance we'll make a dad out of you yet. *Bon appetit*, soldier.

***

1.

Having a baby causes direct damage to the environment. It's the poop, you see. There's no pleasant way to dispose of bundles of fecal waste. The simple act of bringing new life to the planet is essentially another little knife in Mother Nature's back. The sheer amount of waste, bodily or otherwise, that you create and subsequently feel compelled to not have in your home is astonishing. Even if you choose to go down the eco-route, with cloth nappies and waste-free breastfeeding and hand-me-downs stored in the attic, I am sorry to say you will still end up dumping an area of landfill the size of Romford every week. Which is especially horrifying if you live in Romford.

2.

All the clichés about driving with kids in the car are true. Every newspaper strip cartoon or sitcom that features a red-faced dad with his nose against the wheel while his kids squabble in the back seat: accurate. I don't know what it is about the automobile environment that is conducive to arguments, but I can personally vouch for more than a dozen road rage incidents isolated within the four doors of our Ford Focus. Stop kicking the chair. *Stop kicking the chair.* STOP KICKING THE CHAIR OR I'LL DRIVE US OFF THE ROOF OF THIS MULTI-STOREY CAR PARK. You won't say that last one, but you will think it.

3.

Mother's Day is now exponentially worse. Mother's Day before you had kids: "Did you get your Mum a card?" "Shit, no. I'll order one now on Moonpig. There, done. For 90 seconds there we almost had a problem." Mother's Day after you have kids: "No, no, I'll get up and change the baby. You stay in bed, you deserve it. You put your feet up today, it's your day. I'll sort dinner tonight too. It's fine, I don't mind the extra graft, because [grits teeth] you deserve it." Just a reminder, you're going from having to buy one card to buying at least two: one for Mum (you still have a Mum) and one for your partner, who is now also Mum and therefore is newly qualified to receive Mother's Day-related tat. I'm currently trapped in a three-card minimum situation: one for Mum, one for my wife, and one for my wife *from* my kids. Not to sound like a sad old fuck sitting on his own in a puddle of his own piss in a Wetherspoon's on a Monday morning, but... Mother's Day: it's a racket!

4.

It's impossible to relay the cuteness of your kids to others. One of the most entertaining aspects of fatherhood is when your kids' brains fuse together some wonderfully absurd or poetic thoughts, and you think 'That is just so... them!' The downside: no one else cares. Sorry. Trying to tell someone a cute anecdote about something your own kid did or said is like ice-skating uphill, because the cuteness is exclusive only to you and adorability is not a currency that travels particularly well. I remember talking to friends and launching into enthusiastic reportage about the time Kid H told us he'd had a dream about a purple tractor, and halfway through the story I was like, damn, there's no pay-off to this thing.

5.

Whether the clocks go forward or back, you lose. Time is now a meaningless construct, and clocks are agents of deception. British Summer Time? Another racket. You take the hit when the clocks go forward in Spring and you lose an hour of sleep, because you figure, hey, this thing will even itself out when the clocks go back in Autumn... right? WRONG. Your kids' circadian body clocks will still wake them up at the time they always wake up, only now it'll technically be one hour earlier. And no, for whatever reason, it doesn't work in reverse. Clocks are pricks.

6.

A family holiday would be a great potential stress-reliever, if only it wasn't so stressful to organise. It's one of parenthood's great ironies. The rigid routines of childcare take their toll to the point where you'll be desperate to escape and get away from it all - the problem being that 'escape' is no longer an option, because 'it all' now has to go wherever you do. The level of organisation involved for a family holiday is roughly equivalent to hosting the Olympics: there's the logistics of travel with a baby, the potential disruption to sleep routines, the realisation that you don't know how to buy nappies in Spanish ("El... Poopino?") and the nagging feeling that an international paedophile ring might swoop in if you take your eyes off your offspring for one single second. The simple fact is, family holidays can be so exhausting, you'll feel like you'll need a holiday to recover from your holiday. Another cliché to chalk up on the board.

7.

Holidays can only be enjoyed outside of term time, and you will be financially shafted for the privilege. It's not enough that planning a family holiday takes the sort of precision engineering required of a diamond heist - you require the bank balance of a career criminal, too. All Dads remember the first time they tried booking a family holiday in August. First comes disbelief. A rub of the eyes. A refresh of the page. This... can't be right? This is a gouging! A real-life gouging! Then comes denial. You alter the date by one day. No change: the subtotal is still essentially one arm, one leg. Next is anger. This is ILLEGAL. Somebody call WATCHDOG. You're not having this. Delusion: you try and beat the system by inputting your details in a slightly different order. It makes no difference. Forget it, Dad: it's the summer holidays. This is your life now: paying through your actual arsehole for the opportunity to holiday during the busiest time of the year with every other schmuck. One month later, your Instagram is flooded with pics of your childless friends taking photos of September sunsets through empty Sangria glasses on the Cote d'Azur, and you know full well the return flight cost them about as much as six weeks' worth of nappies.

8.

The concept of spontaneity ceases to exist. Remember that great scene in Heat, where Robert De Niro says: "Don't let yourself get attached to anything you are not willing to walk out on in 30 seconds flat if you feel the heat around the corner"? There's a deleted scene where a woman sitting next to him in the cafe chips in and says "I can tell you don't have kids!!!" This imaginary lady is not wrong: with child, everything takes a minimum of 25 minutes. Everything. Short of your house catching on fire and requiring you evacuate, there is no way you're getting your shit together and getting out the door in under 20 minutes. There are always bags to be packed (and one essential element therein will have gone walkabout), spare clothes and toys and blankies to source, bottles or juice boxes or snacks to prepare, and an extremely high chance of a nappy being filled during the home stretch. It might be time to face up to the fact that you are not Robert De Niro in Heat.

9.

Watching kids get hurt is awful. It doesn't matter how careful or cautious you are, you're looking at a solid decade of scraped knees, grazed elbows and bashed heads. It's made extra torturous by the fact you can almost always see it coming in slow-motion yet remain powerless to stop it. The way their little faces crease up, the sad little whimpering that they do. Poor little sods. Every scab is a little medal they wear that effectively tells everyone that their Daddy fucked up.

10.

When your kids hurt themselves on you by headbutting your knee and you feel super guilty even though you were literally sitting still. You are somehow still guilty of an offence. No VAR check needed. There's a crying child in the vicinity and you've got a gormless look on your face and your knees shouldn't be so sticky-outy anyway. Send him down for a thousand years, says the gallery. Fuck.

When your kids accidentally hurt *you* but then *they* start crying and you realise that no one will ever feel sympathy for you ever again. All part of the rich tapestry of life, chief. The sympathy scales are seriously unbalanced and they will remain lopsided for the foreseeable future. Your pain, both physical and emotional, no longer registers like it used to. I could be found bleeding out in my back garden with a smouldering bullet hole in my back with my kid holding the pistol, but as long as he had a sad face my wife wouldn't call the ambulance until after he'd cheered up and had a snack.

You miss them. Always. This is a tough one. The parental relationship starts hot and heavy: for those first few weeks, you don't leave one another's side and you are there for every burp, fart, sound and smile. Then, when paternity leave is up, you have to re-join the rat race and just up and leave. That's not fair? This is an absence that you have not felt in your life before. They sprout up so quickly and before you know it they're walking, talking and breakdance fighting - but you quickly realise that you won't always be there to witness the milestones race by. It's hard not to feel like a part-time Dad during this difficult time, known by some experts as the 'Cat's in the Cradle' period of adjustment, during which even the sappiest father-son melodramas can reduce you to tears.

Pocket money is now entirely under your control. On the surface, you might think this is a fun thing. Your kid is learning the value of money thanks to your guidance and generosity! You can picture them in the newsagents: *One iced bun please shopkeep, and an apple for pater*! In reality, being in charge of the purse strings is a massive responsibility with potentially life-altering consequences. How do you budget this? What's the current rate of inflation? Give too much each week and your soon-to-be-spoiled brat won't ever respect the mantra of a hard day's work for a fair day's pay. Give too little and it's highly likely they'll turn to a life of crime to support their Freddo addiction. Once you start the pocket money program, do you cease all purchases from your own pocket in order to keep the experiment pure? Do you let them spaff their wad on penny sweets and Pokémon cards or do you encourage them to save? Don't forget to factor in good behaviour and punishments, both of which can affect the running balance. It's all a bit too much like doing your taxes. Cuh, they should be paying you, cuh, am I right?

14.

You will come to detest the sound of your own voice. Maybe you never thought of yourself as an authoritarian. Maybe you want your kids to grow up with an encouraging voice in their ear at all times, not a nagging one. That's real cute, let me know how you get on with that. Me, I'll still be here, desperately trying to project authority and shouting into the ether, repeating the same five stock phrases again and again and again to an audience of no one. Your kids will one day develop the curious mutation of selective hearing, meaning they learn to tune you out so effectively they don't even know they're ignoring you. The only person left listening to your repeated refrains - DON'T RUN, I SAID NO, I SAID STOP IT, LEAVE HIM ALONE, LAST CHANCE - is you, and even you know you have no power here.

15.

You have to let them win. Boooooooo. There's no glory to be gained from parenthood, no prizes for coming first, no spoils for the victor. It's long, hard graft, with zero opportunities for showboating, for shame. The fear of being the archetypal 'Competitive Dad' will soften you to the point of surrender: whether it's sports, board games, or video games, the decent - and expected - thing to do is to let the little ones win. Otherwise, you're the twat who made his kid cry because you flexed too hard to make yourself feel better. There's a fine line to navigate on the competitiveness spectrum - lean too far the other way and you're the hyper-aggressive sports encourager screaming thinly-veiled abuse from the sidelines, well on your way to becoming The Worst Man At Sports Day™.

16.

Leading by example is a massive hassle. Well well well, if it isn't the consequences of your actions. Your days of reap-free sowing are coming to an end: when you have a kid, you have to visibly strive to uphold all the basic tenets of decency and responsibility, otherwise you'll be revealed as a massive hypocrite when you ask your kids to do what you say, not what you do. You'll have to apply this to almost every aspect of your life, not just for simple stuff like eating your crusts and putting your shoes away, but big stuff too, like always saying 'excuse me' after you cut one, *or even not farting theatrically at all.* I know! It's basically fascism! You have to become the role model to end all role models: think Head of Year meets Captain of the England football team meets Martin Luther King. Oh, you don't wanna be a goody-goody? BREAKING NEWS: your child was arrested this morning for setting fire to an old lady and told reporters "a lack of a good father figure" was to blame. Think on that as you clench your buttocks.

17.

Going swimming in public pools is a thing you have to do again. Hello chlorine, my old friend / I've come to stink of you again. Eventually, when your kid is old enough and bored enough, you'll no doubt find yourself back at your local swimming pool for splash-based larks. Unless you are a healthy type, it's not likely there's been much cause for you to go to public swimming baths in the course of your adult life, but here you are poolside, towel under your arm, shirtless, moobs in the wind. The swimming industry has resolutely refused to be modernised: one in every two lockers is still busted, there are still thin puddles of rusty-looking water in every changing room, and the floats still have teeth marks in them. Oh, and getting a tired and irritable infant changed from wet trunks into dry clothes in a partially flooded, coffin-esque cubicle while enduring the shrieks of two dozen other screaming kids is literal Hell on Earth.

18.

Your gas and electric bills will skyrocket. This sounds obvious, but an increase in your existing energy bills is not likely to be something that's high on your pre-baby worry list, so you'd be forgiven for not losing any sleep over it. Take it from someone who regularly receives the shaft from The Big Five: kids jack up your bills into a terrifyingly red new tariff, roughly the amount of energy needed to launch a Space Shuttle. It's no mystery why - babies constantly need to be warm, kids need to have lights on - but it's still a bitter pill to swallow, particularly if 'getting your energy bills down' has been high on your list of futile things you've been meaning to do that are impossible to achieve. You'll also need to learn to be less precious about maintaining your ideal temperature in the house, because those radiators are now serving a new, tiny overlord - you will either be freezing cold or sweltering hot, and there's no in-between. The guys over at British Gas are laughing their arses off at you.

19.

Otherwise lovely family photographs are ruined by having you in them. Your family is beautiful. Look at those kids, all smart and dressed up and handsome. And then there's you. Haunting the frame. A face only a mother could punch. A shambling vagrant somehow adopted into an otherwise acceptable family out of pity. Your partner looks like a model, your kids look like they're in an advert, and then there's you, the human cyst, looking like you've been recently exhumed. Here's some advice: if possible, try not to let light bounce off your face and be captured digitally and subsequently printed and framed.

20.

Telling off kids will make you feel like shit: guaranteed. Discipline is required throughout the course of raising children, unless you like having hideous, disrespectful and obnoxious kids. Sometimes it's necessary to raise your voice, and sometimes, in extreme circumstances and when the situation calls for it, you have to really call down the thunder and turn up the volume to let them know a line has been crossed. A verbal dressing down is unpleasant but necessary in order to set boundaries, but it doesn't end there. Adults, you see, have a tendency to carry these extreme emotions with them long after the kids have stopped being upset. The physical side-effects of anger and frustration fume and bubble in your bloodstream until they eventually cool into the form of a gnawing guilt. Did you overstep the mark? How much discipline is too much? Are there better ways you can voice your frustrations? Is a gentler approach likely to yield better results? Meanwhile, your kid has completely forgotten the thing that got you so worked up in the first place, leaving you to wrestle with your aimless, futile rage vapours on your lonesome.

21.

Constantly feeling like you're failing to chronicle the important parts of your kids' lives. This is a slow-burner. So much of being a father is about living in the moment and approaching each day as it comes. Unfortunately this doesn't leave much room for past appreciation. Because the early days of parenthood come at you hard and fast, and because the milestones fall in quick succession - first smile, first laugh, first feed, first step, first word - you rarely have time to look back instead of forward. You'll find yourself engaged in a constant struggle with the unshakeable feeling that you're forgetting all of the important stuff that has gone before. Yes, you can take endless photos and videos and boomerangs, but context has a habit of evaporating over time. Lean into this feeling too much and you might end up with enough photos to create a real-time flip-book and enough video coverage to launch a Truman Show spin-off, but if you're only capturing baby's life from behind a lens then are you really living it? It's a difficult balance to find. Ideally you hire a full-time documentary crew to follow you around and capture your most intimate family moments, but this really only works if you are a Kardashian.

Through no fault of their own, kids will cause a split in your friendship groups: those of you who have kids, and those who don't. You know those sacrifices they say you have to make when you have children? This is one of those. It's perfectly natural to drift from friends who you increasingly have less and less in common with, but kids are usually the catalyst that seals the deal. Parents and non-parents may struggle to make arrangements because they're both living life at a different pace and have priorities that no longer align. Worse, when they do get together, the growing imbalance between them only becomes more and more apparent: it's hard to maintain a friendship when you are both working from a different baseline. It's not impossible, obviously - God knows, sometimes the last thing you want to talk about is your kids - but the cracks in the foundation are evident and they'll only get crackier.

Travelling around metropolitan areas with a pram is inescapably awful. Walking is quite nice when you have a little one on wheels, whether it be pram, pushchair, buggy or Penny Farthing - a nice aimless pootle is a good way to get baby to sleep and stretch your legs. Heaven forbid you ever walk anywhere with purpose, however, because getting around town with any form of wheeled child transportation is a soul-sapping, energy draining experience. The inability to traverse even the smallest flight of stairs will add tens of minutes to your trip, and if there is no lift or ramp then you are shit out of luck. Once I took my kid by pram to Canary Wharf on the Docklands Light Railway to practise a bit of light consumerism, and over the course of one afternoon I had to use 21 different lifts throughout various train stations and shopping complexes. It's a bracing insight into all of the invisible privileges that able-bodied people take for granted, and it'll make you feel bad for wishing someone could push you around in a big adult pushchair all day.

24.

Getting your kids into the stuff you like is a massive hassle and if they don't take to things immediately you start to panic that you have nothing in common with these idiots. As a dad with a palpable interest in music, art and culture, you will not waste any time in trying to imprint your various tastes upon your poor, innocent infant child, way before they have any inkling what music, art or culture even is. Case in point: I watched A New Hope with Kid A when he was two and he had the attention span of a... well, of a two-year-old. It lasted around 15 minutes until he sat on his grilled cheese sandwich and we had to abort. You can make them wear Bon Iver onesies and hang Maurice Sendak pictures on their nursery walls all you like, but you will struggle in vain to get them into a 'scene' before they're even out of pull-ups. It's a collective cultural blind spot all dads have, where we forget that nothing could have been less cool than the stuff our Dads tried to push on us as kids. I'll never forget the shit I copped for taking a Sting CD to Show & Tell.

25.

The Jar Jar Effect: that inevitable moment your kid professes an interest in the worst part of the thing you love. This is the potential risk of premature infantile cultural ingest. Open them up to the world of Star Wars and they might accidentally think Jar Jar Binks is hilarious. Encourage them to use Spotify to discover new music and curse the day they stumble on Baby Shark. Try and get them into movies and lose the will to live the 118th time you have to watch Minions. You brought this on yourself. Sorry kid, we're Amish now and all the stuff you like is against our religion or whatever, I don't make the rules.

26.

You are broke. I thought maybe this one goes without saying, but here I am, very much saying it. Children are expensive. Like, brand new sports car expensive. Like, extra storey on the house expensive. Like, six-week five-star holiday in Bali expensive. 'It's a small price to pay for all the love you receive in return' you say, hopelessly incorrect - it's actually quite a large price to pay. It's hard to pinpoint exactly where the big bucks go, but any financial inquest you fruitlessly attempt will doubtless identify food, clothes, slightly larger clothes than the previous clothes, shoes, toys, days out, even larger clothes and vast quantities of coping alcohol as the main money pits. It's just as well you don't actually consider providing for children to be an unnecessary cost incurred and this is all a big funny laugh, right? Hilarious.

27.

Soft play is actual physical and mental torture. The phrase 'soft play' is the exact opposite of 'hard work', which is actually a much more accurate description of how much fun they offer. The vibe in your local soft play centre is slightly south of 'shrieking torture pit located on picturesque circle of Hades' and prolonged exposure to these dayglo, piss-soaked, foam-packed play-dungeons is liable to shorten your life expectancy by a good few weeks. Resist the temptation to soft play yourself: there's always the looming threat of getting stuck in small spaces - flaps and narrow hatches and slides - that were absolutely not made to accommodate full-grown adult men. I have an irrational fear of getting trapped in a narrow tunnel where I'll hyperventilate and die and one day become an urban legend and the kids of tomorrow will swear they can still hear an overweight wheezing man muttering 'Call 999' and 'Don't tell your mother' as they clamber through the section my depressed ghost is cursed to haunt.

28.

It's actually really hard to keep the Father Christmas ruse under wraps, even just at a practical level. You don't know true fear until you've walked into your kid's bedroom holding a stack of presents... and then you hear them stir. A thousand thoughts run through your head. Do you try to lie your way out, despite the quite overwhelming evidence? Do you style it out, like, 'Santa just left these in our bedroom, he must have got the wrong room, I'm just helping him out!', palpable beads of sweat gathering on your brow? Anyway, some men - naming no names, definitely not me, myself or I - have a problem with letting a fictional festive fat man take all the credit for the best presents. I mean, if it's all bullshit anyway, can't it be bullshit that somehow reflects well on me?

29.

Swearing is unacceptable, which means you're not allowed to listen to cuss-filled music any more. Once there is new life in your home, you will quickly find your musical choices censured, meaning no songs with swearing or overtly sexual or aggressive lyrics. But all the *best* music has swearing and overtly sexual and aggressive lyrics! What is this, East Germany under the Stasi? That pretty much rules out entire genres of music, so that means no hip hop or rap, even if babies cannot understand the spoken word and therefore have little to no understanding of west coast beefs. I'm sorry to say that the only acceptable flavour of rap music allowed in your house for the near future begins and ends with 'Will Smith'.

30.

Your memory is shot to shit. This comes naturally with age, but having kids accelerates your memory loss like a Mario Kart power-up. Maybe it's the sheer volume of important new things you have to make room for in your brain - important routines, new names and faces, potentially life-saving procedures for choking etc - but maybe it's a silent concession within your consciousness that your own memories and experiences are slowly fading out of existence like the photo of Marty McFly's family in Back To The Future. Keep it together man, you just have to remember your name, address and toilet routine long enough until the kid turns 18, then they can put you in a home.

31.

Kids, on the other hand, have an amazing selective memory, and will use it to show you up when it suits them. Oh, sure, you don't remember me telling you to pick up your LEGO literally fifteen seconds ago, but you do remember that time TWO YEARS AGO where I accidentally put your swimsuit on back to front? That figures.

32.

The smallest, most inconsequential grievances, when repeated often enough, will literally drive you insane. Every kid has a specific thing they do that drives their parents loopy. Mine is when I put my kids' pyjama bottoms on before bedtime. I gather up one pyjama leg so they can put their first foot through the hole easily, but they never, ever wait for me to gather up the second leg and just stick their other foot straight into one big long loose pyjama leg, requiring me to snake it all the way through manually. I always say 'wait'. They always ignore me. Every. Single. Bedtime. Realistically, my gather-wait-gather pyjama bottom methodology will only save them around five or six seconds, but that's beside the point. It's such a tiny non-grievance, but I imagine they are accumulating every day until such a point where, one night, they finally overload my broken brain and I run half-naked, cock-eyed and gurgling into the street, desperately pleading with the approaching policemen: "ALLOW ME TO REVOLUTIONISE YOUR PYJAMAS, OFFICER!"

33.

It's a given that you're wiser and smarter than your kids (hopefully anyway), but effectively teaching them what you know is a skill you probably don't have. God bless teachers. Son of two teachers here, hi there, how you doing. Only now as a father of two inquisitive children can I vouch for just how difficult it is to communicate information in a way that is palatable and memorable to children. Knowing the answers to questions is the easy part, but somewhere in your life you got comfortable with problem solving and data gathering and you just plain dispensed with the 'hows' and the 'whys' because you didn't need them anymore. Teaching, or even just imparting wisdom, involves constantly rewiring your brain to repackage information for an audience that lacks the decades of context you take for granted. Otherwise you're just burbling unintelligible ones and zeroes like a fax machine trying to talk to an iPhone.

Having to answer a billion questions a day only highlights how much you don't actually know. You'll hear the word 'Why?' a lot. Maybe more than any other word, aside from 'bum'. You will be stumped at questions you may otherwise consider easy until you actually have to verbalise the answer. Kids have a way of finding an angle on a question that will make you question everything you thought you knew, like 'Why do rainbows exist?' - not 'How are they made?' but WHY do they EXIST - or 'How do cats know what they're saying when they meow?' The other day it took me a good 45 minutes to wrap my head around why the alphabet is in alphabetical order, when there is no logical reason for it to be in the order it's in. Daddy's tired and needs a lie down.

You have to be careful who your kids idolise on the internet. I miss the old, pre-nonce days of television, where you could rely on twinkly old TV personalities to be lovely and kind and encouraging and not twisted old silver-haired sex fiends. Kids today will generally find their first role models online, and because the internet is still basically unregulated and you're never more than a YouTube algorithm or two away from being indoctrinated into the Nazi party, there should be huge alarm bells ringing already. These friendly and well-lit 'like and subscribe' types seem non-threatening at first, but we've seen time and time again that your charismatic gamer types, YouTube idols and TikTok teens do not always have the depth of character to be put up on a pedestal. We let our kids watch Blippi for a while; he's a bumbling yet wholesome YouTube personality who dresses in blue and orange and posts fun videos about soft play centres and local hotspots while singing insanely catchy,

Pavement-esque songs with his musical partner, Nicky Notes. Anyway, it turns out that before he was 'Blippi', he posted a Harlem Shake video in which he shat jets of diarrhoea over his naked pal's bare arsehole. Honestly, have some self-respect. I mean, the Harlem Shake, for Christ's sake.

36.

It's impossible to tell the difference between kids' t-shirts and kids' short-sleeved pyjama tops. If they're not sleep themed then there's no visual indicator to clue you in. There's no difference in fabric or design, yet everyone else in the household seems to have an understanding of what constitutes a pyjama top and what constitutes a t-shirt, and you'd best believe only one of these is acceptable attire at bedtime. No one is talking about this.

37.

Hangovers are especially intolerable. Age makes hangovers worse, but the addition of kids really punch them up to a spicy new level. The responsibilities inherent to parenthood are basically the antithesis of the hangover. Weirdly, fatherhood is the cure to hangovers, or at least it would be if you took it as a preventative measure and not as the morning after pill.

38.

The general nagging feeling that you have no idea if you're teaching your kids the difference between right and wrong, or if any of it is sticking, and although it's possible you're shaping them into well-balanced, rounded individuals, there's always the chance that your kids are on the way to becoming unbalanced psychopaths who will one day cite

your lack of parental guidance in the court case where they're charged for the murder of two dozen puppies. It seems unlikely, but there's no manual!

39.

You must, without question, feign an interest in the incredibly crappy things that your kids love. When your kid gets into a TV show or book or toy line that's deep enough for it to become an obsession, it is your duty to be their captive audience while they enthuse about every last detail. Yes, their happiness is your happiness, I get it. I love that my eldest is into Pokémon. I love that he loves it. I, however, do not love it. Far from it. Yet I still know that a Bulbasaur evolves into an Ivysaur, which evolves into a Venusaur. That is useless information that's taking up space in my brain, like a wet box in a shed. I didn't choose to remember it, it was viddy-ed into my brain, Clockwork Orange-style, against my will.

40.

You'll want to tell off other peoples' kids, but you can't. The primal urge to protect your children from the world, more specifically from other children, will inspire you to do many heroic things, but the paternal justice will have to stop short of policing other people's kids. You know they're being a little shit. They know they're being a little shit. Even the kids' parents probably know they're being a little shit. But you cannot expect to transfer the same parent-to-child authoritarian regime onto a child that is not your own. You cannot be an OmniDad. You'll just have to make do with fantasising about roundhousing kicking the snot-nosed little brat into the middle of next week, then winning a hypothetical fist fight with their dad.

Every once in a while, you'll convince yourself that your kid actually hates you. That's not true, of course. I'm almost certain of it. And yet, it won't stop you from wondering if, deep down, they've realised they're just not really as into you as you are into them. Kids go through weird periods from time to time where they'll be in a constant strop with one parent for no apparent reason, and nothing you can say or do can make it right. Mummy? Oh yeah, she's all right, good old Mummy. But Daddy? Ugh. They can't *even* with that guy. Even babies can shade you and erupt into a tantrum if you so much as enter a room. Obviously you take this massively personally, because how else are you supposed to take it? Your fragile ego is made of glass, and your kid has a never ending supply of emotional stones to throw at it.

Other children's' birthday parties. Is this what you had in mind when you and your partner decided to have children? Is this it? Standing up for three hours, in a function hall, surrounded by 30 shrieking children hyped up on cold chicken nuggets and Haribo? Half-heartedly applauding the birthday boy or girl whose name you already forgot? Sneaking a few stale crisps from the buffet table that's already swimming in spilled Ribena? Putting the least amount of effort into buying them the first sub-£6 gift you see in the toy shop? Doing this, every other weekend, for the next eight years of your life? You could just sneak out. Just leave. Sit in the car and smoke a cigarette very slowly. Drive to the coast. Escape. *Be free.* But no: there's still arts and crafts and pass the parcel and cake and more singing and balloons before you're allowed to go home. Happy fucking birthday, whatever your name is, I hope you like off-brand Lego.

Making small talk with other dads. In my experience, women can meet a complete stranger and within minutes be talking to them like they've known them their whole life. Men, to my knowledge, cannot be coached to do this, even under duress. The bright red 48-point flashing sub-text of any conversation, perhaps at one of the aforementioned birthday parties, or at the school gates, or sitting waiting for a school play to begin, is this: WE BOTH KNOW THE ONLY THING WE HAVE IN COMMON IS THAT WE HAVE CHILDREN THE SAME AGE. This is not the basis for a long-lasting and meaningful friendship. This is the basis for checking your phone harder and longer than you have ever checked your phone.

You may not sleep properly again, ever. This will be well documented in this book, there's no escaping it. Sleep, as you know it, will never be the same again. It's no biggie, just one entire third of your existence thrown out of whack until the day you die. Just a heightened deprivation of a fundamental human requirement. Just the kind of torture the CIA use to make terrorists fear for their sanity. Just a voluntary lobotomy. Seriously though, it's no big deal. Nothing that can't be fixed by a good night's slee- oh, right.

Children are LOUD. Babies get a pass, you can't be mad at a baby for bawling, that's just what babies do. But children will find ear-shattering new levels of sound hitherto undiscovered on the Decibel Meter. You could not create a more effective noise machine if you tried. Kids are loud when they're unhappy, but

frustratingly they're even louder when they're happy - hooting
and whooping and hollering like greased pigs - which only serves
to make you look like a megabastard for asking them to be quiet.
Children left to play unsupervised will eventually break the
sound barrier if not adequately shushed.

46.

**You're going to get fat because kids never finish their
dinner and you'd rather eat their leftovers than chuck
them in the bin.** Children are obviously fussy eaters, and
they're also prone to leaving giant swathes of breakfasts, lunches
and dinners left untouched just because they weren't feeling its
vibe. You, on the other hand, are almost always hungry after a
hard day's dadding. This is not a complicated maths problem to
solve. You could just scrape the leftovers in the food waste bin
and be done with it. You could do that. But obviously you're not
going to do that. *There are starving children in the world*, you'll
say, to no one in particular, as you shovel half a lukewarm spag
bol into your gob, instantly and single-handedly solving world
hunger. You're the food waste bin now.

47.

**Having kids is the fastest way to feel hopelessly out of
touch with the world.** Fatherhood ages you whether you enjoy
it or not: you'll lose a good few years during the baby blur. Grey
hair and crow's feet are part of the deal, but one unexpected and
unwelcome side-effect of being a dad is how effectively it closes
you out of the loop. Being a parent is like pushing pause on the
way you experience the world while you hunker down in the
baby bunker, but the world doesn't stop spinning: entire news
cycles pass you by, you'll get cultural whiplash trying to keep up
with music, movies and TV, and fame's production line churns

through fresh meat so quickly that one day you'll sit down to watch Celebrity Big Brother and not recognise a single face. Wait, they don't even make Celebrity Big Brother anymore? *Fuck.* If you ever wondered why your Dad never seemed to know which was the artist's name and which was the song title, well... it was because he had you.

48.

Parenthood makes you a nervous wreck. I simply cannot comprehend how the male psyche could possibly emerge from fatherhood without permanent scarring. Being a dad amplifies all of your existing anxieties by multitudes. In the early days it's all about physical protection: treating them with kid gloves, swaddling them in cotton wool, planing off the sharp edges of life. Then, as they grow, so do your fears. Will they make friends? Will they look twice before crossing the road? Are they getting bullied at school? Strife is like a box of chocolates: there is an entire two-layered selection tray of worries to choose from, yet you never seem to get close to the bottom of the box. Depressingly, these anxieties don't seem to fade over time, they just become part of your life - they're the jagged edges of the love you feel, but as long as they still hurt, it means you still care.

49.

Routines and rigidity will box you in, and you probably won't like it. Babies need routine and kids need structure, but as grown adults, we are not always used to sticking to timetables and abiding by rules. Nevertheless, you will quickly find yourself in a situation whereby the agenda for your entire day is dictated by someone else, whether it be a bottle-feed, an afternoon nap, a school run or a hospital trip. Living within the lines of someone else's schedule takes some mental adjustment, particularly when that someone else does not respect or is basically unaware of the concept of time full stop, and if given the choice would completely scrap said schedule in favour of eating, sleeping and playing - three pastimes in which you would happily join them.

50.

The inescapable fact that you cannot protect them from the world. You'll have to watch them grow up and suffer through all the things that you suffered through yourself: school, raging hormones, lack of self-confidence, shitty friends, heartbreak, that terrible phase where they go all-in on a band that are objectively shit. Even the most selfless and devoted dads cannot promise their kid a life devoid of pain or sadness, and you'll share every iota of both like a dagger in your heart - when they hurt, you feel it twice as sharply. You can try to harden them against the world as you know it, paint them in multiple coats of emotional resin, but you'll quickly realise that dulling the way they experience the world is not the answer, and that they won't survive unless they learn to experience the lows as well as the highs. It's by far the cruellest aspect of fatherhood: onboarding them into an uncaring world that will chew them up and spit them out without so much as a second thought.

***

There. That wasn't so bad, was it? [Puts finger to ear] Actually... I'm hearing that it was, indeed, that bad. Still, if you're one of the 3% of readers who are still reading after ingesting that mahoosive mudpie of hot, steaming dadhood, you're clearly cut from the right cloth. It's onwards and upwards from here, lads! Alexa, play 'Things Can only Get Better' by D-Ream! The next chapter? Self-improvement. [Record scratch] FUCK.

#4

Make Yourself Useful, You Worthless Sack of Shit!

By now, you should have built a pretty good impression of the kind of handsome man I am: a strapping, bronzed, alpha male, confident and carefree (and handsome), who stands with hands on hips and legs a mile apart in order to leave room for his massive, swinging piece. Girls stop in the street when I pass, lower their sunglasses, bite their lip and say, out loud, to their cucked boyfriends, 'Now there's a guy who's got his shit together', before totally orgasming.

It may come as a surprise to you that I was not always this impressive a male specimen – I was once a pathetic weakling, like you. But I didn't transform into the five-time winner of People's Sexiest & Also Most Talented Dad award overnight, oh no. I had to work hard every day, learning new skills, becoming a better man, and doing all of the exercise things that people do.

Shut up, it's my book.

With a baby in the making and the best part of a year counting down until B-Day, now is the perfect time to take stock of your life, and to make one or more of those huge, sweeping life changes that you've been talking about for your entire adult life. Lord knows you're not going to be blessed with an abundance of free time once your good lady bursts, so it's time to make the most of the weeks and months you have left and figure out what steps you can take to become the dad you were always meant to be. As per the previous chapter, being mentally prepared for parenthood is hugely important, but there are unavoidable practical considerations to Dadhood that you're going to need to tackle head on.

Alternatively, skip this chapter if you're doing just fine, and you're happy with the amount of time you spend in the bookies, completing online personality quizzes or bookmarking Tasty recipe videos with no intention of ever making them. I can't force you to become a better man. That's all totally fine. You do you, boo! I'd just hate for you to realise too late that you spent vast swathes of your pre-baby life clinging to your adolescence, festering in your fading youth, devoting endless weekends to slovenly pursuits, spending your hard-earned cash building monuments to nothing. You might as well stop reading: you've clearly already got it all figured out.

Yeah, that's right, reverse psychology, bitch! I just Tyler Durdened you! Your life is ending one minute at a time, and while I don't recommend starting an underground fight club in order to unleash your frustrations on other directionless men, a little self-improvement never hurt anyone. I look back on my life before I had children, and it's honestly unrecognisable. I'm not saying it was without value, because that's a revisionist way of looking at things, but I am saying two things: 1) I have absolutely no idea what I used to spend all my money on, and; 2) I have absolutely no idea what I used to spend all my time doing. The answer to both questions is probably 'shopping in HMV to build an enormous collection of physical media that'd stand the test of time', which obviously worked out great.

Don't let the same thing happen to you. Use your time wisely. Learn the following new skills. Better yourself. Aim for peak dadness and let the good times roll.

DAD SKILL #1: D.I.Y.

Sorry. You can't put this off any longer. Though I would hate to live in a world where you would need to pass some sort of manliness test in order to become a father, if such a test existed, at least one of the physical tasks would be to perform some basic carpentry. And I would have flunked, bigtime.

D.I.Y. is almost as terrifying as having a baby. It brings me out in a cold sweat. There's something inherently frightening about the finality of it. I am a man of words not a man of action, and I come from a generation that rightfully prefers digital word processing over writing in pen and ink, so if I make an error, I can tidy it up with a simple push of Ctrl+Z and pretend like it never happened - that's a luxury that previous generations never had. But even something as simple as hammering a nail into a wall to hang a picture has to be done with a level of precision that has evaded me my entire life.

You have to measure the mark exactly, taking into consideration the size of the wall, the width of the frame, even the location of the hanger on the back of the frame. Worse, you're expected to hammer that nail in at a perfectly straight angle, not too hard, not too gentle, to the perfect depth, using primitive hand tools that haven't been modernised in several thousand years, in a completely three-dimensional space with no guides or buffers, and with a high chance of bludgeoning your own soft, doughy fingers - *digits which are crucial to doing the job accurately.*

Get it wrong by even a quarter of an inch, and the wonky picture hanging on the wall will be a permanent reminder of your ineptitude. No pressure, but if you mess it up you've basically ruined the whole wall, and there are only so many walls in the entire house, so you've ruined the entire house. You idiot.

D.I.Y. is what dads are for, but - and I really hate to break this to you in this fashion - pretty soon, *you're going to be the dad*. I never had any training in carpentry or metalwork or painting or decorating or plastering when I was younger. My parents were both teachers, so they spent an inordinate amount of their 'spare' time working on lesson plans, grading homework and resolutely not telling me which end of the hammer was the hitty one. In any case, the interior design of our family house was so archaic and old-fashioned, no amount of do-it-yourself that anyone could have done themselves would have made it better. The hideous wood-panelled walls and exposed rock countertops and artex ceilings made the living room look like a back office attached to a strip club. It was the kind of house in which your hair would feel compelled to grow quicker at the back than at the front in order to match its environment.

I remember exactly one instance of painting and decorating in the family house, which was an emergency patch job when I accidentally kicked a hole in my bedroom ceiling in a fit of rage. Kicking a hole in a ceiling sounds impressive, but as much as I'd love to pretend I was a character from Street Fighter II, the kick was performed from the top of a cabin bed, and the cause wasn't a decades-old campaign of violent revenge over the murder of my sensei, but an argument with my older brother about Micro Machines 2.

Then, before I'd even so much as bothered to learn what Polyfilla was, I'd packed up and moved out, off to university and the wider world, without having learned a solitary useful practical skill. Oh, I'd racked up some hours on Pro Evo, let me tell you. I had obscure Region 1 DVDs that'd make your head spin. But hand me a power drill and all I was good for was doing sound effects for robot movements. I still maintain this is an equally valid use of a power drill.

It was the age of Blu-Tack. The Sellotape era. Luckily, it's frowned upon to make structural improvements to student housing, and that streak continued when I moved into rented accommodation. Darn it, I'd *love* to hang some pictures on the wall, but the *bloody* landlord won't have it! Grrr! If it were up to me, I'd probably knock all this through [gestures vaguely towards a wall] and make it open plan with a serving window from the kitchen to the diner! Believe me, I'd love nothing more than to put up some shelves, honestly, but it's against our tenancy contract, which I respect, so we'll just have to continue stacking all our important stuff on the floor and hanging the non-essentials in a plastic bag out the window. So frustrating! Fiddlesticks etc!

The age of Blu-Tack would eventually come unstuck when Vicky and I moved into a ground floor flat under a shared ownership scheme. This meant that we owned a small percentage of the property and paid rent on the rest. And unfortunately for me, that meant that tenants were free to - shudder - make the place their own. Damn.

It's so much harder learning new life skills at age 28 than it is at 18. At least when I was younger I would have been receptive to self-improvement (sure, I'll learn the guitar if it means my chances of sexual intercourse are marginally improved!), but once you complete your formal education, pass your driving test and get your girlfriend to move in with you, there's nothing binding you to apply yourself to anything in particular. It takes a lack of money and an excess of shame to pull you out of your quarter-life slump.

Besides, there's something inherently wrong with living in a flat with completely white walls. It feels like you're squatting in an abandoned insane asylum, although to their credit, even abandoned insane asylums have interesting colours smeared all over the walls. So something had to be done. This was a definite 'I'm Learning A New Thing' watershed moment. It was decided: two floating shelves were to be erected right in the middle of the living room wall, just above the TV. Yep. Just above where everyone's eyes will always be looking. Cool. Brilliant. Loving it already.

I bought the tools from a nearby hardware store, by putting on my 'tradesman' voice and acting like I knew what I was doing. *Thank you sweedheart*, I'd say, doing a Phil Mitchell. *Keep the change my love*. Phil Mitchell would know how to put up a floating shelf. He'd just headbutt it into the wall.

I bought a hefty D.I.Y. manual, which gave me panic attacks, so instead I watched some reassuring YouTube videos for guidance. It was only then that I realised all walls weren't the same. As in, not all walls are made of bricks. This was news to me. Our living room had a plasterboard wall, and I was delighted to find out it was ten times harder to attach anything to a plasterboard wall, much less a load-bearing shelf. Still, I was determined to make my first foray into D.I.Y. a success. Back I went to the hardware store. *Looks like I'm gonna need some 'butterfly screws' for this tricky bit of plasterboard, sweedheart.* I'm desperately hoping that there is only one kind of butterfly screw otherwise my tough guy persona is shot to bits.

Back to YouTube. Watch again. Watch again. Pause. Squint. Watch again. Get the right-sized drill bit. Line up the marks with military precision. Watch again. Bookmark. Watch again. No turning back now. I put the tip of the drill bit to the mark. Closed my eyes. Opened them again, obviously. Then pulled the trigger.

A three inch crack shot out from the hole in an instant. A massive lump of plaster falls to the ground, leaving a gaping pink crater in the wall. I cry. Phil Mitchell wouldn't cry. He'd start honking on a crack pipe.

Nevertheless, I persisted. I could have abandoned my D.I.Y career there and then, but I kept going, against all odds, determined to achieve my goal of becoming a man who had put up a shelf. The successful shelf erector. As it happens, the width of the shelf *just* covered the messy remnants of the first attempt. The shelf went up and stayed up, even though we were terrified to put anything heavier than a plastic plant on it and never dusted it once in fear of bringing the entire wall down with it. I did have a wobble, when it was pointed out that the shelves looked wonky next to the TV, but after a lot of measuring and a bit more crying and the purchase of an actual spirit level that wasn't an iPhone app, I found out that actually, the shelves were straight, it was the entire room that was on the wonk. Vindication! I beat the system!

There have been other... let's say 'attempts' at home improvements. I gamely attempted to put up wallpaper in the bedroom, resulting in the kind of farcical clarting that wouldn't have felt out of place in an episode of ChuckleVision. I assembled a garden bench under duress after discovering it was delivered in a flat-pack box, and it is perfectly sit-in-able despite the fact I had to file down a metal spike that I'd left sticking out of the arse part - y'know, for tetanus! Somehow, in attempting to retie a loose bathroom light cord, I wound up jabbing a screwdriver into a live socket and ended up shorting out the electrics to the entire house at a cost of £250. Cuh, *men!* Am I right?

When we moved into the house we're currently in, we quickly cottoned onto the fact that our lovely next door neighbour was an actual Man Who Drills, and he volunteered to do some of the more difficult D.I.Y. jobs for us in exchange for polite conversation, which was obviously a massive result. He whipped out his hammer drill - nine times manlier and more sexual than your average drill due to its incessant thrusting - and informed me that mishandling it could result in a broken wrist, which was all I needed to hear to step aside. I wasn't a complete bystander, though: I stood underneath him as he drilled, holding a handheld vacuum and hoovering up all his dust while he explained the rules of cricket to me. See? Not at all emasculating.

The point where I drew the line was when it came to putting up a large and weighty mirror in our front room, featuring the approximate size and weight of glass that decapitates people in horror movies. I did my research, made several trips to B&Q and eventually, through a lot of hand-wringing and hard work, got it hung. A day later, upon returning from a family day out, we entered the living room and found the mirror hanging off the wall at a 45 degree angle, straining the hanger almost to breaking point. It was about then when my incompetence at D.I.Y. went from 'embarrassing inadequacy' to 'potentially fatal character flaw', so I did the sensible thing, retired my tools and got a handyman in to do the job to a professional standard. At least then if the mirror fell off the wall and crushed one or more of my children, I'd be in the clear. What a relief!

As it happens, our house has concrete walls - another type of wall! - which is extremely difficult to drill into and super unreliable, so it actually makes more sense for us to use those quasi-Velcro hanging strips. I can't say for certain this factored into our decision to buy the house, but I can't say it didn't. Recently I was diagnosed with early onset of mild arthritis in my fingers, and sometimes I wonder if my brain subconsciously willed my joints to seize up in order to get me off the hook for any more manual labour. Thanks, brain! I'd give you a thumbs-up, but... ow. Obviously I am not the case study for self-improvement of this skill-set: I very much fall into the category of 'Man who earns enough to pay someone to do menial household jobs for him but doesn't earn enough not to feel bad about it'. I still maintain it's not my fault, it's society's fault. Why is practical stuff of this nature not taught in schools? I did several years of woodwork, CDT, Design Technology and whatever else you want to call it, and to date, I have never needed to craft a plywood CD cabinet or MDF key holder in an emergency. Consequently, many, many pictures remain unhung.

Still, I cannot stress enough the importance of learning how to swing a hammer while your home is still baby free - anything to avoid your children witnessing your incompetence first hand. Do a recce to B&Q, get yourself a little cordless power drill set, practice on random bits of tat and build your confidence, brick by brick - soon you'll feel hard as those pointy metal deelies people put in walls. Nails, yeah, them too. Either that, or buy a concrete house next door to Handy Andy and develop a crippling disability. It's all good.

DAD SKILL #2: LEARN TO DRIVE

What's that? You already know how to drive? Brilliant. What's that? You own your own car? That's fantastic. One less thing to worry about. You're officially allowed to skip this bit, superstar. If you can already drive *and* you can do D.I.Y. then congrats, you're just winning all over the place, you must be tired of winning at life, I'm surprised you had time to impregnate your supermodel girlfriend with your solid gold dick.

As you may have guessed, I could not drive at the time of the birth of our kids. No, that's incorrect - I could drive, I just didn't have a car. I learned to drive in my early 20s, just a few years before I left rural Essex for university life in London, where I realised there was no point in having my own car. My only experience of driving in busy London traffic was when I was taken on a school minibus trip to the Barbican to see The Tempest, and my headteacher Mr Brunwin mounted a kerb, took out a bollard and called a fellow driver a "fucking dickhead" in full earshot of all his sixth-form students.

Besides, nobody needs to drive anywhere in London: you either walk where you need to go, sweat your tits off on the tube or stumble into a black cab after a night out and wake up in the morning £85 poorer. I knew I'd have to sell the trusty old Peugeot 306 before I left for uni, it'd have to be sacrificed on the altar of PARTYING, but then it broke down two weeks before I left. I had to pay £1,000 to fix it, then I sold it for £900. I would have saved money if I'd have just driven it off a fucking cliff.

I was right, anyway. You have to have a special kind of death wish to want to drive in London. You have to have a deep, raging anger inside of you, the kind that can only be quelled by verbally abusing a cyclist, or calling a bus driver on minimum wage a cunt. It's physically impossible to drive directly through central London - many men have tried, but they are consumed by madness somewhere around Oxford Circus, the Congestion Charge zone swallowing them whole like the Bermuda Triangle. Abandon hope all ye who enter the Hammersmith flyover.

Take it from me, however: the moment you have kids, a car becomes a necessity, wherever you live. You will wonder how you ever went anywhere without it. For a short while, travelling on public transport with your kid can be kind of cute. Baby's first bus ride! Baby's first train ride! You'll probably get big smiles from baby, and a few approving nods from fellow passengers too. Hey, this isn't so bad! It's sort of like a fun community made up of people who also can't drive! They'll accept us as we are: imperfect, unable to operate a vehicle and unwilling to walk. It's all well and good until the next time you take the bus into town, and it's a Saturday afternoon. Horror of horrors: there's already another pushchair on the bus. If you're lucky, the driver will stop to tell you there's no room for you. If you're not, he'll just drive straight past you, without so much as a sympathetic shrug.

Maybe two buses later you find one where the pushchair spot is free, except it's otherwise full to capacity, and manoeuvring the buggy in place means you're going to upset at least three grandads. Your baby is now doing full-throated crying because it wants you to look like a total scummer in front of the bus people, the kind of shrill, high-pitched scream that says 'My daddy doesn't know how to change me and also he's a benefits cheat!' The passengers from the other day who were cooing over him have gone, and have been replaced with soulless automatons, who shush and tut and push and shove and read gigantic full-sized broadsheet newspapers like it's fucking 1990.

The journey back is worse, because you have to do it with ten tonnes of shopping hanging off your pushchair, approximately doubling it in width, and literally everyone in front of you in the bus queue also has a hulking great Mad Max-style pushchair/war machine. The most stressed I've ever been as a father was the time I had to take a shopping-laden pushchair home on the 45 bus during rush hour while also carrying two oversized helium balloons and a bastard of a headache behind the eyes. That was the moment I realised: for the love of God, man - it's time to buy a bloody car.

I can understand the reluctance to become a Man Who Does Car Things. If you, like me, have little to no understanding of how cars work, how much all car stuff is supposed to cost, or even what the proper car words are to use in conversation, it's an intimidatingly butch arena to enter. One slip of the tongue or stupid question or Star Wars keyring attached to your car key and an evil mechanic can mark you as a rube who'll gladly pay through the nose just to get the whole godforsaken ordeal over with. Of course, car maintenance stuff can be learned, but it is also technically possible to coast through car ownership by knowing the bare minimum - blag your test, buy your car and cross your fingers nothing ever breaks and you never have to speak to another man about car things for the rest of time.

If you're lucky you'll befriend a mechanic or there will be a distant member of your family, perhaps the boyfriend of a distant cousin, with whom you can fast-track a matey back-and-forth a couple of weeks before your MOT. However, if you, like me, never learned a physical trade and possess no useful skill-sets outside of rebooting a router, you're going to have to just bite the bullet and figure out what a carburettor is all by yourself. I know, it sounds so made up! You've got no choice but to watch every single episode of Top Gear ever made as research and develop questionable opinions about the Falklands as a result.

Let's not get ahead of ourselves: yes, a car is essential for travelling with young children with your sanity intact, but more importantly, car availability is going to make or break your birth plan. Picture the scene. It's an unspecified day in the future. The contractions begin. The water breaks. It's time to go to the hospital. Except you never did get round to organising driving lessons, did you? You spent your savings on an Xbox One and a massive block of weed instead, didn't you? Spent your weekends in the pub and down the bookies and getting your money's worth out of Red Dead Redemption 2, didn't you? Shit. You pick up the phone and dial a cab. Engaged. You try again. Engaged. You punch in another number, hands shaking a little. They pick up, but... they've got no one available for an hour. Same with the next number. And the next. Then you realise: it's 11 o'clock on a bloody Friday night. How has this happened? You've had nine months to prepare. *Nine months*. The colour drains from the room as it goes dark, and giant letters spelling the words GAME OVER and YOU HAVE FAILED materialise in thin air in front of you, and the last thing you see before the pregnancy resets is your partner's grimacing face as she silently mouths the words: *I told you we needed a car.*

Look, you'll probably be okay, I don't want to give you the fear. Cabs can work just fine. They worked for us. Both of my kids were born at ridiculously inconvenient times, both in the early hours of the morning. I eventually managed to find a cab both times, but only because I'd done my homework in advance. You have no idea how difficult it is trying to sound out a cab company to provide urgent transportation in the event of childbirth. This conversation is almost word-for-word exactly how it went down for me when I tried to lock in an East London cab firm.

"Hi, I wonder if you can help me. My wife is pregnant and I'm wondering if you can give any sort of guarantee as to your 24-hour availability should we need to get to the hospital?"
[Alarmed] "Your wife is having a baby? You need to go to the hospital?"
"Yeah. Not now though. Probably in about a month."
[Relaxing] "Oh. Congratulations."
"Thanks."
"Call us when it happens and we'll see."
"Will you definitely be here though?"
"Hmm... in a month I'll be on holiday."
"Right. Will someone else be available?"
"Yeah they should be."
"It's just... I called you at about 1am last Friday and it rang off the hook for about 15 minutes until I gave up."
"I wasn't on last Friday."

"I get that. Obviously I need to know for sure, if we need to get to the hospital urgently."

"You can't drive? You don't have your own car?"

"I... no."

"Can't you call an ambulance?"

"Yeah, no, they don't do that."

"I would say... hmmm... yeah, we should be fine."

"Right, again, that's great, but I n- actually, you know what, don't worry about it."

[To me, as I'm leaving] "Good luck!"

Search long and hard enough and eventually you'll find a cab that will get you there, god willing. But here's the thing: getting to the hospital is not necessarily the end of your travels. There's a pretty good chance that the maternity staff will tell your partner that she's not far along enough and they'll send you both home, in which case you're going to need to get another cab back home - and then a *third* cab to eventually take you back to the hospital again. Oh, and the fourth and final cab home when you're all babied up. Let's say that's a max of £20 a pop - that's eighty quid you're never going to see again.

I mean, obviously, eighty quid is nothing in the grand scheme of things, and it's not like you'd have the brass balls to complain about cab fares while your partner is grunting her way through childbirth, and obviously you can't put a price on the miracle of life, but Jesus, eighty quid, that's not an insignificant chunk of change right there, it's fine though, obviously, absolutely fine, no problem at all, it's just... *fuck*.

It's not even like you can cut costs with an Uber because you're definitely going to put your five-star rating at risk if you leak womb juice all over the back seat of some poor underpaid dude's Skoda Octavia. Don't take that chance. Take the plunge while there's still time left on the clock: learn to drive and set yourself on the road to parenthood. Eventually, after weeks and months and countless lessons in which a middle-aged instructor who voted Leave will find a vaguely racist way to teach you the highway code, you can become a capable, comfortable and confident driver. Or at the very least, a driver.

Just be sure to adjust your expectations now you're no longer a young man. Owning a car in your late teens/early 20s was all about status and sex - that filthy little slag of a Ford Fiesta was a penis extension and you know it. Owning a car as a dad, with all the car seats and baby accessories and Michael Buble CDs and empty juice bottles littering the footwells, is basically a form of castration. Nobody has ever attracted a member of the opposite sex while driving a second-hand Vauxhall Astra with Peppa Pig sun visors on the rear windows. There are no aspirational car adverts in which a bickering couple argue all the way to Morrisons while the kids take turns wiping bogies on the upholstery. No man has ever complimented another man about the sheer horsepower of his Renault Espace. No one ever chooses to drive the beige five-door hatchback in Gran Turismo.

Still, the self-improvement is going great. The sooner you get used to the fact that most of your weekends are going to be spent driving to B&Q for tungsten-tipped screws, the better.

DAD SKILL #3: EXERCISE AND HEALTHY EATING

Let me stop you there. I know what you're going to say. *I already exercise and eat healthy.* That's totally cool. No problem at all. Just so I'm clear, let's recap: you're handy round the house, have a no claims bonus of 12 years on your brand new sports car, and you just got a new PB for 10k. Super. Just fantastic. What a magnificent specimen of a human being you are. Yes, that was *supposed* to sound sarcastic. Oh, look at me, I'm not ashamed of my BMI. Oh, hi there, you just caught me eating a lentil salad for lunch and actually enjoying it, unironically. Where the hell do you get off, buddy? Why did you even buy this book? Where's your fucking book if you're so fucking great? TELL US *YOUR* TIPS ON HOW TO BE A DAD.

I'll continue with the caveat that from here on in, I'm only addressing the unfit: the sofa-dwellers, the Dorito-eaters, the stair-avoiders, the exercise-averse, the salad-swervers, the bus-takers, the dairy fairies, the carb-havers, the XL-wearers, the croissant-butterers, the sigh-as-they-sitters, the easily tired, the permanently hungry, the constant farters who always order starters, the cheese-worshippers, the meat-sweaters, the ice cream-drinkers, the pint-smashers, the elasticated-waistband-wearers, the kebab adjacent, the burrito proficient, the friends of Nando, the men and women up and down the country who are just too bloody starving to waste time preheating the oven. These... these are my people.

It shouldn't be news to you that having children is exhausting - you'll know this if you have ever met anyone who has children, because it'll be the first thing they tell you, before they even tell you their name: *Hi, sorry, I must look a state, I'm half dead, my little one isn't sleeping right now, nice to meet you.*

What you might not understand is how deeply this parental tiredness permeates throughout the entire body - it's a sort of cumulative mental and physical exhaustion that goes from your brain right through to your bones. In the early days, when baby is tiny and can't even roll over without soiling itself, it's just about manageable: you can still survive the days and weeks while bleary-eyed and strung out. But when babies become toddlers and the toddling turns into actual physical activity, you're going to need to keep up with them, for their sake and for yours.

Kids have so much energy it's staggering - just boundless reserves of battery power, enough voltage to juice a mid-sized bungalow if only it wasn't highly immoral to hook them up to the mains. They're simple creatures who only want to experience pleasure while experiencing none of the side effects. They want to live every moment of every day, right up until the minute it becomes physically impossible to stay awake, fighting with every ounce of their strength to wring one more minute of fun out of the day's consciousness.

This is why kids hate going to sleep: they don't need to appreciate the upside of a good night's rest, because their recharge rate is lightning fast, like insane miniature Wolverines, and they're very rarely not at 100%. Attempting to convince a small child the benefits of resting, relaxing or being quiet is an illogical act, because they're just not wired for it. Kids are like the bus in Speed - they can't slow down, they can only speed up or crash.

This is why being out of shape right now might potentially be a problem. Question: what's the most shame it's physically possible to feel as a human being? Answer: the most shame it is physically possible to feel as a human being is struggling to bend over to put your socks and shoes on because there's too much middle getting in the way, and your small infant child is staring at you and wondering why you look like you're about to puke. Shitting yourself in public is also not a good look, but for the purposes of this book, let's run with the fat thing.

I know it's not necessarily everyone's ideal to enjoy a fit and healthy lifestyle, nor is it always achievable or realistic, and it's probably the furthest thing from your mind right now. But the thought of being vegetative and immobile while your own kids run rings around you is not a pleasant one: either your children will grow up thinking you can't be bothered to kick a ball around in the garden, or worse, they'll slowly fall in line and adopt your sedentary lifestyle as their own. Parenthood, brought to you in association with McDonald's.

I don't know you, I don't know your quirks or your routine or your lifestyle, but I do know one thing and it is this: getting fit and eating healthy sucks shit at the best of times, but these two things are literally the last two things you are going to want to do when you've recently been anointed a baby daddy. If you value your arteries and you plan on keeping them unclogged - or hell, even if you want to scale back your fitness fantasies and shoot for 'putting on socks without wincing' - then the time to make that lifestyle change is now, now, now.

Yes, I am aware there are people who like to pretend that having children is a workout in itself. Some women, for example, like to use babies as props in their yoga routines, because they are medically unable to stop doing yoga.

It's not a lie to say that the rigorous routines of fatherhood will affect your body in ways you might not expect - positively and negatively. For example, rocking a chunky baby to sleep every night is going to make your forearms grotesquely thick and sturdy like a university rower - I did so much late night cradling with our first kid that my arms wouldn't fit into my coat any more. But then, having arms like Chris Hemsworth and a body like Chris Moyles is not exactly the male ideal, is it? You can't walk around in a vest top showing off your pythons if you also have the pot-belly of Winnie the Pooh and the spindly legs of a chlorinated chicken. I'm sure there are other ways to utilise your large infant child as part of a full body workout, but then you're the madman in the park waving his hefty baby around like it's a 20lb beehive. No. Have some dignity, man.

I've done the gym thing, and it's just not for me. I have been a member of about eight or nine gyms in my life, and some of them I even went to more than once. There was my first gym, located in the Outdoor Pursuits Centre in Harlow, Essex, positioned in full view of the climbing wall - I quit that gym because of the one guy who was always in there pulling a weird smile/grimace while he was working out and one time we accidentally made eye contact.

There was my university gym, in which all the TVs played MTV with the volume up - I quit that one because it was the Crazy Frog era and honestly, who wants to have sex that much anyway? There was the Fitness First in West London where they teased me with the promise of a new swimming pool, coming soon, it's getting closer, look, builders are building it, we have temporary changing rooms until it opens, it's opening in two weeks, imagine: swimming in your lunch break at work, the dream, you're finally going to do it, you're finally going to get the body you've always wanted and it's all down to swimming, and then the week it opened they doubled the membership fee, and honestly, who wants to have sex that much anyway?

There was the little gym near work, which was convenient and cheap and perfect except for the fact that there would always be one or more men from the office in the changing rooms who would insist on doing small-talk with me while they talc-ed their balls off. I will quit your gym in a heartbeat if you have communal showers, or even if you don't have communal showers but there's always an old guy walking around with his wang out: I don't need this in my life, I will take my belly elsewhere, good sir.

I never did find my perfect gym, and I'm starting to think I never will find one where I'm the only member and it costs less than a tenner per month and also it's powered by magic so I don't really have to do anything. I have, however, found a solution that works for me. Running. I'm talking about running. I'm going to write about running now.

I am not an idiot, I am aware of how much I can bore off: if I could see the live analytics tracking the readers of this book, this would be the point you all churn the fuck out of here. There is nothing more likely to facilitate a full-on eye-roll than someone telling you how running solved all of their problems. But, guys: running solved all of my- no, wait, *okay okay okay*, I'm sorry.

Let me try a different sales pitch. Running is intensely private: you can do as much as you want or as little as you want and nobody else needs to be involved or even needs to know about it - all you have to contend with is the runners running the opposite direction who might occasionally give you a nod or a good morning, and that's it. Nobody knows how far you've run or for how long you've been running, so there's no need for macho competitiveness as per the gym, and there's no shame for taking it steady and going slow. Also, if necessary, you can downgrade from running to walking, and it still counts as exercise: I checked, it's legit.

Running is also free: invest in a decent pair of running shoes and a bit of kit, and that's it, that's your only outlay - no more gnawing sense of guilt every month when £50 goes out of your bank account straight into a black hole.

The best thing about running is that it gets you outside, and because you can vary your route, it's as boring or as interesting as you make it. I mean, it's still essentially pumping two meaty leg pistons back and forth repeatedly if you want to get technical, but you can find yourself a nice route - maybe by some water! - and when the mind wanders or you get lost in an album or a particularly good murder podcast, it's amazing how quickly you forget you're exercising.

Granted, it's not exactly going to transform you into Sir Mo Farah CBE overnight, but importantly, running feels like substantial activity and it gets the heart pumping, delaying your inevitable death by cardiac arrest by days, maybe even weeks. Most importantly, it allows you to join the cool running cliques at work and means you finally get to talk in the lingo, measuring distances by 'k' and calling running routes 'loops' and pretending like you might potentially have a pop at the triathlon this year. You would definitely do it if only it wasn't for your *bloody knee*.

So, to recap: run, then keep running, then run some more, then stop. Congratulations: you now have the body of a Greek god. The next thing you're going to want to focus on is the fact that you eat like shit, like a child with no responsibilities, like a recently orphaned teenager, like how Macaulay Culkin eats in Home Alone when his parents go on holiday and leave him behind in a house full of ice cream.

Maybe you are like me and you have realistic goals: you don't exercise because you want to have a fantastic body, no thank you, you exercise because you want to continue to eat like a Wonka Factory golden ticket winner and not feel quite so bad about it. Nothing motivates you to go out running like a delicious, guilt-free Domino's pizza for dinner - every mile you run earns you an extra side!

However, the flipside to that reasoning says that if you stopped rewarding yourself with junk food after running, you wouldn't have to run half as much in the first place. Hmm. Food for thought, as it were. Surely the end goal of any exercise regime is to not have to exercise at all? Otherwise before you know it you're running for fun, eating chard for the taste, casually mentioning to the guy in the smoothie shop that you've already had over and above your 5-a-day today and that this one's just a bonus, getting up early to squeeze in some squats, voluntarily eating *seeds*. We can't have that. You're just going to have to find some equilibrium - I would recommend a little bit of running and a little bit of healthy eating, which coincidentally leaves room for a little bit of donuts.

For maybe the first year of your child's life, cooking an evening meal is just not something that's going to happen, ever, not even once. You will gain two stone minimum: fact. You'll look back on previous Facebook profile photos with envious eyes. Don't sweat it. It's perfectly natural. You've just spent your every waking hour preventing a small suicidal person from dying 1000 different ways, you are forgiven for not wanting to steam a multitude of vegetables.

Ready Meals are made for new parents: become close personal friends with your microwave and ignore it at your peril. Do you want to put Rustlers out of business? Do you want Uncle Ben to have to work into his eighties? Is that what you want? For Christ's sake, man, put down the kale and just put a pizza in the oven. A baby is a free pass for a fat arse. You've got nine months before junior puts a huge dent in your diet just by existing.

I am possibly not the best person available to advise on a nutritious lifestyle. It is too late for me and my waistline: do not weep for me, I am in a better place (a Pizza Hut). But I still have memories of how I used to eat, pre-parenthood. Low-fat pork cutlets. Feta salads. Broiled chicken. Homemade hummus. Curried lentils and pitas and falafel. Inventive pasta recipes, back when you knew the pasta by name and not just by shape. Non-bacon-based breakfasts. Fistfuls of fresh rocket. Eggs done interestingly. Bruschetta as a naughty treat. Fruit for a snack, I swear to god. The foreign cuisine phases - Moroccan tagine! Lebanese mezze! Italian food cooked from ingredients exclusively bought in a Carluccio's on that week you got a tax rebate! It sounds weird to say it now, but: crunchy lettuce. New potatoes instead of chips. Butternut squash instead of new potatoes. Fish for main. *Fish for main!*

But that was a lifetime ago, two small lifetimes ago if you want to be specific. I am now the living embodiment of the 'Before' photo on a slimming drink label. Heed my warning from the future: ditch Deliveroo, stock up the vegetable drawer in your fridge, consider a smoothie for breakfast and attempt to look after yourself while the concept of 'you' still matters. Bide your time, because the era of the thrice-weekly takeaway will come, but the name of the game pre-baby is damage limitation. Fight the fat as valiantly as possible before parenthood dawns and you eventually give yourself over to a lard-based lifestyle.

There are other ways to utilise the weeks and months before baby drama consumes you - like, off the top of my head, preparing for exactly how you're going to cope with your entire life being turned upside down, inside out and flip-reversed - but for now, you can do a lot worse than mastering the fine arts of D.I.Y., driving and discovering what dill actually is.

Oh, and if you have time before the birth of your child, try to develop an uncanny financial nous, amass a flawless knowledge of history, geography and politics, squeeze in some guitar lessons, learn all those languages, finally finish your art history degree and take that trial at West Ham your uncle always said you should go for.

Congratulations, you're now well on the way to becoming an awe-inspiring physical specimen and an all-round Superdad, just like me! You're welcome!

#5

Learn the Lingo: The A-Z of Having a Baby, Decoded

L et's pause and take stock of our journey together thus far. You have to come to terms with the fact you're having a baby. You're in a healthy state of mind. You have proved yourself to not be completely useless around the house. The warm-up is just about over: it's time to begin your education proper. It's time... to learn!

This is the bit of the book that is most like other baby books, and for that all I can do is apologise, but to be fair, you can't expect it to all be fun larks and vaguely appropriate anecdotes. You're having a baby, man! You need to at least know what a few of the words mean! Nodding and smiling and pretending you understand isn't going to cut it as a survival tactic for much longer. You need to get learnt, son. Baby School is in session.

Once you dip your first toe into parenthood, you'll quickly find it is a world unto itself, with its own subculture, its own pricing plan and its own encyclopaedia. The ladies might be forced to take the final exam, but the entire baby industry is fully expecting you to flunk on the revision. They want you to be clueless, so they can swoop in with their outrageously priced conveniences. *Let us take care of the complicated baby stuff with our wide range of products and services*, they seem to say. *Enter your PIN number and absolve yourself of responsibility!* But no. You are a modern man. You promised to be present, to be a part of the process, to help lighten the load. You are just going to have to suck it up and do what you always feared you must: learn and retain a small amount of new information. I know, it's the last thing you wanted to happen. But you can do it. And hey, look, this book is here to help! I'm not here to flim-flam you out of your money, I already have your money!

The Babyverse can be a complicated and confusing place, so read the A-Z below and use every atom of your available brain power to memorise these wacky new terms. One day, you might accidentally use one of them in the correct context, and honestly, the microbe of respect you'll earn is enough to make it all worthwhile.

A

Anaemia

This is a fairly common ailment for women during pregnancy. Mild anaemia is down to a lack of red blood cells, which means it's more difficult to carry oxygen around the body, which can result in the mother feeling tired. And yes, having 'tiredness' be a symptom of a medical condition during pregnancy is not helpful in the slightest, seeing as 'being tired' is a pretty constant factor throughout every single day of pregnancy, and every single subsequent day of parenthood too. It's a shame really, because divorced from context, 'Anaemia' would make quite a pretty name for a baby girl.

Antenatal classes

In layman's terms, Antenatal classes - also known as NTC classes - are parenting classes. They represent an opportunity to be in a friendly environment with other people who are in the same stages of pregnancy that you are, so you all get to be thick together. Common tasks include learning how to put on a nappy (on a baby, not on yourself), bathing (the baby, not y- okay fine I'll stop) and sitting on a cold, hard, thinly-carpeted floor of a classroom while you practice breathing techniques. None of these activities are things you cannot learn by yourself at home, but they can be a great opportunity to meet other people, specifically other parents, who won't mind the topic of conversation being 100% baby-related.

There are some antenatal class archetypes who will be present at every session: there's the couple on your course who'll you get on with like a house on fire; the obnoxious couple who you'll wish were trapped in a house on fire; the couple who are too loud; the couple you can tell won't be back next week; the couple who find the fake plastic poos altogether too hilarious; and the one weird guy with a beard who's there on his own who claims his wife got stuck in traffic but no one's ever met her.

Antenatal classes are non-essential, but when your partner is stuck at home after the baby is born and she has no one to talk to, NTC friends can be a valuable lifeline. Personally, we went to the first Antenatal class to see what it was like and didn't feel the need to go back, but that was probably more to do with the fact we had to change Tube trains three times to travel five stops, which I think you'll agree is a fair trade off for potentially making some friends for life.

Apgar Score

This is a term that is of use for one five minute window, immediately after the baby's birth. Doctors will rate your baby's health after the first minute and the fifth minute to determine whether or not they need any additional treatment. The Apgar Score is marked out of 10, with a maximum of two points awarded per category: skin colour, heart-rate, reflexes and responsiveness, muscle tone and breathing rate. If junior is scoring less than 7 out of 10 after the first five minutes, they may need further monitoring. It's not really something you need to concern yourself with, but Pushy Dads will no doubt use this opportunity to begin being disappointed with their children's test scores from an extremely early age.

B

Babywearing

This is the act of hands-free parenting. Whether it's done via harness, sling or some other ancient contraption, babywearing is a blessed activity that allows you to truss your baby up in an inescapable cloth prison pressed tight against your person, leaving you free to move, to travel, to live. It's great, and as an added bonus, for some reason, men babywearing makes loads of old twats furious, as if having a baby strapped to your chest instead of in a pram represents some sort of failure of manhood. Use both your free hands to flip off these miserable old codgers. Practically, your best option is to check out any local 'sling library' that may operate nearby, where you can rent a sling on a short-term basis rather than fork out for something that will gather dust when baby becomes too large a garment to wear. It is possible to put on a sling yourself, but there are lots of straps and knots and pulleys involved so you might feel comfortable getting your partner involved in any essential holding or hoisting. The small amount of back pain you may feel as a result of babywearing is tolerable and not nearly as bad as carrying around two aching, milk-filled tits all day long, so cram it.

Whether you opt for front-facing or face-to-face baby wearing is your call: with baby facing out, strapped to you like a human GoPro, they get to soak in the whole wide world while on the move, but having them face you allows for maximum booping.

Birth Plan

Women will start work on their birth plan before the piss is even dry on their test. It is like a wishlist for their preferred method of giving birth: where they'd like to do it, how you're going to get there, who's going to be involved and what they're going to be wearing. It is your job to pretend like you have any control over any of this.

Breastfeeding or Bottle Feeding

The choice may not even be yours: if baby doesn't latch onto the nipple, then you might be bottle-bound. Both options will result in healthy babies, but if we're being selfish here - and if you'll remember the title of the book, it's clear that this is the reason you're here - then breastfeeding is more convenient and cheaper, while bottle feeding is less painful for her and more hassle for you. Not that you can ever admit that to anyone.

There are numerous additional benefits to your partner breastfeeding your baby, but just because you don't have to mix the formula and heat up the bottle at every ungodly hour of the day, don't be fooled into thinking you're off the hook. Breastfeeding and all the aggro that comes with it means your partner has a god-given right to ask you to do absolutely anything for the next few years.

Breech Birth

A breech birth is when baby decides to be born ass-first, following your example of how you've lived your entire life. This can present an issue, as it may surprise you to learn that babies are not really supposed to be born ass-first. Heading into the last month of pregnancy, the ideal position is when baby is 'engaged', locked and loaded with its head in the womb and its ass in the air like it just don't care. If you're entering your final four weeks of pregnancy and baby is still ass-first, an obstetrician might try and perform an ECV, an 'External cephalic version', which is basically them prodding and pushing your partner's belly to try and flip your baby into an un-ass-first position, while she is injected with drugs to relax her uterus. It sounds extremely uncomfortable but not nearly as uncomfortable as giving birth to a baby ass-first.

C

Caesarean

An emergency exit scenario, when a vaginal birth is not viable for health reasons, and baby needs to be removed via a small incision in the abdomen. This is kind of like when a door is locked in an action movie and the next shot is of the hero just busting through the drywall next to the door. Okay, it's nothing like that, I'm just trying to dumb things down to the appropriate level. Birth by caesarean section might sound like some Hannibal-esque method of torture but it is relatively common; around one fifth of all births in the UK are delivered by caesarean. The procedure does leave a small scar and is obviously very painful for your partner once the pain relief - and general shock of giving birth - wears off, so she should probably stop doing her ab crunches. That means that you should probably ease up on the exercise too, you know, in solidarity.

Calpol

Calpol is a form of syrupy pink pain relief for babies over 2 months old, and it fixes everything. It's essentially liquid gold. It still tastes great, and even the smell can take you back to your own childhood. Reminder: it is not purple drank and you are not

Flavor Flav. Stop hogging all the infant pain relief and let your sick kid have some, you bloody lunatic.

Cravings

While it's true that your partner may develop cravings for a certain type of food, it's rare that she'll be jonesing for lumps of coal or anything unusual, and it's way more likely she'll be averse to strong-tasting or strong-smelling foods that may cause nausea. Unfortunately, that means the majority of your cooking. Beware also the myth of 'eating for two': although your partner is supporting a second life-form inside her, the recommended additional calorie consumption per day for a pregnant woman amounts to no more than an extra slice of buttered toast, although obviously you should never say this out loud if you value your genitals.

Curry

Some people recommend eating a curry during the last throes of pregnancy to attempt to kick-start the birth process, but one under-reported side-effect of this is that your masala farts are almost certainly going to stink out the maternity unit.

D

Doula

A doula is a professional who is not medically trained - so basically just 'a woman' - who your partner may wish to hire to lend her a helping hand during the birth process. Doulas will have almost certainly been through birth themselves, otherwise they're taking the piss. Their job is to coach your partner through the tough bits, advise where appropriate and lend emotional, moral and spiritual support throughout the ordeal, all of which does tend to beg the question: what the fuck are *you* for? Although helpful, doulas can be prone to overstepping their remit in a hospital environment and as such are often frowned upon by trained medical staff, so if it wasn't for the fact that you will be busy having a baby, it might have been fun to observe the power dynamic between them from the sidelines.

Down Syndrome

Pre-birth screenings are offered to parents to find out whether your baby is at risk of being born with Down Syndrome. For mothers aged 25, the odds are around 1 in 1,200; for those aged 35, it's around 1 in 350; any pregnant women in their late 40s are looking at a rate of around 1 in 10. You won't find out straight away, and instead will face an agonising wait of several weeks before a letter casually plops through your letterbox with the results. This is a pretty good primer for parenthood in general: spending more time than necessary feeling anxious about things that probably won't happen.

E

Engorgement or Expressing

When you become a parent, you will be older and wiser, and as such, you will begin to appreciate breasts on a whole new level. So, yes, although the beginning of milk production brought on by breastfeeding will result in slightly larger and plumper boobs, just know that they will feel like they are full of lava, and you gawping at them will not help. The quickest way to relieve breast engorgement is to express milk by hooking the boobs up to breast-pumps, which are, shall we say, less than sexy. All in all it's a very confusing time for your erection.

Epidural

The epidural is something of a contradiction in terms, given that it is pain relief that takes the form of a big fucking needle in the base of the spine.

Episiotomy

I'm not going to dress this one up: an episiotomy is when the doctor snips your lady's taint from arsehole to fanny. This is to allow for, and it says here, 'widening of the vagina' during birth. Try not to think too much about it. I mean, I know I said it was time to concentrate and to educate yourself, but this is just ridiculous.

F

FADS

This stands for 'Fetal Alcohol Spectrum Disorder'. This is the special kind of way you can fuck up your baby by drinking alcohol during pregnancy. In a nutshell, the mother's boozy blood flows through the placenta to the baby and can affect formation of the brain and organs with lasting effects. The recommended number of units to drink during pregnancy is zero, zip, nada, nothing. If you can imagine such a thing.

You should all be well aware of the irony of pregnancy being the most stressful period of your entire life, and that you're not able to drink through it. Maybe it's time to get to grips with the fact that alcohol is a shitty coping mechanism anyway, and both of you knock off the booze for a bit? And even though *your* drinking won't directly affect the baby, maybe don't be a massive prick and do it anyway?

Folic Acid

I don't know, actually. Let me check. Shit, it turns out it's actually quite important, my bad. Folate, or folic acid, is a vitamin that can help prevent birth defects. As such, expecting mothers may want to eat a diet that features vegetables, fruit, nuts and eggs, or they can supplement their existing diet with folic acid pills, which can be picked up from your local pharmacy. It is actually terrifying how little I knew about the birth of my own children. From this point on, I'm definitely paying attention.

Foetus

I know this one: it's another word for 'baby'. See? I know what I'm talking about! Just make sure you don't ever actually refer to your baby as a 'foetus' though, because it feels super-creepy, and it's usually heard along with the words 'in a jar'.

G

Gas and Air

Precious air I could kiss you, if only you weren't such a gaseous entity! Gas and air is a readily available supply of pain relief that can be honked upon merrily during labour in order to dull some of the more painful bits. When compared to something like the epidural it's not exactly a hardcore drug pipe that's going to take you round the Moon and back, but I have been assured it takes the edge off. You can have a go when no one is looking if you like. You have to get your kicks while there's still time. I once got into an argument with a childless woman who claimed that using gas and air during labour technically didn't count as a natural birth because you were still relying on something with chemicals in it, and in my head I suplexed her through a garden fence. I have to say, it was extremely satisfying.

Guthrie Test

Also known as the heel prick, also known as the first time physical harm comes to your offspring, also known as CALM DOWN LEAVE IT MATE SHE'S NOT WORTH IT. There's a good reason for it, of course, it's not just to satisfy some sadist urge of the nurses in the maternity unit: a needle is pricked in baby's heel and the resulting blood test is essential to catch early signs of an underlying conditions your tot may or may not have. It's optional, but if you don't allow them to do it, there will still be exactly one prick in the room.

My wife used to be a phlebotomist at Great Ormond Street Children's Hospital and regularly used to have to take blood from the children of model Katie Price. This one time, Katie's mum had a go at my wife and genuinely accused her of being sick and enjoying causing pain to little children. So, y'know, that explains a lot about that family.

H

Hair

Yes, we all know what 'hair' is, well done. But did you know that a woman's hair might become either significantly thicker or thinner during pregnancy? This is due to changes in the levels of oestrogen, which can cause the growing cycle of hair to last longer than usual. Alternatively, when a woman comes off of birth control, her oestrogen levels can drop, which might cause her hair to become thinner or even start falling out. Just a friendly reminder that pregnant women live a daily hell that you know nothing about.

Hand, Foot and Mouth Disease

It's not just for cows. Hand, Foot and Mouth Disease might not have a catchy name, but it does what it says on the tin and it's a shitty thing for your youngster to catch. Baby will get a fever and nasty blisters on their - yep, you guessed it - hands, feet and mouth. For information on how to treat it, see: Calpol.

Haemorrhoids

Need more proof that women are superheroes? The absolute sex festival of hormones coursing through your pregnant partner's body is liable to cause all sorts of bladder problems and issues with bottoms both front and back. So, on top of gestating an actual human being inside their reproductive organs, their own body starts falling to pieces. Constipation is common, and piles are just the cherry on the cake, as it were. Sorry, bad analogy.
Remember the other day when you complained because you had a headache then you took one paracetamol and then it went away almost instantly? You are a piece of shit.

Hypnobirthing

Once dismissed as a sort of hippy-dippy birthing plan for people who don't wear shoes or cut their hair, hypnobirthing is actually a very straightforward and sensible option for mothers-to-be who want to take control of their birth. It's all about creating a calming and soothing environment in which to have a baby, using techniques that are designed to ease the tension that can be the cause of so much pain during childbirth. It's just a shame it's tainted with a name that makes it sound like some sort of primetime Saturday night Paul McKenna ITV entertainment extravaganza.

I

IVF

This stands for 'In Vitro Fertilisation' but you don't need this because you're already pregnant. However, the simple act of having a baby - or even just being in the room when a baby is had - means you really should know what this stuff means. Essentially, this is a very complex (and expensive) scientific technique whereby a woman's eggs are removed from her ovaries and are impregnated with sperm in a lab, before being implanted back in the womb. Even then, the chances of falling pregnant can be as low as 1 in 10. You're one of the lucky ones, pal, and don't you forget it.

Induced Labour

The human body is a well-oiled machine, but even the oiliest of machines need a jump-start every now and then. Even though your missus is obviously well and truly up the duff, it's not necessarily a guarantee that baby will come out when it's supposed to. Sometimes they just get so cosy in the little home that you've made for them, they don't want to leave. Another, less cutesy way of looking at it is that it's fucking dangerous for babies to stay in the womb for any longer than necessary, and as their landlord, you need to eject your unruly tenant, like, *pronto*. Inducing labour artificially can be done in many ways, all of which are excruciating: the cervix may be opened mechanically, your partner's waters might need to be broken manually, or medicine might be needed to start contractions. Induced labours are almost always more painful than the regular kind, because baby will need to be monitored more closely, and there are numerous additional health concerns to consider. I'm running out of ways to tell you that you have won the life lottery by being born male, but that doesn't stop it from being true.

J

Jaundice

An extremely common ailment for newborns, jaundice affects around 60% of full-term babies and up to 80% of premature kiddos. It takes the form of yellow skin brought on by a chemical caused by red blood cells breaking down, and it makes your kid look like an off-brand Simpson toy bought from a covered market. It's not dangerous and it usually goes away after a couple of weeks. Brilliantly, one of the ways you can combat jaundice is to put the baby on a windowsill in direct sunlight, like a pie in a Tom and Jerry cartoon.

K

Kegels

Childbirth does tend to leave a trail of destruction in its wake when it comes to the female genitalia - you can imagine that when the Incredible Hulk busts through a door, it doesn't exactly swing on its hinges like it used to. Kegel exercises are designed to strengthen the pelvic floor i.e. the muscles that prevent one from pissing one's self. Kegels can be done pre-childbirth or post, although the latter is almost literally the definition of closing the stable door after the horse has bolted.
You can also do Kegel exercises, because for men these muscles control many things including ejaculation. Arguably that's how you ended up in this mess in the first place, so maybe put your pelvis on ice for a few more years.

L

Labour

You think you know what it is, but you have no idea when it begins, not really, and you certainly have no idea when it ends. Hint: it's longer than you think, and it's also even longer than that. Like the political party of the same name, labour is essential in order to facilitate good things, but it's also endlessly exhausting and frustrating and painful, to the point where, in your darkest moment, you may find yourself thinking, god, life would have been so much easier if I'd just voted Tory/had an abortion.

Let-Down Reflex

Truly, the let-down reflex is a form of ye olde magick and/or witchcraft. It's the physical act of the female body letting milk flow through the breast, and it can be brought on by many forms of stimulus, including baby sucking on the nipple, or, incredibly, hearing a baby cry or *even just looking at a picture of a baby*. You could line up all of the world's foremost biologists and maternity experts and have them explain this to me until their throats are sore, but I'd still be suspicious of them and would follow them home and watch them all walk through a solid brick wall at the train platform at King's Cross and be all like 'Aha!'

M

Meconium

Baby's first shit, so epic it gets a special Latin name all to itself. The Meconium dump is different from your regular baby turds in that it is composed of all the yummy nutrients ingested while in the uterus, like, mmmm, amniotic fluid, bile and mucus. It's dark and tar-like in substance, and though it is claimed it is odourless, this is because no one has ever had the guts to inhale within three feet of Meconium - having particles of this bad boy sucked into your lungs feels like a Spider-Man supervillain origin story waiting to happen.

Miscarriage

Let's get serious for a bit, he says, the words 'Spider-Man supervillain' hovering incongruously just millimetres away.

Miscarriages are devastating. I cannot begin to imagine the distress they would cause to expectant parents: to build that excitement, to have made that bond, and then to lose it... I can only imagine the bottomless heartbreak you'd feel. There's nothing that can be said that will soften that blow, but the fact is that miscarriages are common (up to one in five pregnancies end in miscarriage before 20 weeks) and not necessarily a sign that full-term pregnancies are not viable. Most women who suffer a miscarriage will go on to have a healthy pregnancy at a later date. So it doesn't have to be the end: you just need to keep the faith, bravely put yourself back together somehow and try, try again.

Uhh, I mean... um, cuh, pop culture references, having a baby is just like Game of Thrones isn't it lads, grrr, lads and dads, beers beers beers, football goals etc.

Morning Sickness

Another ailment that only highlights the litany of ways you lucked out by being born with a dick, morning sickness will be felt by most women within the first three months of pregnancy, and takes the form of nausea, vomiting and loss of appetite. There's no real way to avoid it, other than easing off spicy and fatty foods - it's just something that needs to be endured. Literally all you are good for is holding back her hair while she pukes. You did this. It's all your fault. Accept it. This one's on you. Take the L, big guy.

Muslins

Somehow, I was unaware of muslins before having a baby, they just never entered my life. After having a baby, however, I am not exaggerating when I say we couldn't have lived without them. Muslins are basically all-purpose cloths, thin little rags for wiping, soaking, dabbing, washing. They are invaluable. They will become your best friends. You will find it physically impossible to perform any baby-related task without one, and you shouldn't be more than two feet from one at all times. If you and baby leave the house without at least three muslins, you are both coming back caked in god knows what: guaranteed.

N

Nipple Thrush

Do I really need to go into this? Because I really don't want to. The description online features lots of words like 'yeast fungus' and 'white patches' and 'bleeding'. You get it. You regret having a functioning penis. That's the main takeaway here. The message has been received. Go and give your partner a back rub right fucking now. Imagine how long, hard and loud you would complain if there was such a thing as penile thrush.

O

Obstetrician

This is the medical professional who is trained in baby preparation in all the ways that you are not. The obstetrician is the person who does all the regular checks with your partner as her pregnancy progresses, providing prenatal care, postnatal care, all the natals are covered. In the movies, obstetricians are always hunky and tanned male models who look like Chace Crawford and the husband characters always get jealous because they get to go between the sexy wife's legs and [checks notes] give them smear tests.

Orgasms

It's rare, but it's real: around 0.3% of women have reported epic, earth-shattering orgasms at the precise moment of childbirth. Now, orgasms are great, and childbirth is also great, but these two things don't really go together. The male equivalent is you spaffing your pants at the precise moment you pass your driving test. The sensation, unsurprisingly, is caused by intense pressure on the vaginal canal during childbirth, and in some cases is brought on when the baby's head hits the woman's G-spot. A lot of weird shit happens during childbirth, stuff you'll witness with your own eyes that you will never, ever mention again, but splooging on your baby's head is a total mood-killer.

P
Pâté

Another thing to add to the pregnancy shit-list: all the types of food that preggos can't eat. You can, but she can't, which essentially means you can't. And for some reason, the list of banned foods are some of the best foods: liver pâté, honey, sushi, prawns, soft cheese - a mad king's M&S banquet that's now completely out of bounds. Oh boohoo, isn't your life shit now, no prawns for nine months, how will you ever cope? The answer is, you eat them for lunch while at work, where no one will ever ask you accusing questions or start sniffing your clothes for hints of thousand island dressing.

Placenta

Some fun facts about the placenta. Fun fact #1: technically, the placenta is an organ that develops during pregnancy and is passed after childbirth, which is not gross at all in any way, how dare you. Fun fact #2: the placenta is an essential part of pregnancy and it filters oxygen, glucose and other nutrients through to your baby. It's a good guy! Fun fact #3: the placenta can also kill mother and baby if left to its own devices. It's exactly like a heel in the WWE: a crowd-pleasing journeyman providing a valuable service who is nonetheless liable to pivot on a sixpence and go rogue, slamming your loved ones with a metaphorical metal chair.

Some people like to eat their placenta after it has been passed, but I regret to inform you that every single last one of those people went on to be possessed by Satan, and that is an indisputable medical fact.

Plagiocephaly

It sounds like something you'd see in Jurassic Park, but actually it's a medical condition, more specifically the condition of baby having a weird-shaped head. Because babies are barely formed human beings, there's still a lot of their insides that have yet to solidify or knit together, including muscle tone and the skull. So, depending on the position they were locked into in the uterus, your baby may very well be born a Conehead. Either that or they might look like a Dick Tracy villain for a little while. It's cool, they always go back to normal after a little while, just resist the temptation to laugh. Oh, look at you, the big man with his big solid skull.

Postpartum Depression / Postnatal Depression

So, to summarise: the missus went through several weeks of morning sickness and nausea, her hair started falling out, she got haemorrhoids, she suffered a horribly painful labour in which she was split in two like an overripe melon and she has a tiny human being clamped on her nipple while she's being sewn up again. It is a cosmic joke, then, that after suffering through and surviving all of the above, many women may also suffer from postnatal depression (also known as postpartum depression). This is like getting a shit sandwich for dessert after a main course of sautéed turds. Postnatal depression is common (as many as 1 in 5 may suffer it), it can affect all women regardless of how painful or trauma-free her birth was, and it can last upwards of two or three days in the first week of motherhood. This is a feeling that extends beyond the usual 'down in the dumps' mood you might expect to feel after experiencing something as volcanic as childbirth: yes, she'll be exhausted and worried and seven flavours of anxious, but postnatal depression also rears its head in the form of feelings of inadequacy, guilt and hopelessness. I shouldn't need to say it but will: it is your job to be your partner's support system and bow down to the warrior woman she has proven herself to be. If the depression starts to get more serious and doesn't evaporate after a short while, the best thing you can do is take it seriously and speak to your GP as soon as you're able.

Q

Quickly Moving On

Look, I respect you too much to pretend there's an important baby-related word that you need to learn that begins with 'Q' but there isn't, there just isn't, so let's not waste any more of my time or yours and get on with it, shall we?

R

Reflux

Reflux is not the same as vomiting - it's way less forceful and violent - but the end result is the same: liquids dribbling out of your baby's mush. It's generally little more than air and milk which might be regurgitated during burping after a feed, because babies don't really know when they've had enough, and they have a loose little sphincter which prevents their stomachs from holding onto the good stuff. In some cases, they don't even notice they've done it. Total pissheads the lot of them. Being spit-up on is a rite of passage: if you don't have milky white residue on your shoulder at all times, are you even a parent?

Rash

Oho, will you ever become familiar with rashes. Spotty rashes. Red rashes. Angry rashes. Prickly rashes. Placid rashes. Heat rashes. You will be convinced that each and every one of them is meningitis. You know the glass test, right? Push a see-through glass against the rash: if they fade to white under the pressure, it's nothing to worry about; if it stays red and splotchy and doesn't fade, then fine, just this once you were right, it *might* be meningitis. Stop bragging you idiot, call a doctor!

S

Skin to Skin Contact

Understandably, the birthing process is frightfully tense for baby as well as everyone else in the room, so one way of calming it down is to clean it up and plonk it down on the mother's bare chest. This skin-to-skin contact regulates both baby's heartbeat and temperature, and it aids in the production of milk for the all-important first feed. It also makes for a fucking first-rate Facebook profile pic, provided all the goo has been cleaned up first. Attention! Dad job incoming! Skin-to-skin contact can be performed with you too. Slapping your newborn down on your chest will help you bond with your new baby, and it'll release floods of oxytocin - often known as the 'cuddle hormone' by people who probably aren't scientists - into your body that will make you feel high as a kite. So consider that before you coat your entire body in half a can of Lynx Africa before you leave for the hospital.

Sophie the Giraffe

A middle-class baby chew toy that marks you and your baby out as modern sophisticates - she's from France, don't you know! Sophie, or 'Sophie la Girafe' to call her by her official name, is awfully pretentious for something that gets gnawed on by drooling idiots, and there's something unsettling about her dead-black dot eyes, but there's no doubt she's the most high class of all the pop culture giraffes. Sorry, Geoffrey Giraffe, but since Toys 'R' Us went into administration you just have nothing we want.

Stretch and Sweep

The stretch and sweep is one of many methods that your midwife or doctor may perform to try and kick-start and overdue labour. It's not a clever name - it consists of a couple of lubed-up fingers inserted into the vagina and wiggled around to try and get things moving. This is the pregnancy version of twiddling a remote control's batteries to make it work.

Public service announcement: when my wife used to work as a maternity assistant, there was a doctor on the ward who was a stretch and sweep specialist, who was known as 'Bobby Big Hands'. Please consult your local maternity unit to learn of any potentially off-putting nicknames in advance.

Swaddling

The act of wrapping a baby up tightly in a blanket to replicate the restriction they felt when in the womb. Cuh, not very receptive to change, are they? Quit living in the past! Swaddling is quite a lot like making a burrito if the filling was a baby, except the worst case scenario with a burrito is that you might spill chilli beef down your shirt, whereas with swaddling the worst case scenario is your baby accidentally rolls over onto its face holes. So get good at making burritos while you can.

T

TENS Machine

This one stands for 'Transcutaneous electrical nerve stimulation', and I'll never understand for the life of me why they couldn't bolt an extra 'E' word on the end of the acronym to make it a TENSE machine, because effectively its sole purpose is to combat tension and reduce pain. The TENS (ugh) machine consists of two electrodes that your lady attaches to her skin, which deliver a small electrical current that results in a slight tingle. In terms of pain relief, this is very much in the vein of sticking a plaster on an amputated foot.

Lots of pregnancy websites are very careful to caveat the actual medical benefits of TENS machines because there appears to be precisely no scientific evidence that they actually work. However, many of them are keen to mention that "some women find it helpful" and because no man can ever question those credentials it looks like you're just going to have to pretend the robot orgasm machine is definitely a thing.

Twins/Triplets

Hahahahaha unlucky. I am unqualified to comment on how difficult life as a dad would be with twins, or god forbid triplets, but for a rough approximation, maybe take heed of all the warnings contained within this book and then somehow imagine all of them being twice as bad.

There are certainly a number of benefits of having twins, including having two kids via one pregnancy, and combining two kids' worth of stress into one convenient breakdown.

U

Ultrasound

Q: Who's the coolest person on the maternity ward? A: The ultrasound technician. The 20-week scan is undoubtedly one of the highlights of pregnancy. Your partner has to suffer through four months of nausea, hormones and anxiety, but once you hit that halfway mark, you get the mother of all pick-me-ups: you get to see your baby. While it's still in the womb! Via magic! Or technology, whatever. It's still a miracle. Ultrasounds are especially exciting for Dads. The Mums get to foster that bond with baby on an intensely personal level - like a landlord/tenant relationship based on love rather than greed. Outside of a few stray kicks to the belly, Dads don't really get to experience that connection until the baby is born, but the ultrasound is a true gift: a brief glimpse of your little one chilling in its crib like it's a real person with arms and legs and a head and everything. It's like a window to another world - a womb with a view, if you will.

All of these jokes are public domain, you can't sue me. The ultrasound is usually the moment where Dads who haven't quite grasped the magnitude of the situation have the metaphorical 10,000 tonne weight dropped on their head. It's real, it's happening, and you can't ignore the adorable little responsibility any longer.

V

Vasectomy

Well it's a little too late for that. If you're content with making just the one miniature clone of yourself, then you may opt to have your tubes tied with a vasectomy. This is a brief medical procedure in which your vasa deferentia - the ducts which carry sperm to your urethra - are cut and tied or sealed to prevent your swimmers from gaining access to your semen. In most cases, a vasectomy causes a temporary inflammation of the nads, but is otherwise painless. It's a noble and effective method of birth control, and it's reversible if you are chronically indecisive.

Getting the snip post-baby is probably the most sympathy you are likely to receive in the genital pain department, even if it is the equivalent of a last minute consolation goal in a 10-1 drubbing.

Ventouse

Ooh, what's this? 'Ventouse' sounds fancy, like a first-class holiday resort on the Amalfi Coast, or a fine wine that Frasier might drink. Ah, hang on. It says here a 'ventouse' is a hoover that's used to suck your baby out of the birth canal, like something from The Jetsons. Yes, that is considerably less classy.

W

Water Birth

This is almost certainly at the top of your partner's wishlist for her birth plan. Water births have numerous benefits, including but not limited to: less painful contractions, less need for drugs or an epidural, and the general relief of being submerged in water during a genital apocalypse, which, as I understand them, might sting a bit. There are a few small additional risks, like the possibility of baby swallowing water or getting an infection, and that you might get put off jacuzzis for a bit.

Weaning

It's a long way off and not something you need to worry about for a while, but weaning is the act of getting baby off the boob and onto the hard stuff. No, not alcohol: solid food. It's a sensitive subject for many mothers due to the intense personal connection felt during breastfeeding, so don't feel like you need to rush it when you hit that six month mark - this is when babies can tolerate solid food, it's not when they need to go cold turkey on the nips. There are three types of weaning: mutual, mother-led or baby-led. Mother-led weaning will be dictated by your partner depending on her schedule, patience and tolerance for gawping arsecakes who complain about public breastfeeding. Baby-led weaning is letting baby discover the joys of food, but be warned, there will be gagging, choking and lots of mess on your floor. Mutual weaning is that perfect situation where mother and baby both decide it's the right time to quit together. Yeah, maybe don't get your hopes up for that one, or for anything else, ever again.

X

XXX-Rated Sex

I hate to be the one to break it to you, but know this: you are not going to be having any. Yes, you will both still have a sex drive, yes, there's something aesthetically pleasing about a pregnant body and yes, you can still have sex, but it'll be uncomfortable, painful and she'll just want it to be over. So not really any different from usual, in other words. And no, you can't stab the baby with your dick. Guh, read a book, dummy! Oh, you are. Well done.

Y

Whyyyyyyyy

An exclamation common to parenthood that you will frequently utter while on your knees, cursing your past sperm for being so damn efficient.

Z

Zzz

Typically, 'Zzz' is a onomatopoeic representation of the sound that people make when they're sleeping, which is not really something you'll be doing.

There you go, that wasn't too hard, was it? Even little kids know the alphabet. You're smarter than a little kid, aren't you? All you have to do is remember all 60 of these definitions and the 7000+ words contained therein, plus all of the other hundreds of terms I couldn't remember or be bothered to make jokes out of, and you'll make the perfect father! Anyway, it's not like there's going to be some sort of pop quiz that gets sprung on you in the maternity unit and you have to bluff and style it out and you accidentally administer an episiotomy when you should have administered an epidural. Unless you're a doctor, in which case you really shouldn't be reading this book at all.

#6

Wait, What Kind of Baby
Are We Even Having?

Hey champ, how you holding up? Sounds like you're doing great. It's probably fair to say that, by now, you are at least comfortable with the *concept* of having a baby. Thinking about it now only brings you out in mild hives, and you've cut your 'freakout time' down to 30 minutes a day. Great stuff! You're slowly but surely becoming a man! We'll make a dad of you yet! [Insert Gary Lineker Italia '90 turn to camera, mouthing "Have a word with him" to an off-screen gaffer]

The thing is, old buddy, old pal of mine - and I'm being careful to use my quiet indoor voice here so as not to upset you - but it might be time to start thinking of the bigger picture, and that means in terms more diverse than just 'baby'. For instance: did you know that babies come in all different types? Boys, girls, and so on? You don't get to choose the sex, because that would be too easy; no, this piece of crucial information is rather thrust upon you. I know! So impractical!

You'd think that, with all of today's modern computers and such, we would have figured out an affordable and effective way of being able to select a baby's sex in advance, much like how one would select the colour of a new iPhone in a Carphone Warehouse. Okay, there *are* Gender Selection clinics which can use Science with a capital $ to pre-determine the sex of your baby, via a messy-sounding selection process called 'sperm sorting'. It's a very high-end mechanic which uses genetic tinkering to pre-screen for genetic diseases among other things, but you just try telling the doctor you want a blond-haired, blue-eyed 'designer baby' and not feel a *little* bit like a Nazi. Still interested? It costs about £15,000. Oh, I see, *now* it's become morally objectionable. Gotcha.

After 20 weeks of up-the-duff-ness, you and the human baby hod have to go in for another ultrasound scan. This sneak peek gives you a bit more definition on what your baby looks like. Not so much like, 'Oh shit, our baby really looks like Screech from Saved By The Bell', more in terms of 'that's baby's arm' or 'this bit is clearly baby's large melon head'. Ultrasound machines are genuinely the most incredible inventions when in full flow - using nothing more than a supermarket barcode scanner and a fistful of lube, you can see a four-month-old heart beating in the womb. I mean, that's just total witchcraft. Can't wrap my head around it. I still don't believe it's real. Maybe expectant parents are all so saucer-eyed and gullible that doctors can get away with showing the same 90 seconds of anonymous grainy baby footage they've been showing for 40 years, then charge you £45 for the privilege. I'm onto your scam, doctors.

More importantly, ultrasound #2 comes with a special bonus piece of trivia - this is when you can find out the sex of your baby. Whoah. This is massive. This is literally a question you have never been asked before. Do you want to know whether it's a boy or a girl? Pause. Consider. There's no need to blurt out an answer like you're a contestant on a gameshow. What exactly are you going to do with this information? How will it benefit you? There is no right or wrong way to do this. Obviously whether or not you want to find out is entirely down to your personal preference. If you're happy to find out the sex early, go bananas with it, tattoo it onto your arse, shout it from the rooftops - all I ask is that, if it's a boy, maybe take the temperature of the room before making any jokes about the size of baby's wang.

I often think that people who want to know their baby's sex in advance are like the people who sneak an early look at their Christmas presents. Surely part of the fun is in the waiting? The anticipation! The delight of not knowing! Anyway, it's not like you actually get to open your Christmas presents in advance - knowing what you're getting doesn't make you get them any quicker. With months left on the clock and no surprises on the agenda, maybe you start to wonder: are the Christmas presents I'm getting the right Christmas presents for me? What if I actually wanted that *other* kind of Christmas present? What if I wait all this time until Christmas and then when I finally open my Christmas presents, I'm disappointed because it turns out I wanted a PS5 instead of an Xbox all along? That's not very Christmassy.

Information can be a blessing but it can also be a curse. The more you know in advance, the more you worry, the more you'll start to project before the little bugger is even born. I've met pregnant couples who have planned out the entire life of their foetus - name, school, future girlfriend - before it had barely lost its tail. We decided we didn't want to know the sex of our kids while in utero, because had I known we were having two boys all along, I would have spent the remaining months of the pregnancies mired in upsetting flash-forwards, panicking that they would inherit my weak chin and sub-par left foot, both boys getting bullied at school for sporting my own sticky-out ears and flaky scalp. I'd have had a breakdown, like Peep Show's Mark Corrigan imagining the torture of his unborn son growing up in the shadow of his father: "He'll be just like me. It'll be like going through it all again. The P.E. hell, the stolen packed lunch, having to do a little dance and sing "I'm a gaylord" to the tune of 'Like a Virgin', although obviously the tune will be different in 11 years' time." Of course, even if I ended up having girls they would have still inherited my bargain bin DNA, but imagining your own genetic deficiencies on your offspring with the pin-sharp recall of your own awkward upbringing is enough to drive a grown man insane.

You have to have a preference: boys or girls - it's the law. Okay, it's not the law, it's just a question that you're going to be asked at least 1,700 times, so you'd better have a good answer locked and loaded in the chamber as to which you'd prefer. The diplomatic answer to the question - the politician's answer - is, of course: "I'll be happy whatever it is so long as it's healthy". Yeah, no, jog on pal, no one believes you. Wishing for a healthy baby is a given, there's no points to be scored here. I'll have none of that "As long as it has ten fingers and ten toes" bullshit - what, any form of disability would be a disappointment to you? YOU INHUMAN MONSTER.

And if you haven't had time to think it through, what with all the... er... what have you been doing again? Well, then here's a handy pros and cons list for each gender to help you make up your mind. Jesus, why don't I just raise your child for you?

BOYS

Pros

- Being born male basically sets your kid up for life. Statistics show they are more likely to get hired for big jobs and they will be paid more for doing them. They'll likely face very little discrimination in life, certainly less than their female counterparts. It's a sad but inescapable fact: the world is made for men. You've basically hit the jackpot the moment your cell cluster busts out that Y chromosome like a Nando's black card.

- Despite all of the above, you get the privilege of raising a good man, who'll be in a position to affect real change and educate other men about what it truly means to be a man in the modern age. Pass on your liberal white male guilt to your son and let him carry the cross for a bit, yeah?

- Football, WEEEEYYYYYYYYYY

- It's a cliché, but it's also true: boys are simple, straightforward creatures who know what they like and say what they mean. There is very little mystery in raising boys: if they say they want fish fingers, this is not code - it means they just witnessed, saw a picture of, or remembered the existence of fish fingers. It may come as something of a relief. As an adult male, who has presumably learned a few things on this big crazy roller coaster we call life, you will comfortably be able to outsmart and outwit them for years.

- A boy? You're a boy! A man, I mean! So when your precious little Tyson (or whoever) is struggling through puberty and is suffering the (non-existent) perils of being male, you can advise with clemency. Relax: you know where you are with a dick and balls, so to speak. You've been there, man, and you lived to tell the tale. One caveat to this is that no children, whatever their gender, will listen to anything you have to say until they are old enough to have their own children. It's the circle of life!

Cons

- Being a man in the 21st century is demonstrably more complex than it was in the 20th century. In the last millennium, it was enough to know how to kick a football, kiss a girl and drive a Ford Cortina to the bloody pub, grrr! More is expected from boys and men of this generation, and unfortunately it's down to a member of the old guard (i.e. you) to teach your son how to be a better man than you were - and you can't do that unless you're willing to better yourself first. Yes, you're right, this does sound like hard work. Oh shit, are they actually looking up to you? This is a disaster.

- Boys generally hang with other boys, and other boys are the WORST. Because we live in a society - thanks *Tony Blair* - we have to love our fellow man, but tolerating our fellow man's piece of shit son is a step too far. Just you wait until they start school and are able to wriggle free of your influence, into the sphere of other boys, with names like Hugo and Justin and Todd. Ugh.

- There's a certain parental culpability here, in having a boy. If, despite your best efforts, you end up raising a problem child, a rough lad, a bad boy - one of the aforementioned 'other boys' - then I'm afraid you're on the hook for it. "He's just like his father," the old biddies on the bus will tut and whisper. Mum gets off scot free.

- Boys are gross. This is scientific fact. Today I watched as my eldest son pretended to talk with his butt, made fart noises and sang a song about willies which he wrote himself. Something tells me girls don't write songs about fannies.

- They're really bloody loud. Sorry. Little fucking foghorns on legs. Little mobile stacked amplifiers. Portable noise machines. The sound of my boys having fun is roughly equivalent to a high-powered jet engine on your front lawn; when they get upset, the decibel level increases until it's roughly the same as cupping your ear towards a space shuttle launch.

GIRLS

Pros

- If we're talking about the modern world, then it is currently more socially acceptable for girls to be boyish and to enjoy traditionally masculine pursuits than it is for boys to undertake quote-unquote 'girly' activities and be feminine. You can have girls who like unicorns and princesses and makeup and you can also have girls who like superheroes and football and death metal. It's fucked up, because having a little girl who is into masculine stuff is seen as fun and cool and will score you Dad points, but having a boy who's into dolls will still raise eyebrows. I'm not saying these definitions are okay, because they're not, and admittedly this is less a pro of being a girl than it is a con for being a boy, but I'm into uncharted territory when talking about girls if I'm being honest, so just nod and smile so I can move on.

- If you have a baby daughter, she and your lady partner will eventually gang up on you and outnumber you two-to-one, but that's probably what you need to keep your bloody mental testosterone levels in check (so much friggin' manhood!) and it's secretly what you want to make you a more level-headed person.

- At least at first, you get a free opt-out for gender-specific aspects of parenting. Stuff like braiding hair, advising on bras and tampons, anything to do with clothing. This temporary timeout doesn't last forever, but once you dive into the wonderful world of raising girls and start to get good at it, you will glow with the self-satisfaction that comes from being a cool dad who can do all these things and more. I assume. Again, I have no idea.

- Eventually, after years of waiting, you get to play the role of Concerned Father to Dating-Age Daughter - another string to your bow of types of men you pretend to be. You can practice the whole shtick in advance: having 'the talk' to the first spotty teenage boyfriend, playfully threatening him with grievous bodily harm for the lols, alluding to extreme physical violence that will occur if she's not home by 11pm, hahaha, great stuff. Harmless intimidation! Needless macho posturing! It's the role you were born to play!

- Girls are typically less into roughhousing than boys so you might get an extra few years out of your knees. I don't know. Stop asking me, I don't have any girls, I am way out of my depth, just end it, end the section-

Cons

- Christ, I mean, where do you start? All the injustices in the world are laid at the feet of women. Every time a girl opens their mouth to speak up, a boy speaks over them; every time a lady has an idea, a lad will try to take credit for it;

every time a woman dresses less than conservatively they have to endure an evening of being hit on by the shittiest men in the world. How do you even begin to explain the gender gap to your daughter?

- Not to state the obvious, but: you are not a girl, and you have no real idea how the female body works (admit it, you still don't really know where the pee comes out), and you are super scared of wiping the wrong way because the one thing you do know for sure is that this will bring about the end times.

- Women are forced by society to always wear a full face of makeup, "smile more" and grin through the fact that their sanitary products are taxed as 'luxury items'. Hey girl, treat yourself to another fanny bung, you deserve it!

- It costs girls, like, £50 minimum just to get their hair cut. File this under 'I Don't Understand Girls and Probably Never Will' with the rest of this book.

- You can play the hardnut dad all you want: eventually you're going to have to face up to the fact that one day a little scrote with chin pubes called Chris is going to try to touch your daughter with his glans.

Maybe you have a preference, and that's fine. Some men want to have boys to shape in their own image, and some men couldn't imagine a crueller punishment. If you're going to find out, don't get hung up on the gender - and certainly don't take it as a personal slight if you didn't get the result you were after. There are some people, god love them, who actually think you can determine the sex of your baby in advance through technique alone, like some sort of expert marksman - and with 50/50 odds, half of them will think they've been proved right. I can guarantee each and every person who believes this is possible is a terrible shagger.

My friend Ben has four wonderful daughters. He made the mistake of telling this to his mechanic, of all people, in a moment of roadside-breakdown-induced weakness. As if talking to a mechanic wasn't stressful enough already, the guy then proceeded to tell Ben that the reason his wife hadn't give birth to any sons was because, and I quote, "you ain't been fucking her hard enough". The *power* that mechanics have! The *gall*! Standing there with your car keys in their hand - and therefore your balls - criticising *your* swordsmanship! I'd love to stop and chat more about my sexual deficiencies but my electrician needs to criticise my nutsack. "If you want a girl, you make love," he went on to say, in a garage I have to assume was wallpapered head to toe in wrinkly old Nuts Magazine pullouts, "but if you want a boy, you have to *fuck*." As if anyone can fuck you harder than a mechanic can! Honestly, like the secret to fertility is the depth of the thrust or the vigorousness of your penetration; like a baby son is the prize you get for ringing the bell at the back of your wife's vagina like a test of strength machine at a funfair. It's obviously a ridiculous hypothesis, except that the mechanic had four sons. Say what you will about his forecourt manner, but you can't argue with results like that. Maybe he's onto something. Maybe this guy *fucks*. Ask your local mechanic for sex advice and let me know how you get on.

If you choose to find out the sex of the baby in advance - and yes, noted: it *is* horrible when you have to use the words "sex" and "baby" in the same sentence - then there is a very real possibility that your partner may wish to find out at a gender reveal party. This recent invention, a cousin of the far more humble baby shower, is an excuse to have lots of shrieking women and their husbands over to your house, unfortunately while you're still in it. The gathered coven then get to be part of the most exciting moment of your life: when you find out if you're having a baby boy or a baby girl. Because why enjoy a private moment of life-changing intimacy when you can share it with Shaz from Zumba while eating a mini flapjack?

Gender reveal parties still feel like an overtly American occasion, but, like Halloween and Black Friday, the Brits have reluctantly followed suit and fallen into line so we too can have all the things. Perhaps this means it's inevitable that one day the UK will follow suit and elevate a reality TV show villain to supreme executive power, like, Prime Minister Simon Cowell, or Shadow Chancellor Nasty Nick. Baby showers are harmless enough, they're just a transparent excuse for girls to coo over small baby-sized things and eat cakes fashioned into the shape of human shit: normal behaviour. But gender reveal parties are way worse, mainly because *you* have to be involved.

Oh, sure, it's just a bit of fun, right, okay, message understood chief: the 'it's just banter' defence, beloved by all extroverted fun-havers everywhere. What, you don't like sharing massively emotional baby milestones with your mates? Did you even invite them to the conception? Will they be there for the birth, leaving cake crumbs and cocktail sticks and Prosecco stains all over the hospital reception? You'd better hope your face doesn't betray even one iota of disappointment at the moment of truth, otherwise you'll be fielding a series of increasingly aggressive questions from half-cut women you've never met asking why you hate girls and/or boys so much.

Your standard run-of-the-mill gender reveal party usually involves some sort of ceremony whereby you and your partner cut/smash/tear something open to be presented by a colour: blue for boys, pink for girls, because that's just how the world works, get over yourself new-age liberals, never mind the fact that gender and sex are not even the same thing. You get the idea. Slice the cake to reveal a blue or pink sponge. Beat a piñata to death to reveal confetti that gets you one step closer to your first-born. Release coloured balloons into the atmosphere to choke a duck P.S. you're having a girl. It's a concept so simple, even you can understand it. But no. We, as a society, had to make this process bigger, weirder, more confusing, more extra, more white. Hilariously, the Wikipedia page for 'Gender reveal party' is needlessly sassy, claiming "In today's society, the most common demographic taking part in gender reveal parties are heterosexual, Caucasian couples", like that needed to be said.

They're also dangerous. One California couple accidentally set over a thousand acres of rural farmland ablaze during an outdoor gender reveal party that turned into a terrifying wildfire, which is ideally the kind of bad omen you could have done with before you got pregnant. The baby was a boy, in case you're interested, and almost certainly bore the mark of the beast.

Still feel like you can top the gender reveal forest fire? Here are some genuine "creative" gender reveal party ideas from the internet that will make your gender reveal party reveal all the other gender reveal parties to look like shit.

Gender reveal lasagne

"You can now order coloured versions of the Italian staple dish and serve it up to guests in celebration of your baby's sex."
Great, now everyone has to eat a gross neon lasagne while thinking about childbirth. Also, it ain't cheap: *"One gender reveal lasagne for 12 people will set you back £107... but it does include garlic bread and salad."* OH WOW GARLIC BREAD WELL THAT'S ALL RIGHT THEN.

Gender reveal water pistols

"For couples who are willing to get a little messy, you can fill water guns with coloured paint to have your guests shoot at you."
Develop PTSD when you associate this most cherished memory with traumatic gunfire!

Gender reveal bonfire

"Have your family and friends gather around a bonfire and toss in a flame-colour-changing chemical to share the sex of your baby."
What? I'm not going to this, it sounds rubbish, I don't care if it is my baby.

Gender reveal fireworks

"If you're ready to reveal your baby's gender around the 4th of July, then a fireworks display is the perfect choice. Set off fireworks for guests in either blue or pink. Just make sure fireworks are legal in your area!"
Public service announcement: if you can afford to arrange fireworks to celebrate the announcement of the sex of your baby then the sex of your baby is irrelevant. Just saying.

Gender reveal eggs

"Fill eggs with coloured confetti or dye the inside of the eggs with pink or blue food colouring. Have guests crack the eggs at the same time or mail an egg to out-of-town family and friends."
This one sounds like a whole lot of admin for very little return, but I just loved the phrase "mail an egg", like an egg is a perfectly sane and logistically possible thing to either send or receive via the postal service.

Gender reveal punt

"If you're a sports fan, you can buy balls for virtually any sport you like filled with bright pink or blue powder that will explode on impact. You can kick a football or hit a baseball to reveal a big cloud of blue or pink powder."

Hahahaha god I hope you go through this needlessly masculine charade and end up inhaling a bitter, pink cloud of dust, which stains your tears the colour of disappointment.

Gender reveal bath

"For a cute idea, fill a clear plastic tub with water and add a rubber duckie on top. When ready, add a colour-changing bath bomb to the water to reveal your baby's gender to guests."

Imagine explaining this to someone. 'Yeah, so come round at about midday, we're going to make everyone watch us run a bath... Yeah, a bath...Yes, I realise most modest-sized bathrooms can only host four people max... No, nobody has to get *in* the bath... No, a-Actually, you know what, my mistake, the party is *next* Saturday, bye.' [hangs up]

Gender reveal balloon pop

"Put a balloon on a target with pink or blue paint inside. Using a bow and arrow, hit the target to reveal the sex of your baby."

Why are so many of the gender reveals aggressively violent in nature? Burst this, kick that, maim and smash and stab for your unborn child. This one is great if you would like the most tense moment of your life to also depend on you successfully executing a high-pressure feat of sporting accuracy while all your impatient family and friends gather and watch.

Gender reveal card

"Create a pull-tab gender reveal card to mail to your family and friends."

Wait, so I wasn't even invited to a party? Why are you even telling me this? Fucking cheapskate.

Gender reveal confusing trivia game

"Make a 'Bow or Bow Ties?' trivia board. Have your guests ask you baby and parenting-related trivia questions. For example: 'What was the most common baby girl name in 2019?' If the couple gets it right, they get to draw a pink bow or a blue bow tie out of a bag and put it up on the board. Once you're out of bows and bowties, the gender will be revealed!"

... Sorry, what? How does this work again? The trivia does what? This sounds more confusing than 3, 2, 1 with Dusty Bin.

Gender reveal scavenger hunt

"Send your family and fr-"

I'm going to stop you there, that's enough internet for today.

Fine: if gender reveal ideas don't have to be tethered to any recognisable plane of reality, then why not push the boat out and get really creative? Fuck it, I'm going into the gender reveal business. Each of these ideas cost £107 and none of them come with any additional garlic bread or salad.

Gender reveal tattoo

Ask a trusted tattoo artist to ink a portrait of a celebrity on your back, and break out the mirror on the big day. If they drew Bea Arthur then you're having a 'golden' girl, but if they drew Thin Lizzy frontman Phil Lynott then it looks like the boys are back in town!

Gender reveal extreme surprise wake-up call

Have a friend wake you up at 4.45am by yelling the sex of your baby into your face repeatedly with a megaphone. Look at you! You can't believe it!

Gender reveal poisoning

Ingest a huge quantity of coloured glitter in the name of fun, then when you feel your digestive system quivering from throat to arsehole, head to the nearest hork receptacle and rejoice at the sight of your gender-coloured barf and/or shit! Make yourself ill with happiness!

Gender reveal prank

Through careful cajoling, find out which sex your partner would love the most, then fix the reveal so it announces the opposite. Once your partner has faked enough faux-happiness, you can 'fess up and come clean to a chorus of brays and hoots of laughter from your assembled friends - she'll never forget your part in making this most special day extra emotional!

Gender reveal that you already predicted

When you learn the sex of your baby, state confidently that you knew it was going to be a boy/girl and don't back down. See, told you, nailed it, I even said it, remember I said it, like, loads? Act like the prediction is proof of your extra-sensory powers and inherent masculine intuition, and not, say, the product of a 50/50 fucking guess!

Just a heads up if you are already struggling: gender is the easy bit. Two potential outcomes in a scenario you have absolutely no control over? Completed it, mate. For a true test of your mettle, you need to name the bloody thing too.

Choosing a baby name is exactly as torturous as you might imagine. The task is this: find a name for your child that both you and your partner can agree on, despite the fact that there are probably only about three names that exist that meet that entirely arbitrary criteria and you won't even know you've found one until you've cycled through over 3,000 terrible ones, and did I mention that the rules are entirely arbitrary and that the validation process is lawless, and that names you suggest that seem fine will be vetoed instantly as they are revealed to be, actually, quite awful, offensive even to suggest, and that, conversely, there's something wrong with you if you don't like the names that your partner is suggesting, because those names are the names that are perfectly suitable and if the names you suggested are genuine then you must not be taking this seriously at all, let's just name it after your father-in-law and be done with it, God.

I can offer some guidance here, not by offering suggestions but by taking some names off the table - the process of elimination is the fastest route to victory. Think about the names that you associate with bad people, horrible people, people that have sullied their names forever - your Adolfs, your Borises, your Piers Morgans. Here is a list of all the types of names you can strike off your list before you even have to come up with a single one you actually like:

- Famous paedos and celebrity nonces
- War criminals
- Vengeful exes who smeared their name in shit on the windscreen of your brand new Ford Ka

- Any 24-carat twat from The Apprentice whose annoyingly-spelled name (Kris, Darin, Khevin) you will forever associate with failure

- Porn stars

- School bullies, school weirdos, school teachers, school dinnerladies you had a crush on, basically anyone with any association with school

- X Factor hopefuls who got through to judges' houses on the strength of a sob story alone but failed to adequately impress Robbie Williams with their softly-spoken Lorde covers

- Tory politicians and their stupid speccy Tory children

- Names that sound good on a man of 40 but will nonetheless be a burden on a small baby (Bill, Chris, Dave, Alan, Pete)

- Pop culture icons (real). No, absolutely not, sorry, you are not allowed to name your child after your favourite singer or actor, first and foremost because tastes shift like the wind and evolve over time and the stuff you're into now will almost certainly make you cringe in two years' time, let alone ten, but mainly because you don't want to get stuck with a kid named after a high-profile celebrity who, in the years since the baby's birth, got cancelled due to racism/sexism/cultural appropriation/jacking off in public. Do this and you are literally the guy who is currently yelling "BRITNEEYYYY! JUSTIIIIN!" at his horrid fucking offspring in the big Tesco cereal aisle

- Pop culture icons (fictional). Careful now, because naming your child after a character in your favourite TV show or movie series is fraught with peril. If it's a series that's still going, they continually run the risk of jumping the shark and/or turning heel. Pity the poor bastards who loved Game of Thrones so much they named their baby girl 'Khaleesi' only for her to become an internationally reviled hate figure

- Jeff, because you can't call your baby fucking Jeff

Also excluded, of course, are the names you already have in your family; the names you cannot feasibly shout across a crowded living room without having more than one person turn around. Yes, technically I will allow you to choose the names of dead relatives out of respect, but anyone that's still breathing is not up for selection for logistical reasons. Pre-birth baby naming is a weird process if you have friends or family who are also expecting, because you need to stake your claim on your name, like putting a 50p on the pool table in the pub.

You cannot enter into a situation where there are two baby Harrisons or Imogens or Chesneys on the go at once. But also, you cannot share the name of your baby with any other preggos in case they hear it and love it so much they cast off their beloved Jeff and embrace *your* baby's name instead. This is a nightmare scenario. It's baby chicken: who will swerve first? It's not that likely, but you can't be too careful. Better go obscure. No, even more obscure than that. A name so obscure that no one has ever used it. Chorky. Jalf. Granit Xhaka.

If you absolutely must choose a name that you would privately describe in inverted commas as 'offbeat' or 'different', may I recommend the middle name? The middle name is the universally designated location for you to offload all your high-minded, middle-class pomposity - go ahead, drop the 'Tarquin' bomb here if you must, just know that the birth certificate will be the only form it's ever, ever added to.

Equally, the middle name is the perfect place to stash a cool pop culture tribute or movie reference without dooming the poor child to a lifetime of ridicule. For example, I wouldn't be so cruel to have named Kid H 'Marty' after Back To The Future's plucky protagonist (it's practically an invitation for film-savvy bullies to flick him in the forehead), but I am exactly as dorky as giving him the middle name 'Emmett' - it's a reference, but also, it's a nice name in itself so I have plausible deniability if the playground bullies start sniffing around.

Sometimes, however, you just have to let the good ones go. My favourite film of all time is Jurassic Park, but there was no way I was going to be able to call my firstborn 'Velociraptor' or 'Tyrannosaur', so unless I can convince my wife to give birth to two more sons called 'Sam' and 'Neil' I'm just going to have to leave it. (Bonus realisation: I have just now, literally right now while writing this paragraph, realised that Sam Neill's character in Jurassic Park is called 'Alan Grant', and my middle name is 'Grant', so if you squint a little bit or mumble it or don't really pay attention, my name is basically Alan Grant. That's right, I'm retconning my own middle name, and I don't even care if the dates don't add up).

Fine, you want specifics. The baby names book - a whole book of baby names! - didn't yield any results, because 98% of the names within are definitely destined to become freaks. 'Have you met my son Skylar? He's a sex pest, we're very disappointed in him.' Choosing a baby name is a torturous task, because it's one of the only decisions you'll make in your life that is almost 100% irreversible - not unless your kid grows up and is willing to spend, like, £25 to change it by deed poll. Oooh get you, why not change your name to 'Mr Moneybags'? No, it's clear you need help, guidance, a trusty friend with a cheatsheet to crib from. Fine, I'll give you a list of names you can have for your baby, names so great they'll live on in legend, names so amazing they'll open doors and drop jaws.

- Phil

Yeah, that's it, that's the entire list: Phil. Baby Phillip. Pip to his mum, Phil to his schoolmates. You'd never get a serial killer named Phil. Phil is reliable. Phil has a van. Phil is happy to go in goals. Phil will get the beers in. Phil will lend you his hedge-trimmer. Phil will pop round and feed your cats while you're on holiday. Phil will do your plastering and charge you mates rates. Phil will make fake office background noise for you while you're actually on the phone in the pub. Your girlfriend is never going to cheat on you with Phil. There's never going to be a universally reviled media figure or fictional character called Phil. There's never going to be a shit Phil, and even if there is, you can't stay mad at Phil. Okay, the name 'Phil' is starting to look really weird now. Sorry I ruined you, Phil. Either that or 'Mark'.

You're right to feel stressed, this is a lot of responsibility all at once - all because you had sex with a girl that one time. You know what? Maybe the alternative is much more agreeable. You may decide that, for the time being at least, ignorance is bliss. Maybe thinking of it just as 'baby' right now makes more sense.

There's another upside to not knowing the gender in advance. Vicky spent years working as a healthcare assistant on a Maternity Ward and was present during hundreds of births, so I consider her to be something of an expert on the subject. She told me that during the moment of birth, she would do what literally no one else in the room did: she looked at the dad, and at how his face would always break into an enormous smile upon learning the sex of the baby. I always secretly suspected that men were the most important part of the birthing process and now it's confirmed.

So you see, the gender is irrelevant, because the occasion itself is overwhelming enough. Leave the presents under the tree, lad, and resist the temptation to fiddle with the wrapping, because it'll be Christmas soon enough.

#7

An Exhaustive List of Things Not to Say to a Pregnant Woman

L ook at you now, coming on leaps and bounds! Bit of a spring in your step, is it? Growing more confident by the day, are we? Think you're more attuned to pregnant women, do you? Here you are, poised to start a conversation with a pregnant woman, thinking you've got common ground. This should be interesting. Before you start flapping your piehole, please mentally scan this 'do not say' checklist to make sure you're not about to put your massive male foot in it.

"When is it due?"

Don't. Just don't. The first rule of thumb for conversing with pregnant women is to assume they are not pregnant - despite what might seem like overwhelming visual evidence - until they reference it. Because although the chances may seem slim, there is every chance this woman is not pregnant at all, and just a bit bloated. I know it seems like a thing that only happens in cartoons and sitcoms, but I have seen this happen in the wild, and I have never wanted the ground to swallow someone more.

"Was it a surprise?"

Jesus *fuck*, scale it back immediately you madman! This is a statement of war, the verbal equivalent of the assassination of

Archduke Franz Ferdinand - men have been killed for less! What you've done is, you've seen the small person growing inside this poor woman's belly, this precious bundle of joy, this miracle of life, and you've said: "This wonderful child which you're bringing into the world... I am assuming you achieved this by accident, yes?" Note: saying the opposite, "Was it intentional?", is not better.

"How long have you been trying?"

What you hear: a harmless question inquiring how long it took to get pregnant. What she hears: "So, how long have you been letting your husband do big cums in you?"

"How does it feel?"

It probably feels like shit. Next question.

"How far along are you?"

It's not so much the question here that's offensive, rather the fact that whatever answer you receive will inevitably lead to one of the intrusive comments below. There is no reaction you can give to the number of weeks given, other than a polite "Ah!" and a nod. So why bother? This was a mistake, admit it. You wish you were at home, trading insults with anonymous children over Xbox Live. You know where you are with those noobs.

"Not long to go now!" / "Still a while to go yet!"

If only you were capable of perceiving time at the same rate as a pregnant woman. Alas, you are not. Therefore, any and all questions relating to the remaining duration of pregnancy are null and void, and your input is not appreciated.

"So it could literally come any minute!"

And it'd probably be welcomed, if only to end this stultifying fucking conversation.

"I bet you're looking forward to getting it over and done with!"

How incredibly perceptive of you, Sherlock Holmes. Also, you don't know that this woman is looking forward to pregnancy being over, even if she's complaining about the symptoms. She might be terrified of the birth, and everything that comes afterwards. She might be desperate for it to be over. She probably doesn't want to share either of these opinions with you.

"You're so small!" / "You're so big!"

Question: would you consider it appropriate to comment on the size of a woman's body if she *wasn't* pregnant? Heads shaking all around, that's pretty much a unanimous 'no'. Why, then, would you consider it appropriate to ask the same question to a pregn- oh, you already beat me to it, well done you, we got there in the end, no need for me to spell it out.

"Did you know that technically pregnancy lasts closer to 10 months than 9?"

How did you imagine this question landing exactly, in your head I mean, when you asked it? Was it your aim to make this woman feel like her excruciating ordeal is never-ending? Because rest assured, your presence is making every second feel like an eternity. Yes, technically it may be correct, but technically if this woman crammed your own balls down your throat it would be manslaughter not murder, so there are a lot of technicalities flying around right now, aren't there?

"Did you watch the episode of One Born Every Minute where..."

I'll stop you there, there's no need to ask this question, because *all* pregnant women watch One Born Every Minute. It's mandatory viewing for parents-to-be. You're just going to have to put that box set of The Wire on hold for about, ooh, 18 years.

"Have you had any weird cravings?"

Yes, she's probably craving some more interesting questions. Move along.

"Eating for two, are we?"

What she hears: "Eating extra large portions like a fat sweaty hog, are we?" Believe it or not, hormonal pregnant women don't tend to appreciate anonymous strangers commenting on their calorie intake, as strange as that may sound. Women, am I right?

"Are you sure it's not twins?"

If it was intended as a joke: this is not a joke because no humour was detected, please retract. If it was meant seriously: take it as read that the pregnant woman that stands before you has at least a basic understanding of the organism that's growing inside her, and isn't just going to do her homework at the last minute and wing it on the day like you would.

"Do you know your birth plan yet?"

Do you know *your* birth plan yet? Don't like the heat of that spotlight now, do you? Enough with the third degree, Columbo.

"Ha ha, I'm so glad men don't have to go through this!"

Text: Women are good but being a man is great, LOL! *Subtext:* I am so thankful that I never have to suffer any major hardship in my life because I would fold into a pathetic heap if I ever had to endure one fraction of literally any element of pregnancy, pity me and my wretched gender for we know not what we say, LOL!

"Can I touch it?"

Unless you are the man who put it in there or the doctor responsible for taking it out, the answer is almost certainly 'no'.

"Boy or girl?"

Again, not a hugely offensive question in and of itself, but usually a gateway into a whole realm of tiresome opinions about gender that do not need to be heard by any living human being, let alone a mother-to-be.

"What are you going to call it?"

Nani. Yeah, that's right, first name 'Nani', last name 'Yafaqin-Bisniss'.

"Are you going to go NHS or private?"

What she hears: "How much money do you have in your bank account right now?" Whatever answer you'd get, you'd have to pivot to pretending it's the better option of the two anyway, so put your judgement on ice and cross this one off your list, pronto.

"When [distant friend/relative that this person does not know] had her baby, she [painful procedure that this person does not need to hear]"

I know you mean well and you're just trying to make conversation, but telling a story about someone else you know who once had a baby does not qualify as an actual anecdote. You might as well say "I was a baby once".

"Happy birthday! Have a good one!"

Especially don't say this if you have been given a 'Congratulations on your pregnancy!' card to sign at work and you didn't really look at it properly. I definitely have, uh, never done this.

"I think..."

I'm going to stop you there, because this is going nowhere good.

"I..."

Nope. It's not about you. Shut it down.

"But I..."

Shut. It. Down.

The observant readers among you may notice that this doesn't leave you with anything left to say to a pregnant woman. This is intentional. You should not speak to any pregnant women at all. You've already done enough damage.

#8

Sharing Your Baby: How to Break the News and Win at Social Media

The time has come. For 12 long weeks of secret pregnancy you've basically been a hermit, avoiding Big Conversations in person, scaling back your social media presence lest you give up any clues, generally living your life like a character in A Quiet Place, where one unprompted outburst could cost you dearly. But those three months have passed without incident. Mother and baby are happy and healthy. It's time. It's time to let other people be part of your pregnancy. It's time to go public. Oh god. Brace for impact.

There are rules of engagement that must be observed here, protocol which cannot be overridden. You need to structure the pregnancy announcement with military precision - this isn't 'Nam, there are rules. For months you've been operating under the radar, sharing information on a need-to-know basis only, but you're in the big leagues now, son. You think your baby belongs only to you? Think again. Your baby is also a grandchild, a great-grandchild, a niece or nephew, a cousin, a second cousin, a second cousin twice removed, a godson or goddaughter, a new neighbour. It's an asset, a prime piece of family real estate, like a timeshare in Cornwall. Everybody wants a piece of it, and you're duty bound to honour those commitments - or at least, you are if you ever want to find a free babysitter or enjoy a non-awkward Christmas again in your life.

The process of telling outsiders about the tot coming in hot has a hierarchical structure which I would strongly advise you follow to the letter. It starts, obviously enough, with your parents. This is tolerable! Dare I say it, almost enjoyable? You're bringing good news to their doorstep: mother, father, I have finally made something of my life, please downgrade your disappointment accordingly!

This is definitely the most adult you've ever felt in front of your parents, knocking that time you got a County Court Summons for not paying your uni landlord down into second place. No fooling: this is probably the best thing that's happened to them in like 30 years. Milk it, girl! If you can also find a way of telling any siblings or other close family members at the same time as your parents, then it's a double win - just take care not to make the gathering look overly suspicious, in case your drunken uncle thinks it's another intervention. On the contrary, Uncle Derek, it's good news - crack open another Magners!

Telling family is easy. Telling friends is where things get complicated. You may not think it, but revealing a pregnancy is a highly fraught situation where friends can be lost or even made into enemies, depending on the order in which you roll out the information. You knew that, right? Wait. Pause. Tell me you weren't planning on putting out a pan-friendship blast, CCing everyone on the same message? A flat, functional communique that informs all your friends, colleagues and well-wishers of your impending fatherhood at the exact same time, agnostic of status or closeness or BFFness? You idiot. You clown. Thank God I'm here. You almost made the biggest mistake of your life.

(By the way, I'm talking almost exclusively about accidentally offending women at this point, in case that wasn't clear. Men are painfully simple creatures who exist in a drama vacuum, and wish to keep their lives free of social complications. You can tell your male friends about your baby whenever and wherever you like: in person, via WhatsApp, in the pub, on the bus, through a bathroom door while they're having a shit, during a game of pool, at work, during a game of darts, while playing co-operative seasons online on FIFA (at half-time), during a game of poker, during a game of anything really, as long as you do your utmost to avoid making it an actual conversation. Women, on the other hand, can stretch to supernatural lengths in order to be wronged by someone and are capable of interpreting even the sharing of a heartfelt message of love and compassion as a perceived slight from a total bitch, because they just live for messy drama and soap opera shit and Mariah Carey 'I don't know her' gifs. It's not sexist. It's not. You're sexist for saying that. Get out of my parentheses, you sexist.)

The official order for information rollout goes like this:

Order	Recipient	Method
1st	Immediate family	In person
2nd	Close friends	In person, together if possible
3rd	Remaining family	Individual private messages
4th	Primary friendship group unable to attend initial announcement	Individual private messages, being sure to alter the message template so any accusations of copy-pasting won't stand up in court
5th	Outer rim friendship group	Joint WhatsApp group and/or email thread

Last	Work colleagues	Email or in person, optional, do not include your line manager unless you want to have to give them menial updates during every one-to-one you have between now and the birth

Congratulations: you have demonstrated tact in communicating a sensitive subject. You also now have more PR experience than most people who work in PR.

The final piece of the puzzle is the general social media announcement, the mop-up message that's making sure the rest of the rabble are informed. Because really, if you're not telling your distant friends, old school mates, online chums and ex-work colleagues that you're having a baby, why are you even on social media in the first place?

This is legitimately the most exciting thing that has happened to you basically in your entire life. This qualifies as an actual status update. You can't tell me you're perfectly content sharing photos of large greasy burgers and badly punctuated signs with misplaced apostrophes and pictures of your mates pretending to bum various statues but you're having second thoughts about telling the world you're having a baby? No, fuck off, you're doing it whether you like it or not. You're not popular or interesting enough to have a secret baby. You're not Beyoncé.

You need to decide which social media platform you use to get your message out. Believe it or not, the social media platform you choose says a lot about you and the kind of father you're going to be. Oh, you're not on social media, you say? Good one granddad! Next you'll be telling me you don't own a TV and that you're reading an actual paper copy of this book like in the olden days! No, stop messing around. Here's a rough guide to the suitability of each social media platform before you go telling the world and its incontinent dog you got some poor woman up the spout.

FACEBOOK

You've probably heard of it. Your racist nan has definitely heard of it. Facebook is the social media platform to use if you want to get your message out to as many people as you can with as little effort as possible. It's flat and functional and there's a very high chance that somehow two members of your family will end up arguing about Brexit in the comments, but that happens on everything you post to Facebook, so don't take it personally. If you want to get online, get the job done and get on with the rest of your life, you've come to the right sinister corporate media conglomerate. Now with emojis!

INSTAGRAM

Want to tell people you're pregnant, but also, want to show people that you're a little bit extra? Instagram is the visual medium for you. Why use words to express your happiness, when you can use photographs with retro colour filters and Polaroid-style borders? It's the social media platform that says 'Yes, I'm going to be a daddy, but I'm also going to carefully curate my kid's existence via a series of painstakingly staged photographs with expensive props in the vain hope that I'll one day be able to leverage my unwitting child and my general 'insta aesthetic' into some sort of book deal or #sponcon'.

TWITTER

It might be the most effective communication tool in terms of brevity and media cut-through, but use Twitter at your peril. Do you really want to be broadcasting personal information to a user base that's 60% Russian bots? Do you really want to get into an argument with a neckbeard with an anime avatar who'll try to convince you that, actually, you're *not* having a baby? It's not a befitting platform for an announcement of such magnitude. One day, your adult child may ask to see how you broke the news of their birth, and you'll have to dig out your original tweet: "Avin' a baby lol, please RT". And no one did RT, because that's not how RTs work. Still, three likes though, not too shabby.

SNAPCHAT

How are you fathering a baby if you're only twelve years old? Please put down this book and go and find a responsible adult.

YOUTUBE

Wait, you're a YouTuber? One of those people who starts literally every single video with the words "Hey guys!" then spends 18 minutes talking about how you did nothing all day? And you have eight million subscribers regardless? Every thirteen-year-old-girl in the country knows your name? Your fandom actually titled itself? You've not paid for any clothes since 2013 and Honda gave you an electric car and you do your weekly food shop in Waitrose and you live in a Brighton mansion with your model-entrepreneur-influencer girlfriend where you make more money selling "merch" each week than your teacher father did throughout his entire life? You're basically as famous as it's possible to be without ever being in the Daily Mail sidebar of shame? Your daily videos are single-handedly bringing down teenage literacy rates up and down the country? Then yes, you should probably use YouTube for your pregnancy announcement.

LINKEDIN

Ha ha ha ha ha ha ha ha ha ha ha ha ha ha ha ha ha ha ha ha ha ha ha ha ha ha ha ha ha ha ha ha ha ha ha ha ha ha ha ha ha ha ha ha ha ha ha ha ha ha ha ha ha ha ha ha ha ha ha ha ha ha ha ha ha ha ha ha ha [big, deep breath] ha ha ha ha ha ha ha ha ha ha ha ha ha ha ha ha ha ha ha ha ha ha ha ha ha ha ha ha ha ha ha ha ha ha ha ha ha ha ha ha ha ha ha ha ha ha ha ha ha ha ha ha ha ha ha ha ha ha ha ha ha nobody cares.

SPOTIFY

Technically, yes, it is possible to create a public playlist and load it with songs whose titles spell out a cutesy message about how you're about to have a baby. A bit like this:

Y'All Said - *Lil Jaundice*
It Can't Be Done - *Luanne, Luwann, Loo-Anne*
I Proved You Wrong - *Chad Sexington*
Haters Go Home - *The Exxon Valdez Experience*
Because - *Elvis Bontempi*
I've Been With A Woman - *Katy Perry*
She's Ripe - *Tricky 69*
With My Seed - *Sexxx/Lords*
Knocked Up - *Rufus Whingeworth III*
And I Did It! - *Dudes Shouting Constantly*
Baby Be - *Justin Bleeder*
Showin' His Face - *Chef Boyardee*
In September - *The Boujies*
2022 - *The Richard Briers Project*
So - *Crotchface Killah*
Get Off My Dick - *Motherfucker Jones*

Of course, just because you can do this, does not mean you should do this. Under no circumstances should you do this. Look, just be one of billions of faceless drones and use Facebook for Christ's sake.

All that remains is for sir to choose his announcement package. We have a wide and varied mix of social media pregnancy announcements available to meet your needs today, ranging from very reasonable to insanely egotistical. How much social currency is sir willing to spend on this venture?

The Bronze Package

Ideal for: New Dads who don't want to cause any bother

Brief: This is your regular, entry-level announcement package, your Tesco own-brand sandwich, your bland, basic, no frills, inoffensive pregnancy shout-out. The Bronze Package consists of a poorly cropped, black and white 12-week scan picture of your beloved foetus, complete with an uninspiring message to provide context. The post will be warmly received for approximately 8 hours and can expect a smattering of likes before being swallowed up by the mists of the Algorithm and, having been regurgitated into mere ones and zeroes, subsequently forgotten forever. You get out what you put in, pal.

Example: "Me and Teresa are delighted to say we're having a baby! Looking forward to meeting the little one in September! Wish us luck!" Job done. No messing about.

Expected range of likes: Somewhere in the range of 50-70 likes, although you can expect to hit triple figures if you tag your partner and bum likes off her mates.

Typical comment: "Congratulations!" Wow. Don't hold back, guys, I'm getting emotional here.

The Silver Package

Ideal for: New Dads who *bloody love a bit of banter*

Brief: Just because you're having a baby doesn't mean you have to stop having a laugh, does it? I mean, obviously it does, but you won't know that when you choose The Silver Package, a social media engagement experience that's approximately 23% cheekier than our low-end offering. You get the same 12-week poltergeist scan, but the accompanying comment showcases your playful sense of humour, assuring assorted friends and followers that, hey, you've still got it! Fatherhood won't change you! (It will).

Example: "Uh oh, whose [sic] this little guy?? Looks like I've got an excuse to rewatch all the Star Wars movies again! Told you I wasn't firing blanks! PS The Phantom Menace is still shit though!!" You get the idea. Just great content, really top notch stuff.

Expected range of likes: Upwards of 70, plus one share from your Mum.

Typical comment: "Oh no you poor bastard lol! Does this mean no more Curry Club on Monday nites?" Yes, 'Smudger'. Yes, it does.

The Gold Package

Ideal for: New Dads who didn't come to fuck around

Brief: Oho, excellent choice. I see sir is a more discerning social media user. The Gold Package exists in a class above the usual white noise - to use the correct social media parlance, this pregnancy announcement is sticky, yo. Dispense with the uninspiring scan picture and cookie-cutter sentiment and instead upload a well-lit and professionally staged photograph of your significant other holding a cryptic clue that reveals the pregnancy in a clever and not immediately obvious way. The trick is looking like you've not tried too hard - you're just a naturally hilarious and cool couple who love to have fun! That's why you took 47 pictures and an afternoon off work in an attempt to get the right pose.

Example: A full-length shot of your partner holding a round and crusty Waitrose bloomer against her stomach, with the caption: "The bun is in the oven. Rising September 2022." There will be one thicko who doesn't get it, but this is the Gold Package, you need to leave those dumbos behind.

Expected range of likes: 150+ guaranteed. Oh yeah. Influencer numbers.

Typical comment: "I always knew you were a master baker!" There's always one chancer trying to outdo you in the comments. If it starts getting more likes than the main post, nip it in the bud by deleting it and reporting the user for abusive behaviour. Fuck off, *Greg*. This is *my* moment, *Greg*.

The Platinum Package

Ideal for: Dads who extremely work in media

Brief: Behold, the high-end option: the bells and whistles package that shows your fans and followers that you've transferred your professional skills with new media to your personal life - at last! It might cost a little extra and take a small and overworked production company three months to put it together, delaying the actual pregnancy announcement until you make the final edits, but Platinum Package Dads wipe their arses on your simple 12-week scan pics. We're talking an irresistible melange of graphic design, flash animation and custom-coded web apps. Because your baby and your CV are basically one and the same thing, right?

Example: A twee, hand-drawn animated story in the style of Hayao Miyazaki that casts you and your partner as intrepid hipster steampunk explorers going on a brave adventure to exotic worlds unknown, with an original acoustic soundtrack you recorded with an actual Mumford when your families Christmassed together in Cornwall last year.

Expected range of likes: Likely north of 1,000, with more shares than you've ever accumulated over your entire life. It's... it's going viral, isn't it? It's happening. It's finally happening! 2,000 likes now and counting. Phillip Schofield just shared it. 5,000! A producer from This Morning has got in touch and wants to know if you're available for a five-minute segment this Thursday to talk about your viral video. You are. You are very available. Ainsley Harriot just shared it! Etc.

Typical comment: "Bit wanky, isn't it?"

The Diamond Package

Ideal for: DRAMA

Brief: [whispers] Please step this way, sir. There is, of course, an option that surpasses even the Platinum Package. It is one we cannot recommend unless sir is absolutely sure it is appropriate. The Diamond Package pregnancy announcement is a very special pregnancy announcement because it is not a pregnancy announcement at all - it is the absence of one. It requires both parties to go dark on all platforms for a minimum of nine months, unannounced, without so much as a jovial status update or an errant like to place you in the social ecosystem. Then, after sufficient time, and utterly without fanfare: a picture of you with your new child, *which no one even knew you were having.* This is the only way to win at social media: vanish without trace for ages, reappear suddenly with a gigantic bit of news, play it off like it's no biggie, then continue being infinitely cooler and more aloof than the poor suckers who follow you. And then, just like that, just like Keyser Soze walking off his limp at the end of The Usual Suspects, you're gone into the night, spoken of only as myth and legend.

Example: A picture of you with your large actual son, accompanied by the caption: "Had a baby."

Expected range of likes: It doesn't matter, remember? You're not, like, in it for the likes, yeah? You don't, like, assign a value to yourself in that way? Although obviously you'll get an avalanche of likes and each thumbs up and heart emoji and shocked reaction will give you life.

Typical comment: "What the fuck?" That's right, Dad. You don't know me. You don't know me at all.

Made your choice? Good. Now hit that button. Share it. Share your baby. Share your baby with everyone. Even the people you actively dislike. Share your baby. Retweet your baby. Upvote your baby. Self-like your baby. Tag all your friends in pictures of your baby. Comment on your baby. Lean into it. Go on, really *lean into it*. Get used to it. Embrace it. Make everyone else block you. Dare them. Double dare them. Choke their newsfeeds with pictures of your kid. Your baby belongs to the internet now, and social media will probably do a much better job of raising it than you ever will.

You may worry about oversharing information about your baby - every smile, every shart, every hilariously inappropriate new onesie, every vom sesh, every single roll of fat. You are right to be cautious, because social media is made up of people, and people are, by and large, awful. Hitler, for example, was a person. Everyone has a right to privacy, especially small pink blancmange babies who are unable to give consent as to the usage of their image rights. We now live in a terrifying world where it is entirely feasible that a person's entire life, from birth to childhood to adolescence and beyond, can be charted on social media, like some godforsaken episode of Black Mirror. This is problematic for several reasons, potential employment being just one of them. "We'd love to give you the administrator role, Mr Smith, but it appears as per your Facebook page that in 1994 you claimed, and I quote, "Babylon Zoo are my favourite band of all time", so we've decided to go another way."

Try to get your head around funerals in the all-encompassing social media age - why bother with a eulogy when the priest can just scroll through your Facebook wall? "Mr Smith was a good man, an honest man, and he loved his family, as you can see from his profile pictures. He 'liked' Adidas, Marmite, Dr. Dre and Batman. And, if we scroll through his status updates, we can see that, as a young man he- hang on... Babylon Zoo? Seriously? Oh my god. This funeral is over. End livestream."

If oversharing is a concern, and you'd rather err on the side of restraint when it comes to cataloguing your child's entire existence, then I applaud you for a sensible and responsible decision, hopefully the first of many you'll make as a dad. Holding this opinion, however, does not mean you have to criticise those who take delight in sharing pictures of their kids on social media - these are not mutually exclusive positions. How are you going to find fault in someone who is so hyped by the product of their own loins, they feel the need to share that feeling with others? What is social media for if not for that? Don't be a social media spinster.

We've all met them, we all know them: the baby blockers, the infant allergic, the feed purists - the ones who loudly and openly complain that Facebook is all baby photos now, as if Facebook is something that can actually be ruined, as if 'people having children' is an unexpected event in the continuing evolution of the human race. They're the same users who always wang on about how social media "used to be" before "everyone got involved" e.g. back when being an early adopter of a new technology qualified as being a social pioneer. How dare you fill their feed with photos of your miraculous life events - you're spoiling social media simply by being on it and using it as intended!

You can spot them a mile off. Pre-emptively block anyone with more than three of these tell-tale signs on their profile page.

- Profile picture of them the one time they met a celebrity (think more Martin Clunes than George Clooney)

- Vague comments relating to their support of Manchester United (I don't know why, but it's always Manchester United)

- Several quasi-political posts that display Sun-reader levels of understanding and zero context (e.g. "Jeremy Corbyn has done it again! Unbelievable!")

- Multiple shares of funny videos from BBC Three sitcoms and/or Have I Got News For You

- Half-hearted attempts to be part of national conversations that offer no detailed insight into any significant water-cooler topics (e.g. "Just watched the Michael Jackson Neverland documentary. Bloody hell.")

- Minimum three posts per day, every day of the week including weekends, for the last six months, absolute psychopaths

- Always the first to comment on their own posts, answering questions nobody asked

- Always the first to post whopping great TV spoilers, never willing to back down

- No family photos and no personal updates of substance, aside from the odd allusion to familial drama deep in the comments (e.g. "I really wish I could celebrate Father's Day, Barbara, but he knows what he did.")
- Single, obviously

Maybe you used to have similar opinions? Back in your past life, before the b-word? It's entirely possible: social media archives our embarrassing behaviours and charts our lack of progress as human beings like nothing else. And apparently we voluntarily opted in? For reasons that presumably made sense at the time?

Against my better judgement, I signed up to an app called Timehop, a piece of software which asks for your permission to root through every post you ever made on every social media platform you've ever signed up to, before giving you a daily presentation of what you shared online on this day in your own personal history - year by year, every status update, every drunken photo, every thirst trap, every howl into the digital void. It was most definitely A Bad Idea, but I cannot bring myself to delete it because it's too effective in showing me how our attitude to social media has changed over the years. Another way of saying that is "I need constant reminders of how much of a twat I used to be online, and I live in constant fear that even the recent stuff I posted is going to turn out to be just as twatty in years to come".

For example, via Timehop I can see that one year ago today, I posted some pretty run-of-the-mill tweets about the Netflix algorithm and shared a cute pic of my family at the park; four years ago today I had a conversation about Kanye West's album 'The Life Of Pablo' with a Twitter chum; and 12 years ago today I remarked on Facebook that the new Prawn Cocktail Pringles make your fingers "smell like fanny". I should point out for clarity's sake that I would have been 27 when I wrote that, so not exactly a naive teenager. I thank the Lord above that Facebook was not a thing when I was 21, or 16, or - Jesus Christ, can you imagine? - 13 years old. It'd be absolutely mortifying.

The point is, all of social media is terrible, but some of it is slightly less terrible than the rest. Posting album after album of baby photo camera roll probably qualifies as the most sensible way one can possibly use social media - everything else is just drawing rope for you to hang yourself with.

#9

Shit! Contractions!

Why are you reading this, you idiot? Put the book down! Now's not the time to read, it's the time to panic - your partner's uterus is exploding, go go go! There's no time to pack a bag, or put on any clothes, and a cab's going to take too long to arrive - you're just going to have to run straight to the hospital! Don't bother bringing the pregnant one, she'll just slow you down! Shit shit shit shit shit shit shit sh-

That was a test. If you're still reading this, you passed. Remain calm. Obviously as soon as contractions are confirmed, your body goes into emergency mode and your muscles all stiffen and you lose all coordination of your limbs and your brain starts undulating wildly like it's twerking in your skull and the voice in your head tells you that you could still make it to the Dover ferry in under two hours if you stopped for petrol and that you could forge a new life for yourself as a mime on the Parisian riverfront, sending over however many Euros per week qualifies as child support. Resist the temptation to do any of that. You're going to be a father whether you like it or not, you don't want to have to deal with street theatre on top of everything else.

But yes, you're correct, this is very much the endgame. The end of the beginning, or the beginning of the end if you've a flair for the dramatic. This is the point in the movie when it's just the hero and the villain left, standing on a rickety bridge in the lashing rain, and you think, right, this thing is definitely wrapping up pretty soon, might as well put the kettle on. The closing credits are rolling over the end of the first act of your life.

You can't escape. You can't turn back the clock. It's time to step up to the plate and be the man you always knew you could be. The first step is probably checking that your partner is not in too much pain, because you've been stood silently in the hallway for eight minutes with your key in the front door, lost in thought over how much mime you actually know. I mean, everyone can do 'I'm in a big glass box', but where do you go from there? What's the money mime?

Focus! The good thing about contractions - he says, very much without a female reproductive system - is that they're like a little ticking clock that guarantee you won't miss your big appointment. You could set your watch by these twats: the time between contractions is your best indicator on how things are progressing down there. They're like little status updates sent from the nether regions that contain nothing other than the red-faced angry emoji. Yes, as you may have guessed, this is the section of the book where I talk about female anatomy with the kind of unearned confidence that only a man can.

For a more accurate description, I asked Vicky what contractions felt like, and naively asked the question "Is it a bit like a muscle spasm?" She laughed in my face, then went deathly serious, all the love drained from her eyes, and she looked at me and said: "They're *excruciating*".

She showed me a video of a great analogy of contractions and birth, in which a woman placed a ping pong ball inside a balloon and half-inflated it. The contractions are the slow squeeze needed on the top and sides of the balloon to get the large ping pong ball slowly pushed through the tight, elasticated neck. It didn't help that the lady used a pink balloon, which reddened as the neck stretched and the ball crowned. I watched the whole thing with my legs crossed and my sphincter clenched. God bless my hideous male genitals. Contractions are not always straightforward. Be careful you do not fall foul of a hilarious prank the female body pulls on itself, where the cervix pretends it's having contractions when - get this - it's actually not. LOL! What a delightful biological jape! What perfect comedic timing!

These are called 'Braxton Hicks contractions', named after 19th century doctor John Braxton Hicks. I don't know the guy personally, but he sounds like a prick, because I couldn't think of a more annoying thing to put your own name to. Braxton Hicks contractions feel just like regular contractions, and women are more likely to get them in late stages of pregnancy, except they're not actually an indication that the labour process has begun. They're just for laughs! So that's something to look forward to! The fun never stops! Note the over-use of the exclamation mark to indicate sarcasm!

There's no official order of things when it comes to labour, and different women experience contractions in numerous different ways. Contractions are not even always the first indicator that baby is knocking on the door. Often the first sign that labour may be imminent is the 'bloody show': a screamingly literal description of a blood-tinged mucus plug dislodging itself from your partner's cervix. Yeah, the women in charge of naming the things that happened to them during birth really didn't sugar-coat it, did they? Anything to avoid having to say the words "mucus plug" again. You must resist the temptation to say it in your best 'George Clooney in From Dusk Till Dawn' voice ("Now that's what I call a bloody *show*!") because having to explain your rubbish movie references is really not going to help proceedings in any way.

Another indicator that THE HELLMOUTH IS OPENING is your partner's water breaking, which usually happens after contractions have begun. Movies and TV conditioned me to believe that a woman's water breaking was a) considerably gushy, and b) visible to external parties. This is not always the case. For some women, it'll be a small but constant trickle; for others it'll be like a surprise wee - either way, don't expect much of a "sploosh".

The water breaking is your clearest indicator yet that you're getting closer to the main event; with the amniotic sac drained of all fluid, your baby is more prone to infection, sort of like how when you fall asleep in the bath after a few glasses of wine and you wake up shivering and naked in an empty bathtub because you accidentally pulled the plug out with your arse. Like that but serious. It is around this point in the birth process where you must make the following note to self: do not, under any circumstances, be tempted to compare the pain of contractions, or any part of the birth, to a kick in the bollocks. You may be wondering as to the equivalence. I know I did. Zip it, swallow it, digest it and never speak of it. Men have such limited scope in how we can feel pain in our anatomy that 'a kick in the bollocks' is the worst possible thing that we can imagine. Unless, of course, you had to have the old swab up the jap's eye after your lads holiday to Riga turned out to be a ploy to indulge your mate's mate Kev's love of Eastern European prostitutes. I can't speak for that, but I have had bruised bollocks before, as I'm sure have all of you. I've had a football kicked square in the nads from point blank range. I've had a tennis ball launched into my testicles at about 50mph from an automatic service machine. This one time I briefly trapped my nut sack in a fold-up clothes horse (by accident, it wasn't a weird sex game) and almost passed out from the pain.

We all have bollock stories. I know it hurts. You know it hurts. Regardless: don't bring it up. Don't say anything. Unless your balls are about to split wide open and rip right down to your arsehole as a buttery watermelon passes through them, maybe just keep your opinions under your hat for now. Still, it's natural to wonder. Birth is probably worse than a kick in the bollocks. A bit worse.

There should be no need for alarm, because hopefully, you will have planned ahead for this situation. At least, I hope you did? My dude: it was a 100% certainty - this was never one of those 'I'll wing it on the day' type scenarios. You're not winning any cool points for being particularly Fonzie about this. Contractions mark the final stage of pregnancy, where your partner has moved on from nausea and discomfort to actual physical pain, which means congratulations are in order, because you've been promoted from useless nearby well-wisher to actual helpful baby-birthing facilitator. Don't try and be all unruffled 80s high school cool kid about it, Ferris Bueller. Plan ahead! Meticulous, comforting, useless plans!

I recommend you pack a bag ahead of time. The contents of the bag are irrelevant, because in the stressful hours to come, it's totally possible you'll forget to use anything you put in there. Get it packed nice and tight, all lovely and pointless and sat by the door. The contents of the bag don't matter. The bag is symbolic. It says 'If we can prepare ahead for this one thing, maybe we can prepare for ALL the things'. The bag is you. You're the bag. Be the best bag you can be.

Bag Item #1. Music

Spend some time crafting an iPod soundscape of soothing music and whale noises instead of relying on your trusty 'FRIDAY BANGERS' Spotify playlist. You're going to want to take great care putting together a birth mix, because man oh man is there potential for it to backfire. This is the music that will soundtrack one of the most memorable moments of your life; these are the tunes that will be the first things your baby ever hears. So, maybe don't just bang your iPod on random and give yourself over to the gods of shuffle, because I guarantee the one Nickelback song you have lurking in there "for a laugh" is just waiting for its moment.

The musical genre you're aiming for is somewhere between 'inoffensive background music' and 'pleasantly distracting upbeat tunes', which is a tricky mix to nail. Even artists you love can be grating in the extreme when you're trying to push a kid through an orifice. Anything too Lighthouse Family or Leonard Cohen and you run the risk of being the dipshit DJ who's making the whole birth worse, a feat no woman would even think possible. Anything too Taylor Swift or Tiësto and you'll stress everyone out with an unnecessarily high tempo. Yes, you want a playlist of songs you could accurately describe as "chilled out", but what you do not want are songs so middle of the road they'll get on the tits of any person in the room who's happening to endure an immensely traumatic physical experience. Before you know it, you're listening to the inimitable Welsh twang of Stereophonics frontman Kelly Jones, tolerating his "do do doo"s and his "have a nice day"s while you're staring at a mangled, bloody vagina. Birth music is supposed to coax the little bugger out of there, not convince them to crawl back in.

A friend of mine set up a pre-curated playlist for the birth of his first child and he and his wife had to grimly accept the fact that the first song their baby son ever heard was 'Would I Lie To You?' by Charles & Eddie; not a bad song, but not exactly one that says 'Welcome to the world'. Worse still, they relied on the radio for the birth of their second child, only for the *same*

Charles & Eddie song to start playing during their C-section. A cute quirk, or a cosmically-ordained coincidence that forever twins the fate of their children to that of the high-voiced interracial one-hit wonders? Time will tell on that one.

Don't trust the good people of Magic FM to do you a solid - there's every chance your baby will be born to 'Cotton-Eye Joe' and is therefore doomed for all eternity. Get the birth music wrong and you've fallen at the first hurdle; Child Services will be there to evaluate your parental skills before you've even made it to the car park: "Excuse me sir, we've been informed that you engineered a set-list of birthing music that included 'Sex on Fire' by Kings of Leon, would you please come with us?" It's all academic really, because at no point during the birth of your own child will you ever feel comfortable to ask an overworked NHS staff member 'Do you have a spare iPod dock?' Sigh. Just stick it in an empty glass and don't dare complain about 'the acoustics' unless you want it rammed up your hole.

Bag Item #2: Snacks

Food. Sustenance. Energy. This feels like a biggie. A short while after the birth of our second child, Vicky went deathly pale, started speaking in tongues and fainted. It was absolutely terrifying, but it turned out her blood sugar was low because throughout the 24 hours or so of labour, the only things that had passed her lips were gas and air, substances which are famously neither filling nor nutritious.

So, your next bag item should be food-based to avoid such an eventuality. Also, you might get peckish yourself. It's tiring standing around for hours on end, and you don't want to be out in the corridor staring straight through a vending machine when your little miracle is born. 'But my Scampi Fries got stuck in the coil!' is not a valid excuse for missing the birth of your child, and every Scampi Fry you eat for the rest of your days will be tainted with the acrid stench of your failure.

There are no official guidelines as to what foodstuffs are acceptable to eat in a hospital, so you're going to have to use - uh oh - common sense. Case in point: one member of my family may or may not have been told off for knocking back an entire bag of Wasabi Peas during the birth of his son. It sounds obvious in retrospect, but go easy on the umami. Good ideas: energy bars, fruit, anything boring or bland or inoffensive. Bad idea: anything meat-based (do not stop at Chicken Cottage), anything sloppier than a basic Tesco Value sandwich (the NHS frowns on crumbs), anything that's going to stain your fingers or stink to high hell (cradling your newborn child with orange Dorito dust on your fingers is a no-no), and anything that requires you to give directions to a delivery man (sweet Christ man, PRIORITIES). Avoid overly sweet stuff like Haribo - it might feel like a harmless little pick-me-up, but nothing will repulse you more than the consumption of a family pack of flavoured beef gelatine. My recommendation is to cram as many of those yoghurt covered breakfasty oat and nut bar things in the bag as you can. Consider that my official endorsement. I am available for sponsorship if anyone from Belvita is reading.

Bag Item #3: Clean clothes

Sure, why not. There's every chance you're going to be hanging around a very small area of hospital for hours on end, haunting the corridors, stressing and sweating and getting hella smelly. Who knows, maybe it'll be an overnight stay? Sleeping in a hospital bed, or in your case nodding off in a cheap IKEA chair next to a hospital bed, is not comfortable in the slightest, so you can at least bring a clean pair of kecks to make the undercarriage experience a little bit less... soupy.

Pack yourself a clean t-shirt too: not one of your best ones, and not one of your painting and decorating t-shirts, but something in between - a garment you wouldn't mind if it got unspecified birth goo all over it. Also be aware of the fact that when the baby has arrived, you're going to want to take photographs together, and it will probably reflect badly on you if you appear in those photographs wearing your FEDERAL BREAST INSPECTORS t-shirt. Nothing with any slogans or cartoon characters on it as a rule; fast-forward ten years to when your kid asks to see their baby photos and you have to spend 20 minutes explaining what Rick & Morty was.

While we're in the vicinity of clothing, make sure you have comfortable footwear ready to roll, because you are going to be doing a lot of standing, probably more non-stop standing than you've ever done in your life, a veritable marathon of standing up, standing still and pacing up and down the wards. Don't be the guy in his work shoes. Don't be the guy who feels the need to take his work shoes off, becoming the guy in his socks. It's got to be trainers all the way, or slip-ons if you want to make it fashion. Just don't inform your dangerously pregnant wife about your choice of sensible footwear expecting some sort of kudos, because the soles of your feet are not particularly high on the list of body parts she's worrying about right now.

If you really want to score points, pack a whole bunch of knickers and clean tops and sleepshirts for her. It should go without saying but I'll say it anyway: nothing too sexy. God, keep it in your pants you dirty dog, nothing erotic is going to happen for several months, get used to it. In lady pant terms, the bigger and Bridget Jonesier the better. You want to pack her the kind of pants that you could carry your shopping home in.

Round off the bag with fistfuls of other useless essentials. Toiletries, lip balm, hairbands, bendy straws. Paracetamol, yeah, that'll take the edge off. A book, of course: *because reading material will make this go quicker*. A USB charger for some reason. Tissues I guess? Is chewing gum allowed? Um, a notepad and pen? Yeah? It's all good, get it all in there. Overload that bad boy with tat.

Mission accomplished: you packed the bag ahead of time. So, when the time comes and the contraction panic kicks in, you can accidentally leave it by the front door on your way out of the house and not feel guilty. The fact remains: you packed the bag.

The next, fairly obvious, step: you're going to need to get to a hospital. Unless you're planning a home birth, of course. Home births sound great because theoretically you never leave the comfort of your own home and your baby is born straight into familiar surroundings, and if the birth takes longer than expected you can nip into the kitchen to break open the good biscuits. Plus you know the Wi-Fi password.

However, you also run the risk of getting placenta all over the carpet, womb lining getting right in there in amongst the fibres of your shag, and you'll never, ever be allowed to complain about the stain because apparently it's not even nearly the same as the time you accidentally trod dog shit through the house. So it's swings and roundabouts really. Let's assume for the purposes of this chapter, you're giving birth in a nice, reliable, sterile, carpet-free hospital.

If you're driving, you'll need to plan the route - no, scratch that, you'll need to plan three routes: 1) The direct route, straight there, green lights all the way, no bother whatsoever, slotting straight into the empty parking space right nice to the Maternity Unit; 2) The back-up route, which supposes that there will be roadworks galore and traffic on all the main roads, meaning you'll need to find the top secret hidden but super-fast route to the hospital that definitely exists but no one knows about; 3) the

'999 Special Episode with Michael Buerk' route, where the straightforward 10-minute drive to the hospital is rendered an apocalyptic nightmare by a fiery train crash or a hellish bus explosion or a landslide or something. Can you guarantee you'll make it to the hospital when the nation's transportation network falls into absolute chaos due to an impending Mad Max-style scenario? Hey, it could happen. Do your homework just in case - it'll reduce the overall panic in your partner by about 0.4%. Progress!

You're at the hospital now, meaning it's highly unlikely that you'll have a dramatic, soap opera-style birth in the back of a car or a bus stop or a crowded pub full of a colourful cast of Cockneys on Christmas Day.

You're in the right place. Hospitals have got all the equipment for getting babies out of there - the big BBQ tongs, the vacuum sucky thing, the stretchy gloves, all of the things. I'd say you could relax, but we both know that's not going to happen. The first thing you notice when you get to the hospital is that all the employees are freakishly calm and placid, which only has the effect of making you freak out more. This is because, in the nicest possible way, no one there is half as worried about your baby as you are. Of course, NHS staff are the salt of the Earth, and they're diligent and hardworking professionals who toil endlessly in terrible conditions for the good of their fellow humans. But also, they're at work. Think how much you care about your thankless, low-paying job, and transpose that lack of passion onto them. Frightening, isn't it? Even people doing high pressure jobs get complacent sometimes. We've all heard stories about pilots landing passenger planes with stinking hangovers, right? Well, replace 'pilot' with 'nurse', 'plane' with 'small human being', 'hangover' with 'shit pay' and imagine the runway is your life. That's right: the person ultimately responsible for delivering your firstborn into the world goes about the task with as much zeal as you do when tabulating your quarterly sales reports.

This is the start of the inevitable comedown, when the initial 'This is it!' adrenaline starts wearing off and the crushing reality kicks in. You will probably be waiting hours before your partner is far along enough to begin pushing or be induced and the birth can begin. Hell, you could be waiting days. You might even have to go home and come back to the hospital when the contractions get closer together, meaning you have to go back to square one re: bag-packing and travel arrangements. Go back home and try to get some sleep, they tell you, with a straight face and everything.

It slowly dawns on you: having a baby is the most boring exciting thing that will ever happen to you. Maybe you are one of the lucky ones and your lady swans into the hospital with a right old wide-on, bypassing the triage waiting area like a priority boarder to go straight to the birthing unit where the baby will slide out of her like a bar of soap. Probably not, though. You'd better start hunkering down, it's likely you're in it for the long haul.

It's a good thing, really. The birth will take every ounce of energy you both have, so having a brief bit of respite before the push over the top, as it were, is quite welcome. You'll get to sit and chat with your partner and behave somewhere in the region of normal, while still both hyper-aware that your kid is one sturdy mucus plug away from showing his or her face. When was the last time you just sat and talked together, without the distraction of food or Netflix or sleep? Remember when time just seemed to melt away when you were together? Good, because this is not that: I hate to break it to you, but you're going to feel every goddamn hour, minute by agonising minute. A couple of hours of waiting you can handle, it's no more trouble than buying Glasto tickets. But six hours? Twelve? Longer? Ooof.

Bear in mind also the following two caveats: first, you are not allowed to complain - she is, obviously, but you're definitely not - and second, you're not allowed to get your phone out either. Let me reiterate in capitals for added emphasis: YOU'RE NOT ALLOWED TO USE YOUR PHONE. I mean, technically you are, and it's right there in your pocket, singing its little digital siren's song like always. Fiddle with me! I contain the sum of all human knowledge! Just one little play! But think how it looks: what possible tweets could be more interesting or exciting than the impending birth of your first child? None tweets, is the answer. You're onto a loser here, chief. Just do what the rest of us did and secretly check the football scores when you go to the toilet.

It's understandable that you might get bored. It is possible to believe the following two contrasting opinions to be simultaneously true: that birth is a miracle, and that it can also be quite tedious waiting for that miracle to arrive. For example, let's say the second coming of Jesus Christ was announced out of the blue and was scheduled for 3pm. Everyone is psyched! You go to the chosen arena where He himself is scheduled to return, super-excited, well ahead of 3pm to get there in plenty of time. So pumped for Christ! However, 3pm comes and goes, and you're still excited, but there's still no word. It's now 6pm and you're checking your watch and you've been given no official explanation as to why Christ is late, and his disciples are no good, they're just standing around like idiots, waiting just like you. You get to 11pm and you start thinking, 'Come on Jesus, this is ridiculous' - it's not that you're angry at Christ per se, just that His return has been so badly organised, and you haven't eaten anything yet, and come to think of it you don't even know how you're going to get home because the last Tube has probably left.

Then, eventually, 12 hours later, lo and bloody behold: Jesus Christ in the house! When He finally shows up you forget about all the waiting because of the whole general Son of God positivity vibe and all the magic tricks with the wine and bread and all that, but at the time there you were quite rightfully aggrieved at being made to wait so long, and it did briefly threaten to take the shine off the Second Coming. It turns out that having a baby is also quite a lot like attending a Guns 'n' Roses concert.

It's quite possible that during the contraction period you'll have your first encounter with - ugh - other pregnant people. How dare they: using up all the gas and air, getting the slightly larger and comfier looking chairs, generally being one centimetre more dilated than you are at all times - the nerve!

Up until this point your pregnancy experience will have been extremely personal and self-contained, with social excursions like NTC courses as optional extras. Suddenly, before you know it you're in a public hospital, sharing the same facilities as other members of the great unwashed, who are probably called Sharon or Dave or Jordan and their pregnancy is probably just a big scam for extra benefits and it's just a pillow up there.

You don't get this with private healthcare; no one else is allowed to give birth in the same postcode as you, you get all the purest, uncut drugs from the best dealers in the county and the harpists in the delivery rooms are instructed not to make eye contact with you. But no. You had to consistently fail to pick winning scratchcards and thus had to give birth in a *public* hospital on the *National* Health Service. Great.

Our first birthing experience was not really an enjoyable one. Vicky's contractions started at about 1am, which is an incredibly inconvenient time to go into labour if you think about it, and there were very few doctors available so we ended up waiting for nine hours in the triage - that's a curtained-off cubicle about the size of a swimming pool changing room, or a Starbucks disabled toilet. The girl in the cubicle next to us was having a tough old time of things because it was literally impossible to not hear both sides of the phone call in which she called her absent boyfriend a "stupid cunt"; she then told her Mum to "fuck off" before pissing herself, and the wee seeped under the curtain into our cubicle and I got it all over my nice comfortable trainers. They don't tell you that in the other baby books: 'Don't wear your best trainers because you might have to stand in a puddle of someone else's urine'. You're welcome.

There's enough drama to go around without swapping bodily fluids with your new friends. Gas and air is a huge source of both thrills and spills, literal highs and bottomless lows. If you're ruled out for the epidural like we were and you find yourself careening straight for a (*gulp*) natural birth, gas and air is the only thing that's going to get you through.

At first, Vicky couldn't get enough of that sweet, sweet nitrous; not only did it calm the nerves and numb the pain, but it distracted her and made her start blathering the sort of pie-eyed gibberish you normally hear from weed smokers. However, though gas and air may be natural commodities, they are finite as fuck in a hospital environment, and the rapidly diminishing levels on the canister act as a good indicator on exactly when you should start panicking again.

It's not an exaggeration when I say that my beautiful wife honked on a drug pipe connected to a canister the size and weight of something Jack Bauer would have to defuse, and she bled that entire sucker dry. By rights she should have inflated to a comical size and needed anchoring to the ground. You just have to hope the drug pushers in your local hospital have an equally envious supply of nitrous that has clearly been swiped from under the bonnet of Vin Diesel's car.

Hopefully, finally, after seemingly endless inspection of your wife's vagina, a maternity worker will give you the nod and tell you you're fully dilated - in other words, the door is fully open, you're just waiting for the welcome party.

Brace yourself: it's time to move into the birthing ward. You'll go through those double doors a man and come out a dad - although sometimes you might have to go into a lift as well, in which case you'll go into that lift a man and come out a dad (on the way back down after the birth I mean, not immediately after getting out of the lift on the way up: please consult your local hospital's floor plan for the specifics of exactly what you need to come out of to become a dad).

This is it. Crunch time. Baby o'clock. Let the time and date burn into your memory, because the quote-unquote "happiest day of your life" is happening right now, and it's absolutely terrifying. Even if you wanted to run as far away as your piss-soaked trainers could carry you, there's no mime on earth that could adequately convey the array of emotions you're about to go through.

#10

The Birth: "Oh God, WHAT DO I DO?" and Other Questions

This is it. The big one. Remember the breathing techniques that weren't actually for you, and try to stay calm - the one thing this scenario could absolutely do without is a shrieking lunatic melting in the corner. The simple fact is this: in a matter of minutes, there is going to be one additional person in this room; then, in a matter of hours, you're going to have to take that additional person home, and they're going to live with you, eat all your food and upend your social life for at least eighteen years.

Christ. It's a lot to take in, isn't it? Between one swing of life's pendulum to the next, your life changes completely. Tick: immature if well-meaning idiot. Tock: actual father to an actual human being. Tick: no dependencies, total freedom. Tock: grumbling to no one in particular about Tube stations that don't have lifts. BONGGG. The bell tolls for thee.

Obviously you will have had nine whole months of getting used to the idea of your newfound responsibilities, but as you're racing through the maternity unit, following your panting partner horizontal on a hospital bed like in every bad medical drama you've ever seen on TV, it can honestly feel like the pregnancy has passed in a heartbeat - and you haven't even got to the hard part yet. Being in a birthing unit right before your baby is born is like standing at the foot of Mount Everest and preparing to conquer it: yes, it's massively overwhelming and hugely intimidating and really quite frightening, but you know deep down you can give it your best, and what's more, you kind of have to do it now *because you already bought all the stuff.*

First, a home truth: your presence here is not a requirement. To be clear: this is not an invitation to nip round the corner to Dave's Arcade and have another bash at finishing Time Crisis 3. Obviously, yes, you're present at the birth because you're not a complete and utter shit, and because you're supporting your partner through literally the worst pain she'll ever feel in her life, and because it's a miracle to see your own child come into the world - just a few reasons why you would never, ever miss this life-changing, character-defining moment.

However, it's important you know your role: emotional support, hand-holding and... er, that's basically it. Saying nice things and offering a clammy hand to squeeze. Allow that hand to be squeezed and don't make so much as a whimper if she grinds your bones into dust.

During the birth, you are a completely perfunctory person. You need to be there, but you're not actually of use. You're surplus to requirements. Think of yourself like a cushion on a sofa. Yes, everyone has cushions on sofas, but take those cushions away and you can still sit on that sofa - it doesn't cease to be a sofa, it just doesn't have a cushion on it any more.

If a purple space tyrant clicked his fingers and you vanished into a wisp of smoke and ash, it'd be a real bummer, don't get me wrong, a total mood-killer for everyone, but at the end of the day, that baby will still get born. It is a very strange experience being on the periphery of an incredibly intense and visceral experience such as childbirth, because there are horrendous hardships being endured by people you love *right there in front of you*, but despite your close proximity you can't do anything about it. It's a bit like accidentally walking into the finale of a slasher movie and having to stand silently in the shadows while the killer mutilates everyone.

So, to reiterate: be aware of your surroundings, do what you're told by the doctors and trained medical staff, do the bidding of your poor partner and fulfil her every request without question or sarcasm, get the fuck out of the way when necessary (hint: it's always necessary), and get used to the idea of not being in even the top five most important people in the room.

The moment that kid pops out, you instantly become a less important priority, and it stays that way until the day you die. Don't fight it, don't kick against it - give in to it and get used to it. This is the perfect time and place to check your ego, like, maybe forever - leave your am-dram, attention-seeking, woe-is-me, burn-it-all-down self-sabotage bullshit at the door and don't bother collecting it on the way out.

Hey, it's been a while since you did or said anything! Be your partner's cheerleader and offer more words of encouragement. Try something like "You're doing so well!", that always goes down a treat. Maybe deviate on that theme, like "I can't believe how well you're doing!" or maybe even "Who's doing well? You are!" Don't get cocky, kid. Keep it simple. Keep it brief. Don't be afraid to duplicate platitudes. You're not submitting work for Oscar consideration - tell her she's brilliant five thousand times if you like, as long as you get the message across. I stuck to a script something like the above, as I was terrified of saying something stupid or insensitive like I always do.

Areas to avoid covering are: anything to do with timeframe (e.g. "Nearly there!" or "Not long now!") because you don't have a single bloody clue how much longer it's going to take; anything to do with pain (e.g. "Does it hurt?") unless you want to hear in explicit and vivid detail about exactly how much it hurts and where; any random non-sequiturs about anything that happens to stumble into your stream of consciousness (e.g. "Don't worry, I set the Sky+ to record tonight's Graham Norton Show, we can watch it when we're back!"); and finally, anything - and I mean absolutely anything - to do with you or any hardships you might be going through, because no one will ever care about your sore feet, clammy hands, bad back or numb bum. "You're doing so well!" gets the job done efficiently, time after time, with no aggro. It is the Peter Crouch of platitudes - feel free to keep bringing it off the subs' bench.

If there's lots of shallow breathing and rushing around of healthcare workers, and you feel extra-specially useless, then you're probably getting close to hearing those immortal words: "We're going to need you to push". This is it, this is literally it. The legs are up in the stirrups. There's quite a lot of poo, certainly more poo than you were expecting, at any other time seeing that quantity and consistency of poo might be alarming, but the poo is barely registering right now, because: baby is coming.

Everything from this moment is clouded by intensity, and becomes difficult to recall in detail - you'll enter into a sort of fugue state, which does tend to make it quite difficult to later remember any witticisms or observations that might make for interesting reading in a book you may or may not end up writing.

Heed my advice: take a second, the only second you need take for yourself throughout this entire process, and push 'record' in your head. Sear these moments into your brain forever. Be present. Witness heroism up close and personal on a scale you never thought possible. Never forget how lucky you are to have stupid, dangly, convex genitals. Any time in the future you get tired or emotional or feel discontent, remember how much sheer pain your partner went through, how much Cronenberg-ian body horror she endured, how much weight she gained and blood she lost and poo she publicly pooed in order to bring your child into the world. She had to do the hardest thing she'd ever done, birth, so you could both do the new hardest thing you'll ever do, parenting. Don't ever, ever forget it. Technically you will never win another argument as long as you live: this beats all.

If you're debating which end you need to be at for the main event, my advice is to forgo the relative sanctity of the head-end and get in the end-zone where all the action is. Get in the mixer, my son! There's no glory hanging back in your own half, no prizes for playing it safe. Nothing is going to drive home the visceral intensity and the physical toll of this birth more than having a front row ticket to the whole Grand Guignol show. Unless you're likely to faint at the sight of blood like a sitcom character with a slide whistle, I cannot recommend it enough: nobody likes missing the first few minutes of the movie, so I don't understand why you'd purposely avoid the first time your child's skin has ever seen sunlight, gore be damned.

The sight of a baby crowning is one of the most astonishing and unforgettable things you will ever witness in your entire life. For your partner, this has been very real for nine whole months - the connection has been total, the bond permanent, and now, the pain exquisite. For the father, however, save for a few soft kicks and calming whispers delivered through a belly button, this is the first time you can *see* them, the first time you get to feel that palpable connection for yourself.

It's the first time you can truly appreciate the magnitude of the task, the overwhelming physical sacrifice that your partner has made, the sheer size of the fruit of your looms. You'll look straight through the goo and the poo, and the fact there are way more dark blue and purple things than you were expecting, because this is the closest you will ever get to watching an actual miracle unfold. You may accidentally go several minutes without breathing because it all happens so fast. You've been pacing around the maternity unit for hours, maybe even days, dragging your feet and staring at the clock, willing the baby to get a shift on; now, suddenly, in the blink of an eye, it's got one foot in the front door.

Maybe the next push sees the whole head emerge: a sight so simultaneously alarming and comforting and ridiculous it's genuinely a shock to the system. It's a little person! Living inside another person! Like a Russian Doll! You knew this all along, obviously - right? - but seeing it with your own eyes barely computes in the moment.

At this point, the department in your brain that regulates emotions has officially declared emergency measures due to an overwhelming workload and a shortage of staff: it is the most harrowing, wonderful, terrifying and magical moment of your life, and you are not equipped to deal with those emotions individually at the best of times, let alone all of them at once.

A braver and more vain man than I would train a head-mounted GoPro on his own face during the birth and later watch back the film of his own myriad expressions, attempting to extrapolate which emotions were being felt. You're probably looking at combinations of 'heart-stopping fear', 'life-affirming joy' and 'severe fatigue' at a base level, with a hearty helping of 'pride' and just a dash of 'gonna vom' in the mix too. Such relentless emoting takes a gruelling toll on the mind and the body; when the adrenaline wears off, you may feel like you've been physically assaulted by an invisible, face-punching maniac.

Maybe the next push is the last one - once the head and

shoulders are out, the rest of the baby slides out with one final guttural, tennis player grunt. Suddenly: baby! Total baby! Houston, we have a baby! There are medical staff rushing around, clamping this and clotting that, grunting turns to crying, and you may be vaguely aware of nurses talking in impenetrable medi-speak, but it doesn't matter. You have a baby. God help us all.

At this point you are probably so tense you're levitating, but be sure to come down to earth to meet your child. Sure, it's small and completely purple, and covered in a weird white sauce you will later learn is called 'vernix' - a Latin word which literally translates as 'cheesy varnish' - but it's your child! You guys made a person! You created life! You have achieved fatherhood! You have a... oh shit, right, is it a boy or a girl?

In all the excitement and amongst all the paralysing fear, you may, like me, forget to ask what sex the baby is. I was so overwhelmed with the tsunami of tension and so wiped out by the subsequent waves of relief, I lasted a good 30 seconds in a blissful baby bubble before I even remembered that humans came in different types. Congratulations, Mr Reader: it's a beautiful bouncing baby boy/girl [delete where applicable]!

There's no time for smug self-satisfaction, because your first official job as a father approaches: the cutting of the umbilical cord. That's right, the traditional severing of the sinewy conduit that connects your new baby directly to the life-giving sentient blob that is the placenta. It's really not a job you can mess up: you can't accidentally cut off the wrong appendage, because the nurses will have the cord clamped and the instrument in place ready for you to cut, so the whole thing feels ceremonial in nature, a bit like cutting a ribbon at the opening of a new branch of WHSmiths. A ribbon that's made of thick, white, pulsing human gristle.

I won't lie, this bit is gross as fuck. It feels super wrong that the first contact you make with your child is to shear part of it clean off. And don't even get me started on the placenta. That shit is disgusting. Yes, it provided your baby with nutrient-rich blood while it was in utero, but what happens inside the body stays in the human body - I know my colon performs a valuable service all up in my guts but I don't need to see it plopped in a bedpan outside of my arsehole.

I won't go into too much detail, but the placenta looks like someone accidentally sat on a brain then left it in an airing cupboard for a year. It looks like a deflated plastic football that was presumed lost but is found at the bottom of the garden underneath an old fence panel where it's being used as a hostel for woodlice. It looks like an angry bag of offal. It's like a jellyfish made of blood, or a pancake made of lungs, or a cheap raw minute steak dunked in blue ink. I know some people like to eat their placenta, but my first instinct upon seeing it was to Sellotape it to the underside of a frisbee and fling it out the nearest window. Placentas are givers of life, but they're also capable of killing mother and baby, which is all the proof I need that it's the devil's whoopee cushion and you need to have an exorcist on speed-dial just in case.

Some days later, when you have finally come down from your baby-birthing high, you may think back to these alien body parts - the vaginal cheese-wax lubricant, the veiny blood tube, the fleshy demon pizza on the other end - and do a full-body shudder. But for now, all you have to do is *snip*. Don't think too hard about what it is or what it does, just crimp that shit right off. Job done. Hey, this parenthood lark isn't so bad!

Meanwhile, motherhood gets off to a bumpy start: as if giving birth wasn't hard enough, your partner will then have to pass her placenta, which is no picnic either. Even then, she's likely to need 'clean-up' - there's never a good time to hear the words "torn perineum" but it's always a possibility, and stitches could be in the offing too. Basically, the woman you love just blasted a hole in herself so you can one day live out your dream of taking a tiny version of yourself to see a Star War - she needs rest, care and attention.

It is at this point - while the baby is taken aside for checks - that you may feel the most spectacularly useless you have ever felt, if only for a few brief moments. Emotions may get the better of you, and you should let them. The entire experience is a savage whirlwind, a hurricane of high tension and drama - you'll both feel like you've been picked up, shaken around and dumped back on the ground in a completely different state, and even though in this moment the eye of the storm provides some calm, the harsh winds of worry never relent, not really. You are both forever changed: physically, spiritually, emotionally. It's understandable if you want to shed some tears, because the life you once enjoyed is over, gone, never to return. Lie-ins on the weekend. Spontaneous nights out. Relaxing holidays. Disposable income. All ablaze on a Viking pyre that's floating ever out of view. Not always, but usually, it signifies the end of your youth.

And then, the baby returns.

It's less purple than it was before - in fact, it's something approaching a human skin colour, probably the sort of colour you'd turn if you'd been screaming for that long. It's all cleaned up, and significantly less 'glazed' than it was upon exit. It's all swaddled up in blankets and cosy and calm. That's a bit more like it - less 'recently pulled screaming from a bloody exit wound', more 'most liked Facebook photo of all time'.

And then you get to hold it. And, Christ, in that moment, in that single instant, at maybe only three or four minutes old, it unlocks something inside you, something that changes you forever. It is, unquestionably, the happiest moment of your life, you're sure the only moment of your life that has ever really mattered, and you're in it, living it, savouring the first true moment of calm you've felt in days and weeks and months. They are so helpless, so naive and innocent, so infinitely perfect, and yet their world is so small. New feelings rush through your veins: the urge to protect this armful of pointy elbows and skinny legs from the world; the resolve to do whatever needs to be done to give it the best possible life; the certainty that this kid, your kid, is going to be the best kid out of all the kids. You're feeling the truest and most powerful kind of love, and it surges through you like adrenaline, revitalising you, giving you purpose anew - an hour ago you were such a shambles you could have strolled onto the set of The Walking Dead without makeup and not looked out of place, but now you feel ten feet tall and made out of steel girders. This is it. This is what being a father feels like. Hold onto it for as long as you can and try desperately not to let it go.

Now, If you don't mind, I'm ending this chapter here because I need to go and hug my kids.

#11

The 50 Best Bits of Being a Dad

C onsider this chapter an intermission. It's a balm for your soul. You have just been through one of the most intense experiences of your life even though you technically didn't even do anything. The aftermath of the birth is a scary time for a man. You'll have many questions, like 'What do I do now?' and 'Seriously, what am I supposed to do now?'

Your entire life just went through a major upgrade: you have just gone from having 'zero' children to 'one' children, or 'child' if you want to use the correct term. And yes, although you will temporarily be doo-lallied with New Dad Endorphins (science), this blissed-out state is sadly fleeting and will soon make way for familiar friends like panic, anxiety and high intensity sweating.

So, you need a time-out. You need positive reinforcement. You need a metaphorical arm around your shoulder, and a metaphorical voice to tell you that everything's going to be metaphorically okay. I'm happy to be both of those disembodied entities on this occasion. I'm delighted to tell you that the rest of your life as a father is going to contain countless moments of unimaginable happiness, contentedness and love. Honestly, I take great pleasure in doing so: I feel like I'm an X Factor judge telling my group of fresh-faced young lads that they're going through to judges' houses, where a duet with an ex-member of Westlife almost certainly awaits. For some reason I am Louis Walsh in my metaphor.

As men, we don't talk about the good stuff often enough. We tend to think our default setting should be stoic and hardy, that we should stay strong and provide for the family, and that it's the women who are expected to be emotional and goo-goo-eyed and the foremost facilitators of cootchie-coo-ing. Fuck that shit. If you truly open yourself up to fatherhood and embrace it with a full heart, there is so much to it that will enrich your lives.

So, while your old lady and your new baby sleep like it's the first time they've ever slept, do yourself a favour: exist in this little waking dreamworld for a little while longer, practice some much-needed self-care and indulge yourself with the best of what's yet to come.

***

1.

Children are the ultimate excuse for everything ever. Having kids is the real-life equivalent of a 'Get Out Of Jail Free' card. It is the most wonderful thing. It doesn't matter what kind of occasion you want to avoid, even if it was an occasion that you planned - if you feel less than enthused about doing a thing, then you can use your kid as an excuse, and you no longer have to do that thing. As if by magic. The excuse can be as specific or as vague as you wish, because no one will ever question it. Sorry, my kid is coming down with something, I can no longer attend your birthday drinks. Sorry, we had a bit of a rough one last night so I'm going to need to skip your slam poetry meet just this once to catch up on some sleep. Sorry, my child exists therefore I no longer feel burdened to be social in any capacity whatsoever, you're just going to have to find someone else to do my community service.

Displaying your kids' paintings around your gaff makes you feel like a TV Dad in an American sitcom. I love having the kids' artwork pinned on the walls or stuck to the fridge or generally just adhered to any surface in the house. There's something performative about it that makes me feel like a proper stereotype, like I'm living in a single-camera situation comedy and playing a perennially grumpy suburban dad who hates his neighbours and resents his buxom wife but occasionally has to admit he loves his suspiciously old-looking kids [comedy tuba noise]. Having your kids paint a picture of you is also a great way of figuring out how they see you, so hopefully the illustrated you is big and lollopy and smiley and not a frenzied mess of jagged black scrawls and stink lines. Hey, wait a minute kiddo, why the heck have you drawn Mommy holding hands with the Pool Boy?!? [canned laughter]

3.

Proper unconditional love. Including 'unconditional love' as an upside of fatherhood maybe doesn't feel like I'm doing it justice - it should be your guiding principle to everything that follows. To have your kid love you from the moment they first open their eyes should be your only aim and the only thing of real importance in your life. Unconditional love from your children is your power source now, not food or sleep or exercise, and it will inform absolutely every single thing you do. Luckily, it's not a difficult thing to obtain, as long as you're not a huge asshole or you've entered into some kind of emotionally twisted We Need To Talk About Kevin-style scenario.

4.

You get to be there for all of your baby's 'firsts'. Memory is cruel because it only goes back so far. Yeah, maybe you remember your first kiss, your first pint, your first wank. All solid gold. But what about the truly momentous firsts that you experienced as a young child? Lost to the mists of time. Fatherhood gives you the opportunity to experience these achievements second-hand via your children. You get to be there for it all. The first step. The first word. The first time eating solid food. It's a thrill to play the part of an extremely localised historian, specialising solely in the achievements of your offspring. And even though these things eventually become less special through repetition over time, you get to hold onto these memories forever in your own private mind museum (until it's eventually closed for renovation).

5.

It is impossible to think of anything less important than how you dress. Male fashion standards are already pretty subterranean when compared to the expectations around how women dress, but once you have a baby, the arse falls out of your wardrobe and still no one will bat an eyelid. There exists no item of clothing too casual for a new father to wear: pyjama bottoms and slippers for the short trip to the corner shop; an oversized XXL hoodie so shapeless it could feasibly fit a party of four; a faded and yellowing promotional video game t-shirt that accentuates your burgeoning dadbod curves. It's so freeing! It may be several weeks before you venture into a pair of jeans and the suffocation of tight denim on your skin will give you heart palpitations. Let me stay here, I'm so comfortable in my style wasteland.

6.

Getting the first laugh from the baby. Extremely newborn babies are very cute but are essentially just sentient people-shaped blobs. They don't really do anything. What a waste of time! But wait. A few weeks in, and you start to get a glimmer of a smile during playtime. A smile that definitely wasn't fart-related. That was fun-related. So you do whatever you did again. And again. And again. Until, eventually: a laugh! An actual human laugh! Your action directly led to an emotional response from baby that wasn't a cry! It's not just a blob, it's people! Clearly you are smashing the whole fatherhood thing. This micro-validation gives you a hit more addictive than any drug, and you'll spend the rest of your life trying to replicate it.

7.

Also: having someone to laugh at your jokes is just what your ego needs! This little guy gets it! Yeah, him, the emotionally stunted one-year-old who still craps himself on a daily basis! It is incredibly easy to get a laugh out of an infant child, and it is very easy to convince yourself you are a comedic genius when you're in their company. Any material based on or around bums, poo or wee is going to *slay*. In case you were wondering, this is absolutely where Dad Jokes come from: the bar is set low and stays low, even when your kids outgrow it.

8.

Father's Day is like getting a whole extra birthday every year. Now you're cashing in your chips! From now on, for one day in June, you get to reap the benefits of Father's Day, a day specifically designed to benefit you, a father. For 24 hours, the kind of VIP status that only a small amount of money could buy.

Maybe it comes in the form of a humorous card (I hope you like football or golf or jokes about farting because there is a 98% certainty that's what's on your card) or a fancy beer or a morning lie-in, or all of those things. Gifts are nice, but honestly, it's an honour and a pleasure just to *be* a father and to be able to spend the day with your family. Please collect all gifts in advance on the gift table, gift-giving will commence after the lie-in.

9.

You now have a special licence to smile at cute little kids on public transport without feeling like a weirdo. Lookit that little smasher on the bus. Going to give him a cheeky little smile. Classic kiddywink. And bless, that adorable wee girl sitting on her daddy's knee. Might throw her a wink. It's all perfectly legitimate, because, look, I also am in possession of a child, therefore I cannot be considered an oddball or a possible baby snatcher. Parenthood, am I right guys? We're all in this together, etc! It's all fun and games until you catch yourself smiling at a little kid on the train and you realise you don't have your own kid with you acting as your nonce shield and for a split second you worry the kid's dad might fill you in for being a massive paedo.

10.

Being welcomed home by screaming maniacs who literally worship you. Many times I have come home carrying all the stress of a hard day's work, only to be greeted by my hysterical children who will literally yell my name and run the length of the house as fast as their little legs can carry them to thwomp satisfyingly into my gut. And it's only Tuesday. There's honestly no feeling quite like it. It's almost worth leaving the house for.

11

When you let them beat you up in a play fight and it doesn't even hurt because you know that if it came to it you could take them easily. It's not really a flex you should be proud of, but you've always got it in your back pocket should there be any doubt. It wouldn't even be a contest. A hypothetical rabbit punch to the ribs should just about put it to rest. Maybe next time you'll think twice about hypothetically engaging me in a tickle fight, you little punk.

12.

Parenthood means your opinions on any subject suddenly have more heft to them. Being a dad is an extra special argument qualifier, which you can wear like a special big boy badge of honour. Try this out for size, it's the perfect opener to any vaguely controversial or hot-button conversational topic that might pop up: "As a parent, I think..." You can add whatever bullshit you want after the ellipsis, it doesn't matter, people will still pay attention to your opinion and give it credence, at least relatively compared to anyone in the conversation unfortunate enough to be childless. Finally, a seat at the grown-ups table. True, your opinions on everything are still terrible, but at least people are *listening* to them.

13.

No one can stop you dressing your kid in frankly ridiculous clothes for your own amusement. If you want to dress up your infant child like a moustachioed pirate for laughs, then you do so. If dressing your baby up like Yoda makes you feel good, you should do it. If you want to put your kid in a giant hotdog costume then it is your God-given right. I want you to do that. I want to see those pictures, and so would other people, because dressing up a child in ludicrous costumes for the sole purpose of making adults laugh is never not hilarious. It is a fundamental cornerstone of good parenting.

14.

Cuddles. Yeah, that's right, motherfucking cuddles. Real men love cuddles. Real men ask for cuddles and give cuddles and pursue more cuddles at the cost of all else. Introducing cuddles into the life of a man who has led a largely cuddle-free adulthood is like giving a thirsty man a long glass of water in the desert. When you pick up the kid and hold them close and nuzzle them in your nook, both fitted together like snap-to-fit building blocks, you can feel the good juju fizz inside you. Note: hugs are not cuddles. Don't flop your arms around me and kid me you're down to cuddle. It's a full-body thing: arms and legs need to be fully wrapped around the body and suspended above the ground. When done right, there's no place you'd rather be. If Donald Trump's father had cuddled him even once, the world would be a very different place.

15.

Being able to easily bullshit your way out of any discussion with your kids using verbal gymnastics or actual proper deceptive behaviour and gaslighting. This is a special treat, applicable only to adults: as a father to children, you get to say one thing and do the other and there's literally nothing anyone can do to stop you. Practice what you preach? No thanks, what's in it for me? I mean, there's no need to be nasty with it, like, don't eat all their Soreen and act like it never happened, but sometimes a man has to protect his own hypocritical self, you know? So you can roll out the old classics like 'Don't spoil your dinner' while also completely ignoring your own rules and boshing through a pre-meal Twix, because, actually, adults need a much higher daily calorie intake than children, so go off. Didn't know that, did you? Didn't even know what a calorie was. We can do this all day. Looks like *I* win this round, small child.

16.

You get to pass on your musical tastes to your children, whether they appreciate it or not. From the moment you started trying for a baby, you had probably already mentally fast-forwarded to this precise moment in time: the moment where you get to force your kids to listen to the music that you like, in the vain hope that they'll like it too and eventually grow up to be [sniggers] as cool as you. It's tempting to think of yourself as a sort of wizened old John Peel-esque figure, curating amazing playlists of obscure landfill indie bands and LCD Soundsystem deep cuts for one extremely nonplussed listener. I once had a mini breakdown in the car when Kid A asked me to turn up the radio when 'Don't Look Back In Anger' was playing because he said he liked it. He's me! He's basically me! Never mind that the musical landscape will be completely different by the time your kids are old enough to appreciate music as an art form; never mind that there aren't really 'scenes' any more, or recognisable 'tribes' for them to belong to. They *will* like The Strokes, dammit, they will.

17.

You get to give them the haircut you always wanted. Alternatively, if they get a bad haircut, ehh, it's not like it's your problem.

18.

Discovering that the kids of today still play with the toys you played with as a kid. When was the last time you thought of Fuzzy Felt? 25 years ago? 30? Fuzzy Felt is still there, in classrooms and charity shops and libraries, kicking it old school. The sensory nostalgia is immediate and overwhelming. I am happy to report after lengthy play sessions with my boys that Play-Doh technology has not really advanced past the Play-Doh factory, which is still the daddy. Ravensburger are still dropping board games with the best of them, while Playmobil sets still have that unmistakable '70s aesthetic and all the figures have kept their porn star bowl cuts and still dress like Wes Anderson characters. For all the whizz-bang appeal of your Fortnites and the other digital murder simulators, you just can't beat the classics. Maybe one day you'll let the kid play with them, too.

19.

Fatherhood forces you to be more comfortable with your own company. Having a kid and expanding your family is great, obviously, it's why we're all here, but it does also have the knock-on effect of making you appreciate your alone time all the more. Time to yourself becomes a precious commodity, and because it was so scarce, I found that I learned to be a lot happier when I was by myself. In general, your expectations for what constitutes an acceptable use of private time will relax quite considerably: you may find you no longer need digital distractions to keep you occupied, just silence, a good book and maybe a sandwich. I can't stress enough how important it is to practice good mental health and to carve out little private moments of zen where you can find them amongst all of the madness.

20.

Sometimes it's fun to play the old geezer card. You spent your entire youth being lectured by old gippers who couldn't wait to tell you how different things were back in their day. Well, compared to your kid, now you're the whinging old fart, so you might as well lean into it and do your bit, even though you know full well that the rapid advancement of technology in the 21st century combined with inner-city gentrification has meant your upbringing was comparatively luxurious compared to previous generations, and that your dad, Grandad, old Gam-Gam lurking in the corner over there, could bring down the whole house of cards if he so wished with no more than a simple flex of his childhood ration book.

21.

Kids make for a great patsy. Let's say you accidentally spill food on yourself while eating breakfast. A big old jam stain right down the front of the old work shirt. The day is not ruined, not when there's blame that can be apportioned. That's right, now you're a responsible father, you can blame your kid for the stain and say they hugged you before you left the house. Bloody affectionate kids! Grrr! It's a totally legitimate excuse that hurts no one, and it might make your boss picture your kid hugging you, which makes you look like a bloody good guy. No downside at all to this one. No chance at all of being rumbled, the stakes are too low. Besides, what are they going to do? Fire you for having adorable children? See you in court! I'll be the defendant with the Marmite smear on his collar, which was also caused by my kid.

22.

When your kids ask you questions, you get to pretend you're incredibly smart and wise and worldly, even though you're still that same scared little boy who's worried he'll be outed as a fraud, wait, this is turning into a bad one. And yes, if you're wondering, this book *is* a kind of therapy for me, thanks for asking.

23.

Bath time is fun, weeeeee. Bath time is yet another leisurely pursuit that we as adults let slip from our grasp, for shame. Sure, we literally outgrew baths some time ago, but did we have to outgrow them spiritually too? Having smelly kids who require constant bathing will help you recapture some of that lost youth spent getting prune-fingered in the tub. With nothing more than a splash of bubble bath and a few crappy plastic bath toys, early evening can be transformed into an aquatic adventure par excellence, complete with naval battles, soapy beards and occasional cleansing. It's time to get wet like we did back in the good old days.

24.

You will laugh longer, harder and deeper than you ever have in your entire life. For all the horrible shit you will go through as parents - and there is a *lot* of horrible shit - you will still frequently find yourself helpless with laughter at the insanity of daily life with children. This is partially due to you lowering your general standards for what is funny, and the heightened sense of on-the-edge hysteria that bubbles beneath your surface, but still: LOLz is LOLz. I've had booming laughing fits over the most ridiculous situations, the kind that genuinely leave you wheezing and sore, and I never had that before I had kids. Of course, we cannot rule out the possibility that I may have just lost my mind.

25.

Fatherhood totally counts as a proper life achievement and if you are so inclined you could never seek to achieve another single notable thing in your entire life and you would still be considered a fully functional member of society. You're a father to a human child which makes you a real person and there's nothing anyone else can do or say to make that untrue. For all intents and purposes you are technically a valued member of civilisation, and you've got the kid to prove it. Wherever it is. I'm sure it's fine.

26.

There are some genuinely brilliant kids TV programmes these days that you can watch, guilt free. One of the biggest concerns you'll have as your kid grows up is how you're going to prevent them from becoming a square-eyed screen slave, because across proper telly, streaming services and YouTube, the entertainment options are almost limitless. Thankfully, there are plenty of shows that are suitable for kids but basically made for adults that you can all enjoy together, or hey, no judgement, even on your lonesome. Many a time I have been sat watching the amazing series Teen Titans Go! with my kids before realising they both left the room around 45 minutes ago.

27.

Having a kid of school age is quite a good excuse to relearn some of the stuff you forgot. Back in the dusty recesses of your mind exists a treasure trove of useless information that you learned at school once upon a time ago and filed away post-exam once you no longer needed it. But when you start flicking through some of your kid's school books, it all comes flooding back. Long division! Verbs, adjectives and prepositions, oh my! Ancient Aztec civilisations, ox-bow lakes and photosynthesis! All of this stuff is still useless and has no practical application in the real world and you can't ever let your kid know this, but it's still fun to revisit education as an oversized man-child, effortlessly absorbing elementary-level information as an adult like Will Ferrell squeezed into a tiny desk in Elf.

28.

Dairylea Dunkers are back in your life, and it feels so good. There's something unsettling about seeing a lone adult eating a Dairylea Dunker, or an off-brand equivalent. The dainty little breadsticks. The laughably shallow pot of cream cheese. The brightly coloured foil wrapping. It's not a manly snack, like beef jerky or Pepperami or some other aggressive meat-based stick. Dairylea Dunkers are a snack for children. And yet: you have children. You share a fridge with children. Therefore: if you want to eat Dairylea Dunkers in the comfort of your own home, safe from prying eyes, then you can dunk to your heart's content. As long as there's a small child in the vicinity at the time of purchase, the assumption is that you are treating your kid with a savoury snack, not that you are an uncultured swine with a busted palate who enjoys processed food made for toddlers.

29.

Soft play is like fun baby jail. The best way to get kids exercising without realising they're exercising is to take them to soft play - a garish, multi-colour prison yard in which your offspring can fling themselves around at breakneck speed, while you can be safe in the knowledge that since every possible surface is padded with several inches of thick foam and netting, it's literally impossible for them to come to harm. Okay, *significant* harm. Chuck the kid inside, get a latte and some Rocky Road and enjoy a few blissful minutes of respite staring at your phone while they slam themselves silly in the bouncy house of screams. If you must get involved yourself, just remember: soft play is a workout. In my experience, 20 minutes of unfettered exploration and adventure in a multi-coloured kingdom of crash mats is roughly the equivalent of one joyless hour of cardio at the gym.

30.

Paternity leave rules. On the one hand, paternity leave is desperately needed in order to stabilise your life as a new father and find your post-birth equilibrium. On the other hand, it's three weeks off work: woo, and indeed, hoo. Chain your basic paternity leave together with some annual leave you should have been saving and you might even be looking at a whole month away from your desk. A month! That's probably the longest you've ever had away from spreadsheets and memos and Karen from HR slurping her coffee. It's basically a holiday. An entire paid calendar month in which you will not be required to wear a collared shirt or trousers. 30 days in which you don't need to worry about where your swipe card is. Four weeks in which you can finally see if your face suits a goatee before deciding that it doesn't, but at least now you know! This 'paternity' thing might not actually be all that bad!

<h1 style="text-align:center">31.</h1>

If you wish, you can now argue with your significant other through conversations with your child, and it won't technically qualify as an argument. Attention passive-aggressors, this one's for you. If you get stressed out with your partner and need to communicate some harsh truths, you can totally use your innocent child as a convenient conversation conduit. "Mummy said she was going to do the washing up, didn't she my little love? Because Daddy's already done three loads today already, hasn't he sweetheart? Silly Mummy must have forgotten!" It's no argument, you're just having a chat with your child! If pressed on it, you could read the transcript out in court and be confident you'd walk. Tone? Jovial. Language? Appropriate. Aggression? Passive. Verdict? Not guilty.

<h1 style="text-align:center">32.</h1>

Young kids form the weirdest, most hilarious obsessions with household objects, and it's adorable. The old cliché about kids ignoring the toy and playing with the box is true, but it's also true that really young kids often bond with bog standard household objects that really shouldn't qualify as toys at all. Kid A had a bizarre love of vacuum cleaners as a toddler, and would stand next to one with his arm around it posing for a photograph like he was on a date with it. Other kiddies may get hot and heavy with the remote control or start to develop intense feelings for your water bottle, while the £49.99 V-Tech Kids Speak & Spell laptop you bought for them remains in its box, devaluing by the second.

33.

The first post-baby 'date night'. Once you get comfortable enough to leave your little one in the care of a good babysitter, you can re-join the human race and indulge in some normality for just a short while - and it feels divine. Food from the shittiest dive restaurants will taste like a Michelin-star feast; crappy movies at your local fleapit cinema may as well be Palme d'Or winners screening at the Croisette in Cannes. Just a few stolen child-free hours can temporarily remind you that you are still your own person and you still exist outside of your relationship and servitude to your child. A word of warning, though: it's likely you will fall asleep in your local Odeon, because the combo of a comfy chair and darkness is irresistible to your ailing body.

34.

When they finally fall asleep. It might take them an age to get to sleep, and they might only be asleep for seventeen minutes, but by jingo, when kids sleep, they *sleep*. You'll learn to recognise the signs that they've finally nodded off: the little twitches that tell you they're dreaming, the heavenly breathy noise they make when their sleepytime breathing regulates, the extra five pounds of deadweight they seem to put on while slumped on your shoulder. When it finally happens, and they lie there doing little miniature snores with their mouths wide open, it's so damn beautiful you almost want to wake them up so you can do it all over again. Almost. But not quite. Bonus points are scored when they fall out of bed and end up in a pile on the floor yet, somehow, remain utterly asleep despite being folded like a towel. You have to scoop them up and put them back in bed, so you get to be their silent protector, which is a bit like being a low stakes superhero.

35.

Getting compliments from strangers is the absolute best and stays with you forever. Though I can't quite bring myself to recommend that you comment on a total stranger's parenting skills, I can say that every time a stranger *has* chucked a parenting affirmation in my direction out in the wild, it has been gratefully received. Because the thing is, parenting doesn't offer much in the way of genuine feedback or external validation. Young kids can't say thank you (and even when they can, they won't) and friends and family members are always going to shower you with praise, whether you deserve it or not. So, to be on the receiving end of a voluntary compliment from a complete randomer who has no stake in your kid whatsoever is quite lovely and can really make your day.

36.

Kids have no pretence: what you see is what you get. Decades of interacting with adults builds up bad habits, and often you need to run words through various filters (sarcasm, subtext, passive-aggressiveness) to decode what's actually being said. Kids are blissfully simple. If they want an ice cream, they're going to ask for an ice cream. No manual needed. Furthermore, if they enjoy that ice cream, it's literally going to be all over their face. They go all in when they enjoy something, but will tell you straight up if they don't. When Kid H eats an ice cream, he closes his eyes and blocks out everything else, to the point where you can't even talk to him until it's finished. I wish I could enjoy anything the way he enjoys ice cream.

37.

Playing with toys is now socially acceptable - no, scratch that, actually encouraged. Adult men have to be careful with how they label their belongings. They're not toys, they're 'poseable figures'. They're not toys, they're 'collectables'. They're not toys, they're... they're... fine, it's Voltron, it's fucking Voltron, okay? He's made up of lion robots from the future, does that sound like it's for kids? No, it sounds like it's for The 40-Year-Old Virgin. Man-babies, I have a simple solution to your problem: just have a kid! Now you can play with as many action figures as you want - and provide the accompanying sound effects - and any adults in the vicinity will give you doe eyes and go 'Awww' and say things like 'He's such a good dad', even though you used to do all this stuff by yourself when you were The 38-Year-Old Virgin.

38.

There's something primal about being a protector. I do not abide by gender stereotypes, and if this book has taught you anything it should be that modern dads can be all things: quiet, loud, nervous, confident, utterly incapable of DIY or dead handy with a hammer. But one thing I think that is universal to all dads is the feeling that overcomes you immediately after the birth: that urge to protect your kid at all costs. That's the great leveller, that is. It's a powerful feeling that lifts you up, keeps you going and informs everything you do. You'll find reserves of strength - both physical and emotional - that you never knew you had. The other side of the same coin is that it's also heartening to be needed by someone so helpless. It's awfully egotistical but it's also not untrue.

39.

You get to be a pal and a confidante. Kids tell you everything. Absolutely everything. Maybe 5% of the things that they tell you is stuff you actually need to know. The other 95% is literally just a list of things that have happened that they observed happening. Nonetheless, it's a nice feeling when they're young and they let you in on every single aspect of their life. Make the most of these moments where you get to be the human sponge that soaks up their word vomit before they turn into surly teenagers overnight and you have to find out their innermost feelings by following them on Instagram and decoding their cryptic hashtags.

40.

You get to leech off of your kids' happiness like a vampire. Although you are still your own person and are capable of feeling joy that is unrelated to your children, essentially, when you break it down, their happiness is your happiness. It's pretty much a 1:1 deal. So when they're happy, you're happy. And thankfully, making kids happy is pretty easy, it's route one stuff. Their happiness can be bought for the price of a bag of sweets or a new LEGO figure or even just a bout of tickling, and the moment they crack a smile, you can feel the good vibes race through your bloodstream. If I could hook this feeling to my veins I would, were it not monstrously immoral and scientifically impossible.

41.

You are responsible for giving your kids a personality and sparking their imagination. If you just focus on teaching your kids the fundamentals - eating, sleeping, not walking into traffic

- then chances are you will successfully create a little monotone droid in your image who may one day go on to be a Halifax branch manager. The fun part of fatherhood is found past the fundamentals, where you get to teach your kid how to be fun. What a responsibility! It sounds like an overwhelming task, to create a personality out of thin air, but it's easier than you think: just by being your own fun self, and using your imagination to spark theirs, you're slowly adding to the giant tapestry of influences that will one day shape who they become. So, go big on mad, impossible bedtime stories; tell them terrible jokes; request they pull your finger. They'll thank you for it one day.

42.

There's nothing more satisfying than feeling a child's weight on you. I cannot explain this. I can only say that I am never more comfortable or at peace than when I have my kids' weight on top of me. This goes back to the early days, when I would let them sleep on my chest as babies, clinging to me like big clammy hot water bottles. As they get older, I let them climb me like a tree and ride me like a horse. Even now, I am never more zen than when they sit on me for cuddles. You get to feel like their world, a rock for them to cling to. My theory is that this is the closest that a man ever gets to feeling like a pregnant woman, even if just for a minute at a time.

43.

Pets become more special. Look, we all know that household pets are basically a dry run for any couple who might one day want kids. If you can keep a cat alive, you can keep a kid alive! The problem is, when said kids arrive, the pets do tend to fall down the pecking order a little, and during the baby years, they may even become an annoyance - the last thing you need is another mouth to feed or tiny ego to sate. However, when your kids get old enough to appreciate the animals that live under their roof, the pets get a stay of execution. You get to see how the kids love them and are fascinated with them, and if you're lucky you might remember a bit of that yourself. For example, our two idiot cats have tested our patience to breaking point over the years - the great flea infestation of 2009, the dead mouse in the shoe incident of 2015, the unbroken streak of puking up hairball turds on our cream-coloured carpet - but because our kids are now old enough to properly pet them and enjoy them, they finally feel like part of the family. (The cats, not the kids).

44.

Routines and rigidity can be good for you. Not to sound too much like Monica from Friends, but sometimes rules can be helpful - they help *control* the fun. So, although the constant and mandatory routines that are inherent to parenthood might feel like a bummer, eventually you come to realise that life is so big and sprawling and overwhelming that often it helps to have a framework to work within. The unchanging nature of feeding times, naps and school drop-offs/pick-ups give your life a structure to build on, a foundation which rarely falters. And honestly, when you're exhausted and braindead and barely holding on to consciousness, sometimes it's handy to have a few red lines in your life that get you up and out the door.

45.

Building forts! Just a reminder that building forts is awesome and every weekend that passes by in which you do not build a fort with your kids out of cushions and blankets and clothes horses is a weekend wasted. The ultimate goal is to build a blanket fort so immense and powerful that you can climb inside it and be hidden from the outside world and fall asleep in a world of pillows and be found six hours later, dangerously cosy, long after the search party gave up hope.

46.

Imparting wisdom to your kid and actually seeing it land and take root. Passing on a philosophy to your child is like the most satisfying trophy unlock you can imagine. I cannot over-express how thrilling it feels to give your kid some life advice and then eventually see them exercise it without any more undue influence. It is how I imagine it feels to watch a bill become law. It might be something simple like 'The label is always at the back of your pants' or it might be something more complex like 'Make sure none of your friends are feeling excluded at the party' but every time your kid acts on something that you taught them, your heart explodes like a cardiac glitter-bomb.

47.

Rainy days in. Oh, let me count the myriad pleasures of a grey day: a warm radiator, a crowded sofa, a blanket, a crap film on Netflix, a barrel of cheap popcorn. If you're lucky you can double your money with a free nap. Outside is overrated.

48.

Your house becomes a home. Another frightful cliché, another inescapable truth. Your house becomes the backdrop to the creation of memories that will last a lifetime, so it's inevitable that the walls, window sills and doors take on more meaning. There will be stains that tell stories, door frames that track growth spurts, gardens that double as playgrounds. Yes, life at this point is basically a framed embroidered platitude; always remember to live, laugh *and* love.

49.

Two words: organ harvesting. Because I am equal parts lazy and open-minded, I asked my wife Vicky what she thought the best bit of having kids was, expecting something profound and heartfelt and lovely, true to form. "You've got a couple of kidneys right there when you need them," she said. I scanned it for sarcasm and it came back negative. *And that was her first suggestion.* Then she got up, said "Maybe I should write a fucking book" then left the room without saying another word.

50.

You have a purpose now. A reason to get up in the morning and go to work. A reason to work on becoming a better man. A reason to leave behind a better world than the one you entered. Granted, you probably should have been aiming to do all that before you had kids, but you have extra motivation now, because your kids are watching. Having kids completely disrupts your life, of that there's no doubt, but once you start to find order again and re-join the rat race, those kids at home strengthen your resolve and reinforce your principles to such a degree that you can shrug off the sort of petty bullshit that used to ruin your day in order to focus on the big picture. There's something wonderfully straightforward and freeing in knowing that you will always have one priority above all else, and that anything or anyone that dares to stand in your way can basically get sideways fucked to infinity and back.

***

That's about the size of it. You've got all of this good stuff coming to you and more. Unconditional love. Cuddles. Parental pride. Mostly though you're in it for the excuses, and man, do those tiny humans deliver on the excuse front. Whether you're attempting to skive work, skip out on social engagements or even just avoid undesirable small-talk with a stranger, kids are your key to being less available! Honestly, after the birth of my first kid, it's a miracle I was ever seen in public again.

#12

The Drive Home

And we're back in the room. So that just happened. You just became a father. A hearty well done and a slap on the back for you. Post-birth is the ideal time to do some high quality basking; the perfect opportunity to really hunker down and bask, bask lovingly in the new family you helped create, bask like a shark, really buckle down and get absolutely basked in the glowing aura of your baby. No, I don't really know what basking consists of either, but that's probably what you're doing right now; just sort of sitting around, finding your breath, trying to erase certain unforgettably vivid images from your mind, making cooing noises every fifteen seconds, just generally wallowing in new-found fatherhood. Equal parts pride and PTSD. Take five. Readjust. You've earned it. *Dad.*

Now, WAKE THE FUCK UP: you have barely strapped yourself into this terrifying rollercoaster and the lofty, dizzying highs that await on the horizon are only matched by the plummeting, stomach-churning, vomit-inducing lows yet to lurch around the corner. Still, thank god you voluntarily signed up for this rollercoaster, right? It'll be a laugh, they said! Hahaha, they said! It'll be the making of you, they said! Life is a rollercoaster just gotta ride it, they said! Get bent, Ronan Keating.

It's a confusing situation you find yourself in, post-baby-blowout. What are the rules now? What happens if you close your eyes for five minutes? Are you, like, allowed to go to the toilet? At what volume are you supposed to talk in the company of a newborn? I think I read that babies' ears are super-sensitive, or they're deaf or something, one of those must be right? Can you check your phone yet?

It's not immediately clear, the hospitals don't have pamphlets or anything, so you just kind of have to fumble your way through it and hope that anything you accidentally do wrong is more of a cute and humbling *faux pas* than a jaw-dropping atrocity - charming and delightful Hugh Grant-esque bumbling fumfery and not, say, getting busted with a massive prostitute. Get used to this feeling of helplessness, because fumbling through things and hoping for the best will quickly become your one and only coping strategy. Welcome to parenthood!

The truth is, you barely have time to bask in anything but your own rank body odour, because hospital staff, overworked and underpaid as they are, are not blessed with infinite patience. There is a congested tail-back of angry little miracles stuck behind you in the hospital traffic jam, honking their horns and cussing you out while they wait for the lights to go green. Once the nurses are happy there are no health risks to mother and baby, you are on a ticking clock until you officially are no longer their problem and they can handle you with all the grace of a ruddy-nosed publican kicking out an incorrigible drunk for puking in a pint glass.

The timing was fortunate for my wife and I as we were allowed to stay in a maternity suite until the following morning (no continental breakfast, poor TV reception, weird smell in the hallway, would not recommend this B&B, two stars out of five). The thing is, it didn't matter how exhausted we were, or what time of day or night it was, because 'wired' was winning out against 'tired' and the adrenaline that was still pumping through our veins put paid to any planned naps or regimented sleep shifts. We didn't much feel like making small talk, and when baby is asleep you are very much encouraged to leave it asleep, so we did the only rational thing that two new parents could do in that situation. Without sharing so much as a word, we lay together on a single mattress on the floor, held each other closely and watched Under Siege, the 1992 action thriller starring martial arts mannequin Steven Seagal, in full, on mute, on the tiny wall-mounted hospital TV in the corner.

Under Siege gave my life structure for one hundred and something minutes. As long as Casey Ryback was straight up murdering a bunch of guys with kitchen knives, the world made sense; when Tommy Lee Jones and Gary Busey had their evil plans thwarted by the guy they thought was "just a cook", I understood how we are all more than the labels that other people give us. Even on mute, this movie has *layers*. And as Under Siege moved towards its exciting climax, the tension was twofold: not only did it count down ever closer to the terrorists achieving their goal of, uhh, stealing a boat or whatever, but we were acutely aware that we didn't really know what we were going to do when the movie was over. How can I possibly assume the role of father? Am I really ready for this? What would Steven Seagal do? Well, the Steven Seagal of today would probably eat his feelings, but an in-his-prime early nineties Seagal would undoubtedly man up and get the job done. Birth was just the beginning - actual parenting is required, now and in perpetuity, and you've barely had a chance to change your pants. It's like running the 100m sprint and having race officials tell you at the finish line that you need to keep running because you've just been enrolled in the marathon. It's the equivalent of Seagal stepping off the boat on his way home from Under Siege and immediately boarding the train from Under Siege 2: Dark Territory. Sorry Steve, *it's in your contract.*

Leaving the relative comfort and sanctity of the hospital is frightening. As long as you're in yelling distance of someone in uniform, there's a safety net there to catch you in case of fuck-ups. Take that safety net away, and, what, you're supposed to figure out how to fix your fuck-ups yourself? Or not even do fuck-ups in the first place? Is that what parenthood is? Just people blustering through life with no previous experience, learning by their mistakes, praying to avoid calamity, trying desperately to keep their offspring alive by any means necessary? The answer is yes, that's exactly what it is, at least at first: panic and survival. Honestly, it's a miracle human evolution got this far and the species didn't die out when the first caveman couldn't figure out how to put the car-seat in.

The drive home is another test of fatherhood. It's a challenge that's both physical and mental, and yet it scores you precisely zero seconds inside the Crystal Dome. This is around the moment the sudden realisation hits you: holy shit, cars are... they're terrible and... and driving is... it's incredibly dangerous! Human bodies are little more than squidgy sacks of barely-contained guts and offal, and automobiles are screamingly violent, weaponised hunks of metal! And anyone can drive them! Including you! How is this allowed? The fat cats of Big Auto will have a lot to answer for next time you accidentally back your Ford Focus into a dustbin.

Think back to what your massively racist driving instructor taught you. Slow and steady. Gently does it. Ease off the clutch. Black people can't drive. Okay, not that last one.

There are real stakes to driving now - although you can't quite bring yourself to be the guy who buys the 'Baby on Board!' sign to affix to your rear windscreen, there is very much a Baby that is, quite literally, on Board, exclamation mark. Compare the sedate drive home to the Fast & Furious homage that was the drive to the hospital and vow to change your ways: you entered this extortionate hospital car park a boy racer, and you left it a kerb-crawling granddad, completely bypassing the middle ground of being a grown man who drives at normal speeds. You have officially been downgraded from Will Smith throttling his Porsche 911 Turbo in Bad Boys to the Fresh Prince cruising his car in 'Summertime' ("Leanin' to the side but you can't speed though / Two miles an hour so everybody sees you").

You can drive with your nose practically pushed up against the wheel if you like, but it's not just other road users you need to be cautious of - it's emotional outbursts of your own making. My pal Ben, he of the four daughters and the sexually aggressive mechanic, told me that the first time he had to drive his baby home from the hospital, he burst into tears behind the wheel - because his newborn didn't have any friends. Now it's entirely possible that there is a very serious testosterone imbalance inherent in the man's genes, but by and large, this is the future that awaits you: entirely illogical and unreasonable thoughts that hit you without warning. Jesus Christ man, you're not even home yet.

Your first act upon returning home is an obvious one: make everything 8000% more tolerable by putting the kettle on, thereby solving almost all of your problems. The second thing you'll do, which won't take you much longer to realise than it'll take for the kettle to boil, is come to the conclusion that your house is full of crap that you don't need. It's funny how bringing a new life into the world, but mainly into your living room, will give you a new perspective on everything - and that perspective is 'I should probably cut down on the amount of things I own that could feasibly get stuck in a baby's windpipe'.

Scan your house again, Terminator red-eye style. Everywhere you look is a potential catastrophe in waiting: piles of dangerous shit that could topple over and crush a small person; furniture that could easily cause fatal injuries to a wee one; collapsible clothes horses likely to lop off little fingers. And what's with all the edges and corners? Since when does everything come with edges and corners? What used to be a humble coffee table is now a razor-lined forehead exploder that your idiot child is one day going to find irresistible to headbutt.

If you're a child of the nineties then you, like me, probably played a lot of Tony Hawk's Pro Skater. It was an insanely addictive videogame par excellence, and prolonged exposure to it had two main effects. Firstly, it was liable to cause teenagers from Bromley to suddenly develop an interest in Papa Roach and NOFX; more importantly, however, was the side-effect one developed when one turned off the PlayStation and ventured out into reality. I found that I'd spend so long staring at the game levels and mentally thinking two or three moves ahead that when I'd go outside I'd start to see the real world in terms of skate lines and geometric objects: a kerb that grinds into a long rail, an ollie from a bench onto a wire fence, that sort of stuff.

All extremely unhealthy, I'm sure you'll agree, but bringing home baby reminded me of this affliction, in that very soon, when you look around your house all you are able to see are the sharp edges and outlines, only instead of viewing the world as a playground in which you can kickflip to your heart's content, you're cursed with seeing your surroundings as an infant deathtrap. This sort of angst-ray vision can develop into a superpower over time, mainly to be deployed when you enter a friend's home or any unfamiliar and therefore hostile environment. You can scan rooms in seconds for dangerous surfaces and objects: a table edge at head height here, a precious trinket or expensive video game controller stored below waist level there, literally anything made of glass, you goddamn childless amateurs. You may start to feel like a Secret Service agent doing a sweep of a room before the US President can enter it, although I suppose the current President is probably more likely to shit himself in public than your baby.

These new-found abilities to assess your environment for danger might give the impression that you're some sort of Super Dad, with your finely honed reflexes and your parental intuition that borders on premonition. You've seen the YouTube videos of the Super Dads: the ones who catch their falling kids without breaking their stride; the ones who use ESP to prevent an accident that didn't even get a chance to happen. They're like Spider-Man and Daredevil all rolled into one, if Spider-Man and Daredevil were driven by fear and powered by anxiety and didn't catch any criminals because they were co-parenting and spent too long wondering if the missing dice from the Game of Life box in the downstairs bookshelf will one day be discovered and subsequently lodged inside a tiny oesophagus. Get together with other exhausted Super Dad friends to compare parenting techniques and you're basically the Dadvengers. The Nervous Wrecks-Men. The League of Extraordinarily Tired Gentlemen.

Because, you see, there are dozens, if not hundreds of things in your house that can legitimately kill your kid. Not the cheeriest chapter, this, but hypothetical horrors such as these power your anxiety like Superman and the Earth's yellow sun. Look around and you'll find that, actually, a modern human domicile is just as dangerous as an Indiana Jones-style Aztec tomb laced with man-traps. Check off these potential killers as you see them:

- Plug socket (death by electrocution)

- Light cord (death by strangulation)
- Window blinds (death by, yep, you guessed it strangulation)
- Stairs (death by falling down stairs)
- Stairgates (death by poor D.I.Y.)
- Small upended foot-stool (death by Million Dollar Baby)
- Coffee table, corner (death by accidental blunt force trauma)
- Coffee table, glass (death by shattered glass)
- Coffee table, coffee (death by third-degree burns)
- Door, hinge (death by finger removal)
- Door, handle (death by eye-gouging)
- Bed (death by smothering)
- Bed (death by falling out of)
- Bathtub (death by drowning)
- Toilet (death by flushing self down toilet, maybe)
- Toilet (death by, shit, apparently kids *can* drown in there, Jesus)
- Dishwasher (death by consuming delicious looking laundry pods)
- Washing machine (death by rinse cycle)
- Harmless household firearm (death by being American)
- Window (death by curiosity)
- Hairdryer (death by burns, parents' own vanity)
- Knives left on edge of kitchen counter (death by stabbing)

- Microwave (death by slim chance that you might accidentally microwave your baby and put your ready meal in the cot, the same way you might absent-mindedly leave your wallet in the fridge)
- Balloons (death by choking and or introduction of foreign body into lungs)
- Bins (death by consumption of hazardous waste or half-eaten burrito)
- Paint (death by lead poisoning due to consumption of paint chips)
- Sharp-edged framed photos of babies (death by irony)
- Bookcase (death by a good old-fashioned crushing, like in the '70s)
- Humidifiers (death by fungus and/or spores)
- Carpets, apparently, at least according to the National Center for Biotechnology Information (death by microtoxins)
- Cribs and playpens (wait, seriously?)
- Yes, cribs and playpens (death by climbing and falling, bloody hell)
- Babywalkers? (death by skull fractures due to stair falls)
- Toy chests?? (death by suffocation)
- Plastic bags (death by suffocation, fucking hell this is grim)
- Batteries (death by swallowing batteries)
- Magnets (death by swallowing magnets)
- Money (death by swallowing coins)

- Pretty much anything that shouldn't be swallowed (death, just death, so much death, around every corner, how does anyone even survive)

- The Grim Reaper's Scythe (is relentless, he comes for us all, even the very young)

- Hold me (only if you hold me)

So, as best as I can make out, by following all known safety advice, you can avoid all of these life-threatening accidents by living in a ground floor flat with no doors, windows, carpet, bed, furniture or toilet. Ironically this sounds quite a lot like a tomb.

Full disclosure, this section started off as a comedy bit, but I'm now genuinely anxious that I live in a death house, surrounded by objects designed to facilitate fatality. This feeling has been elevated considerably by the fact that just this week, while away on a work trip, my wife informed me that two houses on my street, literally situated a stone's throw away from my actual house where I live with my family, burned down due to a single faulty electrical appliance. Like in an episode of Casualty, or Doctors. *Burned actual down*. No one was hurt, thank God, but I am slightly on edge. I own many electrical appliances, for example. Are they faulty? Are they?? DID I SIGN MY OWN DEATH WARRANT WHEN I SWITCHED THE KETTLE ON???

None of this is helped by the fact that safety advice is inconsistent from source to source, and in many cases, measures you take to protect your kids from stuff can actually end up being more dangerous than doing nothing. For example, safety covers for plug sockets are now considered to be a bigger risk than an open socket, because the unregulated covers disable the protective safety shutters built into the sockets themselves. So buying protective covers for plug sockets could be a death sentence. Just tell me what to do re: plug sockets, guys! Decide between yourselves! Next you'll be telling me that 'flammable' and 'inflammable' mean the same thing!

It can't be that hard to agree on consistent safety advice, surely? It's like how every once in a while, the National Heart Attack Association (or whoever) decide to change up the song that you're supposed to sing to help you perform CPR at the correct tempo; they stumbled on the perfect BPM with the Bee Gees' 'Stayin' Alive' (both contextual and funky) but then they changed it to Queen's 'Another One Bites The Dust', presumably for shits and giggles. Was 'I Just Died In Your Arms Tonight' by Cutting Crew too on the nose? Just tell me what to do re: chest compression speed, guys! Find a song and stick to it! I've been pounding on what used to be a ribcage for fifteen minutes straight because I keep getting over-enthusiastic during 'Bohemian Rhapsody's head-banging section.

Your best option to ensure your child is ah-ah-ah-ah stayin' alive (see, it's fun to joke about infant mortality!) is to get into the wonderful world of child-proofing, a process in which you slowly ruin your house and subsequently your life by making all available adult amenities marginally less accessible. Measures include little pop-open clips that ensure Junior can't get into any drawers, rubber baby bumpers that soften any sharp edges around the homestead and lockable stairgates so they can't accidentally tread off the landing onto thin air before plummeting to their doom like a sleepwalking Wile E. Coyote.

Individually, these small daily inconveniences are just about tolerable, but after a while they may start to make you lose your mind - trying to open a fiddly little toilet clasp in the middle of the night with a full bladder is torture I wouldn't wish on my worst enemy. Of course, as soon as you spend a small fortune on decking your home out with safety clips, crash mats and security gates, you'll realise that a much cheaper form of babyproofing was available all along - rather than protecting the baby from the house, you protect the house from the baby.

That's right: throw its ass into baby jail, also known as a playpen. The house can remain pristine at all times! I mean, yeah, your kid is going to grow up with the same spatial issues as your average flamer on D-Wing, but the house looks great!

Okay, fine, it's unlikely your kid is going to be immediately threatened by any of the things on the household appliance death list, unless you have fathered a child who is a direct genetic progeny of Mr Bean. Nonetheless, it's important to be on guard - it sounds obvious, patronising even, but don't leave the baby unattended, even when they're asleep.

Babies are so blissfully incapable that they can roll onto their face and suffocate if not properly cared for. I discovered this early into fatherhood, when I was home alone with our firstborn. He was sleeping peacefully in his Moses basket, and otherwise at a loose end, I figured it'd do no harm if I set him down beside me while I booted up some videogame footie. Yeah: Daddy's reward for doing 25 minutes of solo parenting. I thought I could have it all. Naturally, as soon as I was through on goal I was punished, as my son sweetly flipped over onto his breathing holes, causing me to flap about and quit in a mad panic, forfeiting the game 3-0. No harm was done, but I barely avoided relegation that season. Also the baby was fine I guess.

Although the 'accidental self-asphyxiation' stage doesn't last for long, young kids retain that unintentional death wish for several years and continue to stumble through life like Buster Keaton, comically risking their lives before avoiding certain death by mere millimetres while you suffer cardiac arrest just out of shot. Sometimes it's breathtaking how fearless they can be. We recently returned from a lovely family holiday to the Norwegian fjords, including a coach trip up the kind of winding mountain roads that invite anxiety nightmares. Once at the mountain's blustery summit, the stunning views were spoiled somewhat by Kid H, who immediately started trying to *climb over* the flimsy barrier standing between him and a 1500 metre fall. The suicidal act was obviously shut down in seconds, but, Jesus Christ- I mean, for fuck's... [throttled 'calm' voice] We're on a mountain, buddy!! We don't want to fall off mountains do we!!! Try not to kill yourself while Mummy and Daddy are on holiday my precious angel!!!!

That high altitude episode was a good reminder to always stay vigilant, but for the sake of your poor, racing heart, you will also need to make peace with how accident prone kids are - it's just part of the gig. At first, you will want to wrap them in cotton wool, and treat even the mildest of boo-boos with the utmost urgency. Every scratch or scraped knee or dry patch of skin represents your complete and utter failure to parent - panicked and unnecessary trips to A&E will not be uncommon.

Then, eventually, when you realise that extremely young children are incapable of understanding safety advice or learning any life lessons or avoiding repeat injuries, after the fourth, fifth, sixth accident of the day, the sympathy does start to feel rather surplus to requirements. Go ahead and judge me. You'll understand soon enough. Every "I told you so" you can't say; every eye-roll you have to suppress. You'll understand all of it.

To get a sense of what the average day in injuries looks like, I decided to chart all of the injuries the children of the Gray household sustained over a period of 24 hours. Please understand I am documenting this for educational purposes and resist the temptation to call Child Services on me.

- **10.05am:** Kid A 'accidentally' clotheslined his younger brother off his feet during play, grazing his elbow

- **11.23am:** Kid H tripped and fell on an uneven paving slab in the garden, grazing his knee (fair enough, this one is on me)

- **12.35pm:** Kid H slipped on a water slide in the paddling pool and landed face first in the water, which I have to admit was hilarious

- **12.42pm:** Kid H fell on the steps to the water slide and landed awkwardly on his ass-bone, boy he's having quite the day

- **1.00pm:** Kid A, still wet from the paddling pool, slipped on the floor in the downstairs toilet and hit his head on the porcelain toilet bowl, prompting a frenzied discussion on whether or not there was a dent in his forehead ("It's going in! It definitely looks like it's going in!") until a large Looney Toons-esque bump appeared

- **4.55pm:** Kid H bashed his head on the protruding handle of the living room door for maybe the 50th time this calendar month

- **6.16pm:** Kid A bashed his head on the wooden crossbar from his bunk bed - yes, the same one that's been at the same height for over two years, genius

- **Total preventable injuries:** Seven incidents of varying severity. And believe me when I say this is a relatively quiet day on the watch.

The worst injuries, however, are the accidental ones you inflict on baby yourself. It can happen: an unintended pinch of belly flab; a corner of a nail catches some skin; a thwacked head on a doorframe - all grade-A ways to fast-track feeling like shit with a starter of guilt and a suspect side-order of child abuse. It's the weirdest feeling, having to explain to your partner how you are responsible for a cut or a scrape - what isn't being said, but is otherwise highly visible in 10-foot neon subtext above your head, are the words I PROMISE I DIDN'T DO IT ON PURPOSE. It's the same feeling you have when you have to walk past a police officer on the street, and your gait unaccountably becomes 35% more shifty.

It's the injuries that occur through horseplay that feel the shittiest - the ones where the direct and only line of responsibility points only to you, punishment for committing the sin of fun. Now listen, I love chucking my kids in the air. It's good, clean fun (and it's free!) that's enjoyed by all (except my wife) and it's the kind of thing you can only do when you have very young kids, unless you enjoy the odd hernia or back spasm.

One of my favourite photographs of me and Kid A was taken in the local park when he was 18 months old, and I'd thrown him so high into the air, by the time I'd caught him he was 19 months old. It's harmless, no-risk entertainment. What, you think I'm going to *drop my own kid*? What kind of hapless, cack-handed twat do you take me for? [looks to camera]

One time. You drop your kid ONE TIME and suddenly you're the kid-dropper, the flapper at large, Mr. Can't-Catch-a-Kid, Big Daddy Butterfingers, Sir Drops-a-Lot, Senor No-Catcho, Hot Potato Jones, not to be trusted transporting children or large fruits or expensive vases.

It wasn't a drop, so much as a fumble, but we're splitting hairs at this point, because the most important thing to remember is it wasn't a clean catch. It was Kid H who I dropped, on a bright summer's day out in our garden, and despite myriad factors that could exonerate me - the sun in my eyes, a kid who didn't understand that kicking his legs out might affect the catch, general concerns about Brexit playing on my mind - I take full responsibility for the fact that I threw him in the air but only half-caught him, and he subsequently flopped awkwardly onto the (soft, lush, bouncy, verdant) grass.

I'll never forget the horrified look on Vicky's face, matched only by the gawps on the face of her cousin and her cousin's boyfriend, because obviously when you drop your kid for the first time you have to do it in front of an audience. Face burning red I apologised profusely, calmed the crying child and made my excuses ("They're basically made of stone! He's fine, look, he probably enjoyed it! It's nothing compared to what Brexit will do to him!") but I think that may have been the last time I tossed one of my own children more than a foot in the air.

Still, it just goes to show that the excess of caution and worry that you take home from the hospital slowly gives way and is replaced with a more relaxed, lackadaisical, irresponsible approach to parenting, at least if you're anything like me. Find a middle ground between incapacitating fear and 'he'll only run into the road once'. Stay on amber alert just in case you miss the Big One - the three seconds you don't pay attention that just so happen to be the three seconds your child finds a live grenade in the garden - but rest assured, bumps, bashes and bruises are all par for the course.

Oh God, this sounds weird and child-abusey, doesn't it? Read the 10-foot neon subtext: I AM NOT ADVOCATING HURTING YOUR CHILDREN. Please don't call Child Services on me.

#13

How to Get a Good Night's Sleep*
*sleep not guaranteed

Sleep used to be the thing you did after dinner and before breakfast, and sometimes after lunch. Sleep used to be malleable and would bend to your will. Out all night? Sleep late! Exhausting day? Go to bed early! You were a sleep slut, dipping in and out of consciousness without a care in the world. Naps. Lie-ins. Sporadic dozes when it suited you. Sleep used to be functional, forgettable, a formality. I regret to inform you that it is clear now that you slept on sleep.

Now? Sleep is unattainable, intangible, unreliable, mercurial. Sleep is the thing you crave the most but also the thing you're least likely to achieve - a precious commodity that you'd do anything to obtain. I keep waiting for someone to write a dystopian sci-fi drama set in the near future where the human race is permanently exhausted and sleep is the most valuable substance known to man and illegal naps are traded on the black market, which, incidentally, sounds like exactly the kind of shit screenplay I'd try to write at 4.15am while unable to sleep.

Make no mistake, lack of sleep is the hardest part of having a baby. Oh, all the other parts of having a baby are hard too, but usually when you have a tough day you get to collapse onto a bed at the end of it and push the reset button - being denied that all-important fade to black reset takes some getting used to. Sleep is such a core tenet of your day-to-day existence, so integral is it to your daily survival, that removing it is likely to make you feel like you're going insane.

Sleep deprivation completely upends your sense of logic and reason, frazzles your brain, sends your emotions into overdrive and genuinely makes you despise the childless. You will become obsessed with sleep and your lack of it. Everywhere you go and everyone you talk to, you will feel compelled to apologise for the fact that you aren't sleeping - as if it wasn't immediately obvious from the shambolic appearance, shuffling demeanour and thousand yard stare.

I sympathise, but it is important to note: nobody else cares. This is your punishment for bringing life into the world - it's your rock and your rock alone to push up the hill, and even if they wanted to, no friends, family members or random sympathisers are going to be able to contribute meaningful shift work.

It's not just the nights that are affected - the days stretch long and blur into one endless smudge of half-recalled events, featuring conversations that may have been imaginary and meals eaten at ungodly hours from irregular dishware. Everything feels more laborious when you've pulled an actual all-nighter - imagine the fatigue of a drawn-out hangover minus the fond memories of the fun that caused it. Even the simplest tasks are rendered almost impossible due to a near total lack of comprehension, coordination and vocabulary.

You will genuinely forget things you previously thought unforgettable - immediately after the birth of our second child, someone asked me my age, and I had to *guess* because I couldn't remember how old I was. Even worse, I didn't immediately realise my mistake and carried on thinking I was two years older than I actually was for around four months. Ordinarily it would be great to suddenly regain two years of your life, but new babies have a habit of making you feel like you've aged several decades, like an impatient Nazi drinking from the wrong grail.

Time means nothing during those initial weeks and months after the birth. Without the usual prompts of workdays and weekends to guide you, and with day and night being pretty much one and the same in terms of schedule, life feels like being stuck in that weird pocket of Chrimbo limbo between Boxing Day and New Year's Eve where no one knows what day it is. That, but without the Quality Street.

As the days roll on and you're still lost in the woods of sleep-deprived hysteria, you begin to fear the night, like a character in The Blair Witch Project driven insane by nocturnal activity; the moment the sun starts setting, you're counting down to an overnight haunting punctuated by various bouts of loud shrieking and snot-encrusted weeping.

I'm here to tell you from the future: it gets better. You can't tell, but I said that with a straight face. I myself was once a hopeless case, strung out, sleepless and zombified, even more useless than my pre-baby state. But look at me now: I'm literally writing the book on parenting! Fine: I'm writing a book on parenting. Semantics. I'm living proof that you can endure the sleeplessness and come out smiling on the other side, not fresh-faced exactly, but relatively well rested, coherent and looking significantly less than half dead - maybe only one tenth dead.

If that sounds good and you want to feel like there's light at the end of the sleep tunnel, then you're going to want to remember these three crucial pieces of advice.

STEP #1: DISPENSE OF ALL TIMELINES

A simple one: don't expect there to be a cushy, reliable timeline that applies to your baby's sleep schedule. It is the most infuriating piece of baby wisdom but also one of the most accurate: all babies are different. Conventional advice suggests that babies start to sleep through the night regularly after around six months. The thing about babies, though, is that they bloody love to upend convention and disrupt the norm, like little snot-nosed Apprentice contestants. As soon as you get that six month timeline stuck in your head, you have a point on the horizon that you're actively willing to get closer - and when it inevitably doesn't materialise, you'll start to lose faith and that's when you'll start to doubt your methods. There's nothing wrong with changing tactics every now and then, but new approaches often take an age to bed in, if you'll pardon the quite excellent pun. Consistency and stability is what ultimately gets results - flipping switches in a radioactive panic like a Chernobyl scientist isn't going to win you any awards.

I appreciate it's difficult to ignore the status quo, and it is natural to assume your baby is, somehow, broken, like, sometimes, maybe they come broken? Like from a store? This feeling of inadequacy can be tempered by external factors, such as other people and their other babies.

You cannot be tempted to compare your baby's sleep progress with that of other babies: this way jealousy lies. Many a time I have had to smile through gritted teeth as friends, family members and co-workers have told me how their baby is already sleeping through the night; only occasionally have I let my true feelings show (additional advice: resist the temptation to call the baby a "little fucker" to the mother's face as I once did).

Again, the refrain: all babies are different, bro! There is zero value in judging your baby's progress against other babies. If it comforts you, I have a theory which says all babies that appear to be more developed than my baby at any given time are definitely babies that have peaked early and they will all grow up to be dumbasses who might one day be lucky enough to polish my famous and handsome baby's expensive leather shoes on his lunch break from delivering a critical speech at the UN to bring about world peace. A few sleepless nights is a small price to pay when it comes to long-lasting and meaningful international diplomacy, so you enjoy your eight hours, *Karen*.

The idea is to throw out the clock that's mocking you from the wall; wipe your arse on the stupid calendar. Not literally, of course: that would be uncomplimentary to one's anus. Metaphorically, I mean. Get used to chaos and instability. Get cosy with unpredictability. Give yourself over to the madness. Embrace the night. You know, like Batman. You're basically Batman now, nocturnal and restless and lawless and driven by rage. Be more Batman. Read the bedtime stories in a gravelly, threatening voice if it helps. It certainly punches the Mog books up a few notches.

The secret to cracking a good night's sleep, then, is to flip the script and turn the tables. The key is not to wait for the baby's sleep to improve, but to teach your body how to get accustomed to less sleep. Thankfully, this is something that happens naturally, regardless of how well your baby sleeps. Slowly but surely, and without conscious signal from your brain, your body is already adapting to shorter, shittier, more scattershot nights, meaning you're already on the right path. No need for a clock: the time is half past Batman, baby!

I have been guilty of all of the above (apart from the arse-wiping). I was that mug, submitting my complaint to my son's mother six months and one day after his birth, asking if she still had the receipt. It took me a long, long time to get used to the idea of not having a date to work towards. If you're told that you might have to wait over a year for something, that child-like reaction instantly kicks in: *but that's basically foreve-her-herrr.*

I struggled with that concept, because I am utterly coddled by technology and require a progress indicator to tell me how long I have to wait for something - even if I've only completed 10% of the total, that's maths I can work with. Tackling the baby sleep equation is like doing sums but half of the numbers are question marks, you can't tell the difference between the 1s and the 7s and emojis are apparently part of maths now.

It is impossible to predict an end date, and anyway, it's not like as soon as baby sleeps through the night once, that's them asleep every night. That's part and parcel of the frustration with raising a child - progress rarely sticks, and you'll take baby steps backwards almost as often as you will forwards. That's famously the whole deal with baby steps. It'd be mega weird if babies could take huge strides from birth, just lunging wildly around the playroom. They're small for a reason. I would say that over the first five years of having kids, I could count the number of proper unbroken nights' sleep on one hand. To be honest, I can't even remember the first time my kid properly slept all the way through the night. During those first six months of turbulence I had put an uninterrupted night's sleep up high on a pedestal and heralded it as this mythical, impossible achievement, and now it's been and gone and I don't even recall it happening.

The irony of it all is, of course, that even when your baby does sleep properly, that's not a guarantee that *you* will. I have jolted myself awake in a panic at 3am because there's no kid sleeping in my bed next to me, which has in turn woken the sleeping kid up in the next room. That is just... (*chef's kiss*). When the time comes and you finally accomplish the unaccomplishable feat of a full night's sleep, it's extremely unnerving at first: you wake up groggy, as if from a coma, expecting some horror to have occurred throughout the night, wandering through your eerily quiet house like a scene from 28 Days Later.

The cosmic joke is that even when your kids have figured out that sleep is great, the fact remains that you have spent the last few years training your body to wake up frequently in the middle of the night; on the rare occasion where I am travelling overseas or sleeping at a friend's house, I am physically unable to sleep in past 5.30am. Script flipped, table turned: now *you're* the one who's broken. Which is progress of sorts, I guess?

STEP #2. EMBRACE THE FACT IT MAKES NO SENSE

Sleep training is incredibly frustrating for many reasons, but mainly because it is a clearly defined scenario in which there is an easily achievable outcome that is to the mutual benefit of all parties involved. Look. I'm tired. You're obviously tired. If you go to sleep, you get what you want and I get what I want. It's quid pro quo! Win-win! There is no downside here! As an adult you get used to negotiating sensitive situations where people want different outcomes - being able to broker a deal between opposing sides is truly a fine art. But sleep? Sleep should be an open goal. Why are we arguing? Help *me* help *you*! Embrace my logical approach, tiny human!

The bedtime routine makes no sense either. Newborns, you don't need to worry about: they will sleep anywhere, at any time, on anyone or anything - the kicker is that they just prefer short snatches of sleep instead of bed-busting snoozefests. In the early days, all they do is sleep, at times pre-determined to be most inconvenient for you.

It is truly impressive how newborn babies can fall asleep in the most uncomfortable positions known to man: lying down, sat up, in the crook of your arm, bent backwards over your knee, sandwiched between two thighs, lying precariously balanced on your stomach. Usually, they will be pressed tightly up against either you or your partner, which is enough to paralyse you with fear: even the slightest movement, dead arm or twitching muscle could mean game over. Be so brave as to fart in bed next to a sleeping baby and it's back to square one, no sleep for you, you lose, good day sir. No, it's when they're a little older that the real fun with bedtime begins. Once upon a time, in the past, the child carers of old got together and decided in their infinite wisdom that the way to get kids to go to sleep at night was to make bedtime an event. Before this decision, children were just chucked in a damp haystack in an old barn and told to shut the fuck up until the sun came up: harsh, but also, fair.

This ancient method, decided the child carers of yore, was deemed unacceptable. The new bedtime routine would be full of pomp and theatrics. It would be - gulp - fun. The precious little children were to be dressed in bright and colourful clothes known as 'pyjamas' for the night - clothes that no one other than themselves would ever see, clothes which would be shed the moment the children wake up. Before they were to rest, children would drink a ceremonial pre-bedtime drink of warm cow's milk, a delicacy deemed beneficial to a good night's sleep despite the fact that curdled dairy can take 4-5 hours to leave the stomach. Then, when the children of old were in their old-timey beds, the adults were to remain. Where before the grown-ups would extinguish the flaming torch and immediately abscond to the drawing room for brandy and cigars without so much as a word, now they were to assist the children on their way to the land of nod by - you're going to love this - reading them fascinating 'bedtime stories'; astonishing tales of magic and fantasy and derring-do that would fire up the children's' young minds precisely before they were expected to slumber. Let me know how that worked for you guys - it's little wonder you were all off your tits on snuff. Thanks for the routine, you silly old twats, I'm glad you all died of plague.

You may long for a similarly old-fashioned approach, but tradition - and a series of robust modern laws protecting children against forms of abuse - dictates that the softly-softly bedtime routine is the way forward. And yes, you are absolutely correct - in making bedtime a special event, one so special it is to be repeated every night until the end of time, you are essentially making bedtime something worth staying awake for.

In the first days of parenthood, you can dispense with the stories: babies have no understanding of story constructs or narrative thrust, they don't give two runny shits about the Gingerbread Man or his motives. They basically already wear pyjamas all day every day, like a recent divorcee, so all you have to do is zip them into something called a 'sleep sack', which is exactly what it sounds like, hoist them up onto your shoulder and rock their world for anywhere between 10 minutes and 1 hour of gentle swaying, bum-patting and - critical, this - absolute, Mission: Impossible-vault-style silence. Lay them down gently, and voila: mission achieved. Until they wake up, which will be after anywhere between 10 minutes and 1 hour. Frequently you will spend longer trying to get the baby to sleep than the baby will actually sleep for. This cursed ratio cannot be predicted, only feared, and the process is known in academic circles as 'A Waste of an Evening'.

Eventually, baby starts developing and grows older and becomes more demanding of bedtime, heralding the introduction of bedtime stories into the evening routine. The fantasy is that your little cherub will be relaxed and inert while you fill their snoozing head with charming stories, ensuring a safe passage to dreamland. The reality is your child has somehow grown to allergic to sleep and will lie and fidget endlessly, hyper-awake, with eyes open wide and finger buried deep in nose, immune to your mechanical rendition of a fairytale that, generously, probably fucking sucked when it was written two hundred years ago.

My kids recently took a shine to a book of kiddified wellness readings, nice little soothing descriptions of relaxing scenarios like sleeping on a pillow of clouds and chasing butterflies through rolling meadows. But because the kids inevitably don't go to sleep when they're supposed to, I frequently find myself thrashing violently between *calmly whispered descriptions of ocean waves gently lapping at your toes* and INCREASINGLY HUFFY INSTRUCTIONS TO CLOSE YOUR BLOODY EYES, which doesn't feel very Rancho Relaxo.

Bedtime is often more exhausting for you than it is for the kid, and you will frequently find yourself reading stories through drooping eyelids. I have found that if you are tired enough and the child refuses sleep ardently enough, eventually you will slip into a semi-comatose state while reading, where the brain disengages and the mouth literally starts going off book. Often I've found myself jolting to attention in the middle of slurring a sentence that is absolutely not on the page in front of me, so God knows what random stream of consciousness I've been filling the kids' ears with. I also frequently make myself laugh when slipping into automatic reading mode - accidental spoonerisms, like referring to the Toy Story twosome as 'Wuzz and Boody', are commonplace, but I had to stifle a giggle recently when I accidentally referred to a cartoon octopus's many 'testicles'.

Ideally you want bedtime stories to be interesting enough to capture the attention, but boring enough that one doesn't mind falling asleep halfway through: it's a real tightrope walk. Vicky reads to our boys with gusto, doing all the character voices and everything; in comparison, when Daddy does bedtime, a far more disinterested and monotonous tone is adopted, in the hope that the vacuum of sleep is preferable to my ceaseless droning - Jackanory it ain't. Sometimes the bedtime reading material might seem appropriate to you but might fill your kids' heads with nightmares; I can still remember choosing a bedtime story and Kid A asking me, his little voice trembling with fear: "Are there any crabs in this one?" This is a concern that he had never mentioned once before, and never did again.

I thought I had cracked it when, one night, due to a sore throat, I decided to dispense with the stuffy old book and prop up the iPad, playing the movie Cars 2. Instant results: sleep within 10 minutes! Bless those under-paid, overworked Pixar animators! The next night, the set-up was exactly the same, and sleep was achieved within 15 minutes: not as good a result as the first, but still a win. Cars 2! Who knew!

We repeated the routine again, and it was now apparent that Cars 2 was the only thing that worked, indeed, it was the only thing that was requested - it became as fundamental to bedtime as the bed itself. But then gradually, night after night, sleep was resisted for an extra five minutes here, an extra scene there, until eventually, whole hours would pass in the company of Lightning McQueen and his stupid hillbilly friends, and the film completely lost its effectiveness as a pacifier.

I began to despise Cars 2; watching it was to suffer a most painful form of endurance. It is, by some distance, the worst movie Pixar have ever made. It is also, as I would eventually find out, extraordinarily unsuitable for young kids. After the first 30 minutes, the 'spy movie' genre pastiche kicks in proper and cars start murdering each other with machine guns - one car is crushed into a cube, while another is visibly tortured and explodes screaming in a giant ball of flames. What the fuck happened to 'You've Got a Friend in Me', Pixar? I can honestly recount the first 30 minutes of Cars 2, word for word, scene for scene - I can't remember my wife's birthday, but I can recall every line Mater the redneck tow truck has ever said. My relationship with Cars 2 feels a lot like Stockholm Syndrome: it held me and my son captive, but given the choice to choose an alternative method and escape, I returned to its clammy clutches every night for many months. Cars 2. *Not even Cars 1.* Eventually we left Lightning McQueen to rust in hell, and returned to the good old written word, which didn't work either, but at least it didn't work while not being Cars 2.

So you see, nothing about bedtime makes any sense: the stories, the milk, the flamboyant night wear - it's all seemingly for nought, but it's all you can cling to in a complete black hole of logic. At least you knew where you were with the haystack.

STEP #3. FORGET YOUR OLD LIFE, IT'S NEVER COMING BACK

So, you've got this far. You've completed step 1 and have accepted the fact that proper sleep probably isn't going to happen for a while. You've even managed to wrap your head around step 2 and have accepted the fact that everything about bedtime is backwards and nothing works and everything is futile and- anyway, you've done step 2.

If you are finally to become one with the night and become The Ultimate Dad, you must eventually come to terms with step 3: accept the fact that you will never again sleep as well as you did before you had a baby. Never again. Never again. [Turns up the reverb for effect] *Never again.*

It is hard to come to terms with. It literally hurt me to write those words. You will delude yourself that you will one day rediscover your sleep mojo. But it is a fundamental truth inherent to parenthood: the glory days are over, pal. Everything from here on in will pale into insignificance when compared to the long luxurious nights and languorous mornings you used to have. You remember them: they happened in the past. And unless you happen to be hiding a nuclear-powered yuppie car from the '80s in your garage and value the friendship of an eccentric white-haired old scientist who feels like he should probably be on some sort of watchlist, you can't go back to the past. You can't fast-forward, you can't rewind, and the lack of a functioning pause button is kind of the whole problem. I certainly wouldn't recommend the extremes of the eject button either, unless the thing that you want to be ejected from is 'your own family'.

Get used to it: you are stuck in the boring old present, where everything moves at an interminably normal speed, and all negative consequences have to be endured in real-time. You can dream about your past life all you like, if only you were afforded the opportunity to be asleep in the first place.

I sense tension in you. I can see you still think you will one day sleep like you used to. 'Maybe in a few years, when they start pre-school', you seem to be saying with the facial expression I am imagining you pulling. Buddy, I've been there. I wish it were true. But sleep is a harsh mistress, and she obeys nobody's rules.

As we covered in step 2, this is no place for logic or reason: having a mad one up to your elbows in a sandpit all day does not necessarily equate to a proper night's sleep, even though it absolutely should by all reasonable metrics. The longer you hold on to the misconception that you will one day be able to reclaim your sleep, the more disappointed you will feel when the Nyquil-dosed carrot on the stick dangles eternally out of reach. Refusal to accept the inevitable only prolongs the delusion. You are literally daydreaming.

My advice? Let the past be the past. Slip on your rose-tinted glasses and reminisce how your life used to be; remember it fondly, but keep it locked in a box that is clearly labelled 'NOT TO BE REOPENED UNDER PENALTY OF TORTURE'.

There are many, many things you used to do, which you can no longer do. For example, lie-ins. Oh sweet merciful lord, those wonderful weekend lie-ins - sometimes facilitated by excessive boozing, sometimes by sheer laziness, almost always accompanied by a half dozen episodes of Friends. I swear, the first eight hours of programming on Channel 4 every Sunday for the best part of a decade was taken up with wall-to-wall Friends marathons. The One Where Joey Done A Thing. The One With All The Haircuts. The One Where Chandler Keeps Making Gay Panic Jokes That Didn't Age Well.

It didn't matter if you were only half-conscious while watching, or your attention was rightfully taken by whatever lard-soaked buttie you had decided to inhale as recompense: these were disposable days that were designed to be enjoyed from beneath a duvet. Don't be sad you can't have them anymore; just be grateful you ever got to experience them in the first place. There are some third-world nations where Friends is not even broadcast on a free-to-air TV channel, if you can believe that such an injustice exists.

Oh, and naps! Good Christ: how could you forget naps! Those heavenly little pockets of power sleep that topped you up when you were feeling drained. The sheer, obscene luxury of sleep... during the day! I have had naps that I would genuinely consider to be better than sex. I have had naps about which I could write sonnets. The kind where the sun dapples through the curtains, which are moved sporadically by a soft, cool breeze; the kind with a gentle soundtrack of distant road noises, undisturbed by people or responsibilities; the kind where your extremities go toasty and you can *actually feel yourself falling asleep* and you just let it happen, because it's a Sunday man, what the hell else are you going to do today? It's not like you have [leans into mic] KIDS OR ANYTHING.

Vicky and I developed a powerful system in the early stages of our relationship, whereby we would both return home after a hard day's work (me moving around some HTML code, her doing actual life-saving work at a children's' hospital), cuddle together on the sofa, put on one of the several dozen series-linked episodes of The Simpsons from the Sky box and give ourselves a half hour of beauty sleep before dinner. The Simpsons Nap, as it became known, was an integral part of our daily routine - it was our way of scrubbing the day clean, of expunging ourselves from emotions and thoughts we didn't much want to bring into our home.

I am so glad when I think back to that time in our lives that we practiced self care before we even really knew what self care was, and that we were able to be comfortable enough in one another's company to just shut the fuck up for 22 minutes. These days, of course, I couldn't pay you enough for a Simpsons episode's worth of quiet time each day. But it's fine. Don't be mad at the old, napping you. Separate your past self from your current self, and fondly bid the old you adieu as the new you waves goodbye from across an ever-widening ocean of responsibility.

Overcoming these three mental hurdles should help you get your head around your new sleep situation, but the cold, hard truth of the matter is that the secret to getting a good night's sleep is that there isn't one. Technically, you can move the goalposts and change how you qualify a 'good' night - you can suffer weeks on end having awful nights of broken sleep, but the upside is that when you eventually emerge from the endless shit nights to be rewarded with a few hours' sleep, it'll feel way better in comparison. You're only kidding yourself, but whatever works, chief.

I can't stress enough how important it is to manage your sleep expectations in the first year. Be prepared to be hurt, physically, mentally and emotionally. Work sleep prep into your nightly routine: strategically place any necessary muslins, nappies, paper towels and cups of water somewhere near the bed so you don't have to go hunting for them in the black of night. Train your brain to shut down on command, so that you can take fragments of sleep where you can get them: awkward sleep, micro sleep, uncomfortable sleep, sleep with the sun up.

All of this advice does not mean you have to become a morning person. Perish the thought. Being awake before 6am is achievement enough in itself, you don't have to do a 5K before the sun comes up to make it count. When we were pregnant, I used to imagine what an ideal morning would be like once we had kids: my beautiful wife and I would wake from our slumber in our over-sized bed in an over-sized bedroom (note: not our actual bedroom), smooch and flirt a little, then two tiny heads would poke around the doorframe, and we'd say 'Haha, come on in you little scamps!' and they'd bundle on the bed and we all cuddle and laugh, HAHAHA HAHAHA HAHAHA and everything would be so fucking great forever because for some reason my fantasy home life is like an insurance advert.

Snap back to reality. I am woken at 4.45am by Kid A, who has requested my presence so that I may turn on a light that he is quite clearly capable of turning on himself. My wife is still asleep, scorching the ceiling with her Godzilla snores, next to my youngest, who climbed into our bed at around 11.30pm and currently has his feet next to my wife's head. There are clothes, clean and dirty, all over the floor, the door, the drawers. No one is laughing or cuddling, and there will definitely be no flirting.

Clearly this is not what I had in mind when I would fantasise about a future with kids, but it's still what I signed up for. It's reality, and it's happening to everyone else too.

As I write, I'm just now coming out of a major sleep slump that has lasted about two weeks. First of all, our youngest developed a spot of athlete's foot, which meant an itchy toe of all things would keep him awake; still half asleep, he'd beg us through tears to scratch it, even when we were already doing so. Then, just as the fungus subsided, he got a viral infection and started throwing up at night, meaning we'd constantly wake up with every small cough or shift in his position.

As naturally as night follows day, no sooner had the youngest recovered from his sickness, the eldest started vomiting. That's right, they tag-teamed the germs, passed on the puke baton to ensure blanket coverage throughout all of half term. All of these extra inconveniences were just additional layers upon existing layers of inconvenience: the usual developmental changes, the fears of the dark, the detachment anxieties. This two week period of constant broken sleep, of being continually woken by retching, crying, screaming and complaining every single night, pushed me to the edge of my limits, maybe even more so than those first few intense months of parenting. My frustrations would boil over and my emotions would run hot. On many nights I would rant and rave and stomp and swear, all while still in that weird, unregulated buffer space between sleep and consciousness, displaying the kind of inexcusable diva behaviour I wouldn't dream of indulging in on my worst day, the kind of behaviour that makes me feel like a stranger the morning after.

Other nights, I have woken up, and with nowhere to put the intense and continued frustration I was feeling, would break down and sob, crying "I can't do this" over and over, as close to a prayer as a non-religious person like myself will ever get. It has been a struggle. Right here is where I cannot overstate the importance of talking this stuff through with your partner: emotional openness and honesty can be a literal life-saver, particularly in times of trouble or periods of great stress.

And then, last night, with no warning: sleep. When I needed it most. Maybe an accumulation of six hours, not exactly unbroken sleep, but unbothered. No puke. No screaming. No wet nappies or monsters in the cupboard or rogue fungus. Just sleep. No morning naps needed. When I woke up, the sun was shining. I felt so invigorated, I sang 'You're The Voice', 'Kiss From a Rose' and 'I Don't Wanna Miss A Thing' at full volume while the bemused kids watched on, slightly afraid. So far today, I have done a kitchen full of washing-up, cleaned the cat litter tray, put the bins out and sorted the recycling, swept the floor, tidied up the garden, finished some computer admin, treated the family to breakfast at a local museum, taken the kids to two separate adventure playgrounds, played a full family 50cc Grand Prix in Mario Kart 8 Deluxe (I won, not bragging but I am the superior player in every respect), took on a four-player River Challenge in Super Mario Party, made lunch and finished writing this very chapter you're reading now. It's like some weird sort of caffeinated high. Having a long tall drink of sleep when you've been gasping in the desert for days is like being given superpowers, even if they're only temporary.

That is the secret to a good night's sleep: you recognise it *after* the fact, and make damn sure to appreciate it once it's happened.

#14

The Most Places I Have
Slept In One Night

Never let it be said that parents with young children should give up on achieving their goals - you just have to get a bit creative with the goalposts. If you're a little more realistic with your accomplishments, given your new-found parental responsibilities and everything, you can still push your boundaries and become the best at whatever you want to do, as long what you want to do involves things in or around your own home.

For example, in 2017 I achieved a new personal best in the field of 'Most Places Slept In A Single Night' with a record-breaking score of eight locations slept in or on over the course of one sleep cycle. This is truly an Olympian achievement of which I, and by proxy my entire family, should be very proud.

Sleep with little ones is always a bit of a lottery, although I suppose even the lottery has a one in 14 million chance of winning. A better analogy is to compare bedtime routines to bus timetables: they're both extremely erratic and unreliable, both are capable of ruining your entire day, and the frustration you feel as a result is utterly futile. Just because the bus turns up on time on Monday, does not mean it'll turn up on time the next day, or the next day, or even ever again, in fact, tomorrow you might be waiting at the bus stop for three hours until the bus finally arrives only to decide it doesn't even want to be a bus any more, it's going to be a Ferrari instead, and there's no room for you at all. The bus is your kid, by the way, in case that wasn't clear.

Putting two kids to bed every night is an exhausting process, probably the equivalent of running about twelve marathons, which is why I make sure to carb-load every evening in preparation for the following day. The sleep situation changes constantly depending on routines, developmental changes and whether or not a butterfly has flapped its wings in Hong Kong, but the set-up at the time was that we had Kid A asleep in his bed upstairs, and a young Kid H tentatively asleep in his pram in the front room. My wife and I would divide and conquer and take one kid each, then reconvene on the sofa once the job was done. And that's where the story of my greatest achievement begins...

***

LOCATION #1: THE SOFA

You don't need a baby to appreciate a good sofa, but parenthood makes you realise how critical a piece of furniture it is - way better than, say, that stupid bookcase you have, full of stupid books that you can't even sleep on. If you make that impossibly dad-like "OOOooooooomph" sound when you crumple on your sofa like a lead weight, then congratulations: your sofa is worthy.

You don't necessarily know it at first, but this is where your sleep cycle now begins. As soon as buttocks hit fabric, your arse sends signals to your brain that are the equivalent of that "Toot!" whistle sound they used to have in old-timey factories to indicate the end of the working day. Every muscle in your body clocks off as soon as it senses prolonged contact with high quality upholstery. Quittin' time. All that important stuff you were going to do this evening? Anything that involved firing up the pistons in your legs and tensing your stomach muscles to sit up? Yeah, no. Forget it. The sofa has you. Technically you are now its property. It actually says this in the DFS small print. It's fine though, because you couldn't resist even if you wanted to. That's what that theatrical exhaling actually is: all the resistance just breezing out of your very being. Your body is ready. Ready for motherfucking *beddy-byes.*

This is just one of the ways you will eventually end up like your parents. Remember when you were younger and you were literally full up to the eyeballs with vigour and energy, and every night the dreaded words "Bedtime!" would feel like a death sentence? Remember how you used to be amazed at how your dad could fall asleep anywhere? Even in the middle of a conversation? That's you, that is. You're Dad now, and it happened so gradually you didn't even notice. It's just one of life's cruel jokes. Maybe the hairline hasn't fully receded yet and you still don't really understand Scott Walker records and you are capable of watching television without having a one-way argument with characters from EastEnders, but you now have your old man's ability to turn off the lights and go dark like a power cut.

My dad, like your dad and every dad who has ever dadded, had his own chair, in which he would take brief naps, the brevity of which seemed impossible to you at the time. These were naps so short - literally the ten minutes between Mum announcing "Dinner will be ready in ten minutes!" and dinner actually being ready - they flew in the face of all known sleep science. My Dad honestly popped to his car during my wedding party for a micronap in the driver's seat.

It took Teenage You at least an hour to properly wind down at night and about another half hour to squeeze your spongey brain free of all the vivid imagery it soaked in during the day: video games, TV, girls, sport, comics, Crunchie bars, blue skies, green grass and jumpers for goalposts. But Dad? Down like he'd been hit by a tranq dart in the neck. And do you know why? It's all in the chair. The chair knew what your dad really needed to get him off (unlike your mum, lol), namely a brief, uninterrupted period of time in which complete comfort was provided to defrag every atom in his exhausted body. That's you, now. You are that collection of knackered atoms. And your beloved sofa is your recharge point.

So there I am, stuck to our beautiful brown sofa like a magnet on a fridge. Choosing a brown sofa was no accident, by the way, for reasons that I really shouldn't have to explain. Rest assured, if any area in your living room is white, off-white or even just a sort of inoffensive sandy beige hue, in around 12 months' time it is going to look something like a zoo habitat, with hay and seeds and hair scattered everywhere and dung smeared all over it.

The time is around 9.30pm, post dinner, which was frozen pizza, obviously, because 80% of all meals consumed in the early years of parenthood are "a pizza". I bet a dad invented pizza. It's the most 'Dad's doing dinner' meal of all time.

No sane man can go to bed at 9.30pm - with your sleep pattern all shot to bits, there's a very real danger you'd wake up before midnight, *technically on the same day you went to sleep*, and your deflated brain would implode from the confusion. However, you are quite obviously frazzled from a hard day doing whatever it is that you do. So what can you do? You stick it out. How? By pretending to watch a film or an episode of television that you honestly couldn't give a crap about! Check*mate*, society!

For all intents and purposes you're still a perfectly functional member of the public, consuming mass media and partaking in the national conversation. Really though, you've switched on a colourful rectangular light in the corner of your living room which you'll try your best to ignore for the rest of the evening. It's a foolproof system.

I can still remember the first time my wife and I made it all the way through an evening movie after the birth of our first son. For a long while, evenings were always punctuated with baby cries over the monitor: with frequent trips upstairs, the pause button on our remote control never saw so much action. We were so happy when we managed to consume an entire motion picture, with our eyes open for the entire duration, we literally high fived each other over the end credits. That film was Escape Plan, starring Sylvester Stallone and Arnold Schwarzenegger.

I can tell you now, with the benefit of hindsight, that Escape Plan is not a good movie. Remember that show Prison Break, which you stopped watching after they broke out of prison at the end of season one, thereby painting the show's writers into a prison of their own making? It's like that, except it has Sly and Arnie in it and also that chap who played Jesus for Mel Gibson. But managing to stay awake and attentive, absorbing all of the film's rich character detail and complex plot twists (they escape, or DO THEY?), felt like a major achievement. We may have been the first people ever to enjoy Escape Plan unironically.

I can't remember exactly what we were watching on that fateful night, but it was no Escape Plan. I stuck it out for as long as I could, attempting to stall my drooping eyelids by forcing them to focus on a smaller, handheld glowing rectangle firing AMOLED rays and inane tweets directly into my brain. No dice.

It's now almost 10pm, and I'm into the window of acceptable sleepery. Believe it: this is happening. Sweet, beautiful sleep. There is no better feeling than the moment when your brain decides to stop fighting the war against sleep, lays down its weapons and submits. It's an especially illicit thrill when you're somewhere you're not really supposed to be asleep i.e. a sofa. If you're lucky, you have an unspoken agreement with the person you're sharing the sofa with that says it's totally cool if you need to slip into unconsciousness, as long as you're not in the middle of a conversation or dinner or heavy petting. It's settled: the lids are down. Oh yeah. That's the stuff. Sleeping on the sofa. For a bit.

TOTAL SLEEPING TIME: 25 minutes

LOCATION #2: THE FLOOR

You may notice over the next few paragraphs, the language I used to describe this particular sleep station is significantly less enthusiastic than that used for the sofa. That's because it's the floor. There's no dressing up the floor - it's just the floor. No one can get excited over the idea of sleeping on the floor. Floors were very much not designed for sleeping on. No one puts cushions on their floor. If anything, I'd go as far as saying that floors were explicitly designed to be so uncomfortable, no one would ever want to sleep on one. My parenting hot take is this: the floor is a shit place to sleep. Don't sleep on the floor.

Kid H had woken up, somehow sensing his father was fast asleep via the genetic superpower all babies have. After a quick feed, the only way he'd go back to sleep was to be placed on the beautiful, comfortable sofa next to my wife, where just minutes earlier I had been sleeping as soundly as a horrible overgrown man-baby. Time to move it or lose it.

You might think I'd be annoyed at being displaced. Incorrect: because I am a mature grown-up, I act like a responsible adult and sleep on the floor instead. This is very much an opportunity to teach a Lesson with a capital 'L' about knowing your new place in life, in the new order of things. Your own comfort ranks now so low on the list of priorities it's hardly worth mentioning. You fall asleep on the sofa entirely at your own risk, because if that baby wants some sofa real estate for itself, it's not going to have to put together much of a cogent argument to get it. Besides, if it makes baby happy, it makes you happy - and if it makes baby sleep, it means you can sleep too. Just not there. Down *there*.

To be clear, no one has made me sleep on the floor at this point. I'm not a dog. I have fractionally more self-respect than a dog. This was me trading down my post by my own choosing, and not in the same way that managers do when they get fired and have to tell everyone in the office that they're "moving on to exciting new opportunities" through gritted teeth.

The cycle of sleep was already spinning at this point - to wake myself up and start paying attention to whatever terrible thing we put on TV would be to jam a metal pipe in the spokes. 'Why don't you just go to bed?' I can hear you saying. Oh, GREAT IDEA. Thanks so much for your input, but you're grotesquely naive, and not just because you're talking to a book. If I go upstairs to bed, who's going to lock up downstairs? My wife? Holding a sleeping baby? She's going to put dry food in the cat feeder, is she? Bending over and rattling the box of Go-Cat like a fucking maraca in the baby's ear, yeah? Nice one. No, the only viable option here is to suffer through the broken sleep cycle together. As long as one parent is awake, the other parent cannot simply disappear to the bedroom. It's an unwritten rule of being a dad: you can't just sub yourself off for an early bath when you've had a rough game - you have to wait for the gaffer to give you the nod.

So: the floor. It's not great sleep you're getting down there, let's be real. There's not much glamour on the carpet, with the chewed-up Cheerios and what I can only assume are raisins. There is some comfort to sleeping on the floor, just not in the literal sense. First of all, you're never going to be asleep on the floor all night, that's just not physically possible. Even if you wanted to do an all-nighter prone on the deck, your spine won't allow it and will try to violently escape from your body in protest. The floor is only ever going to be a short-term solution, so the only way is up.

Secondly, because you are technically already occupying the worst place to possibly be asleep that isn't in the bath or on a live railway track or in a bed with Piers Morgan, no one is going to wake you up and move you on. You're in a safe space. No one will ever object to you sleeping on a floor, unless it's a floor in someone else's house and you are Robert Downey Jr in the '90s.

This is what the rock bottom of sleep feels like. You can get a good 20 minutes of sleep on the hard floor of rock bottom before your muscles start spasming and your skull starts throbbing and your hips start to grind into powder. Anything more than that and your body starts to contort like a funhouse mirror and you become overly conscious of your own skeleton and you start to panic that your spine might turn into a giant Nik-nak and you might die, leaving a gnarled and twisted corpse behind like something out of The X Files. It's cool though, because baby is sleeping well up there on the sofa. Good old baby.

Okay, you do feel a bit like a dog. Maybe people *should* put cushions on the floor.

TOTAL SLEEPING TIME: 19 minutes

LOCATION #3: MY BED, OH THANK GOD, MY BED

When I was little and incapable of drawing the day to a close by myself, Dad used to tuck me in tight under my covers, and every night without fail, he'd whisper "Good old bed. Best place in the world," and that would always, always be the last thing I'd hear before I'd drift off into dreams about Garfield or whatever stupid shit I was into at the time.

That ethos has very much stayed with me for life. There honestly isn't a place in the world I'd rather be than in my own bed. Tropical island paradise? I sunburn easily. Solid gold palace full of gyrating Beyoncé clones? I guarantee you I will find a way to kill the party vibe and make everyone feel awkward. The factory where they make red Doritos on 'Free Dorito Day'? Sounds like fun but there's still a long commute home afterwards to think about, and I'm doubtless going to be clogging the toilet of the train with all that saturated fat working its magic through my lower intestine.

I probably need better fantasies, but I don't care: my dream holiday would be to go to bed for two weeks. Home base. HQ. My respawn point. (Thinking about it further, I would settle for the golden Beyoncé palace if my own bed was included as part of the deal. And throw in some Doritos while you're at it).

In our family we've always subscribed to the 'bed is best' theory, so when crotchety babies won't sleep in their own cots and we've long since upgraded from the sofa, there's always an open invite to the family bed. We started off small, with an old mattress that could just about handle two adults on it, with the option to add one small child in the middle providing that one party (me, it was always me) reduced their occupation to approximately six inches of space on the edge of the bed. Which was, fine, obviously, totally, totally fine, except when the small child started to become not-so-small and the saggy mattress felt like it might fold into a sort of deadly bed taco every time anyone rolled over.

It was time to invest in a bigger bed. The biggest bed. Literally the biggest bed we could find. We now own a Super King-sized bed, which is comically large, roughly the size of South-East Anglia and second only in the official mattress size rankings to the mythical Emperor, which is the kind of mattress only actual

Emperors and clinically gigantic NBA stars have. It is the most expensive noun that I have ever bought that wasn't a house or a car. The family bed is now a beautiful, bouncy square, as wide as it is long. Fuck me, it's glorious.

Carrying the mattress up my stairs and fitting it through my bedroom door is legitimately one of the hardest things I've ever had to do, like a Crystal Maze physical challenge but one where you don't even get a sniff of a pony trekking weekend in Cornwall as a reward. I felt like Sisyphus, or Ross from Friends. When I'd finally got the divan bases down and the mattress in place, I organised the rest of the furniture around it, like a big sweaty game of Tetris. I can't describe how orgasmic the feeling was when I squeezed the final bedside table in place next to the bed with less than half a centimetre of room left between it and the wall. It's no exaggeration to say that our bedroom is now probably around 80% bed. Imagine an indoor trampoline with loads of clothes chucked on it and a phone charger poking out the side. My bed is better than your bed. Best place in the world.

When you and your partner finally make that weary decision to sack off the day and attempt an actual night's sleep, it can be bitter-sweet. On the one hand: bed. *Yes mate.* But on the other hand: effort. *Ugh.*

My routine is torture: carefully carry the baby up to bed, set him down in his own cot without waking him, find the two cats (which are inevitably hiding because they are total bastards), shoo them downstairs, turn everything off, lock every door and close every window, set the cat feeder for the morning and clear the cat box of turds. Only then can I start my own actual bedtime routine and hope with all hope that by the time I'm done, tip-toeing around the creaky floorboards and brushing my teeth like I'm in that silent vault in the first Mission: Impossible movie, the kid is still asleep and my bit of bed hasn't been gazumped. (Life advice: if you don't want half this aggro, live in a bungalow and suffocate your cats).

When you've already slept in two locations over the last hour, all of this activity has to be done on low-power mode and through strained eyelids, so you're traipsing through the house like something out of a George Romero movie. Dad of the Dead. Yawn of the Bed. It is agony and lasts eight hours and you hate it, but you do it, because of the reward that awaits: the Super King. That massive, sprawling acre of comfort. Singing its springy siren's song: *voulez-vous coucher avec moi, ce soir*. Yes please. That's a yes from me. I will do your bidding, my King.

Going from sleeping on the floor to sleeping in your bed is like dying and going to heaven, where the floor is obviously clouds but the beds are even fluffier, memory foam clouds. After a hard day of keeping both your child and yourself alive (great job!), you will be capable of sinking into that bed so deep, it'd take a full crew of grizzled yet highly-trained professional frogmen to recover you. It's like falling into a really lovely hole.

I can now fall asleep in the time it takes for you to even think about suggesting dropping a hat. My record for going from nought to asleep is 0.0 seconds. I know you think that's not possible, but I'm living, sleeping proof that it is. Believe that if I'm getting into bed with you after a long day and you have something on your mind, you're going to be discussing it with a log that looks like me.

Buying this massive, oversized bed was one of the best decisions I ever made, but it took time for me to realise that ultimately all I had done was buy more square footage of bed not to sleep in. Inevitably, the baby stirs from his cot and is given an upgrade to the bed, with free reign to sprawl in the centre, relegating me back to my standard six-inch exclusion zone. Maybe your baby will be like mine and slowly rotate throughout the night, until he's somehow sleeping horizontally between you and your partner, the middle bar of a capital H, where he'll unconsciously manage to kick you in the face several times.

You never forget the first time you get woken up by being kicked, quite hard, in the face by an infant; the only pain equal to it is how much it stings when you realise sympathy is fresh out of stock this late at night. The really fun bit is when you get so used to getting kicked in the face, your body doesn't even feel the need to wake you up when it happens, so you wake up in the morning confused at your giant throbbing head and a busted lip like you got the crap kicked out of you in a dream. Being repeatedly kicked in the face while unconscious is actually a pretty good metaphor for parenthood, as it happens.

The sooner you realise that you don't own your bed any more, the better. The instant you got your wife pregnant, you gave up the deeds to that very bed you were doing it on. It's a communal bed now. You own shares in it. You're a minority stakeholder. You're like the caretaker who lives in the school.

But man, my dad was right: bed is still the best place in the world, and I love my bed only slightly less than the kids who are always in it with me. Screw you, floor - we have a new leader!

TOTAL SLEEPING TIME: About three hours

LOCATION #4: MY INFANT SON'S SMALLER, LESS GOOD BED

I don't know what your favourite crustacean is, but mine is the lobster. Somewhere in a lobster's delicious DNA is an enzyme called telomerase, which prevents their cells from damaging when they're regenerated. What this means is that essentially, lobsters are immortal, because getting older does not increase the chance of them dying. Although they can still be killed by predators or by disease or from their own environment, when left undisturbed lobsters can theoretically live forever. I feel a kinship with the lobster, because we have a lot in common - left undisturbed, I can theoretically sleep forever. Key word: 'undisturbed'. I have sadly never been able to test my hypothesis.

I keep no precise record of how long I sleep in my own bed, but it almost certainly doesn't feel long enough. If no one woke me up, I could sleep through until the next visit of Haley's Comet, or at least the next decent Arctic Monkeys album. Unfortunately, as has become the norm, a call comes out over the monitor from Kid A's room, although really, by now the call is so loud and clear, I could hear it through six-inches of titanium with earplugs in.

Kid A and I have reached an impasse in this regard. He knows that if he wakes up in the middle of the night and calls out my name, I'm duty bound to come in and check on him. Conversely, I know that if it's the middle of the night and the quickest way to get Kid A back asleep is to climb in with him in his smaller, notably less good bed, I'm usually going to be too shattered to object. You can't just pull the brakes on that sleep cycle, prop yourself up at 3am and start reading a book of fairytales like you weren't just dreaming about Beyoncé clones. It's impossible.

The proper solution would be to force myself awake, read him a soothing story until he drops off again, then quietly retreat back to the sanctity of The Big Bed. I could do that, yes. Maybe while I'm sleeping overnight in Fantasyland I could also buy a massive tub of military grade Fairy Dust and see if that does the trick too. Get real. I'm sleeping in the kid's bed. I've been demoted again.

In truth, if you work hard at it, the transition from one bed to another can be pretty seamless. On nights where I've been woken from a particularly deep sleep to cross the landing, if you videotaped me, you'd watch the footage back and I'd glide bleary-eyed from one room to the other, pillows under my arm and my feet dragging behind me like Scooby-Doo following some sausages nose-first in his sleep.

That's testament to how streamlined I've made the process of bed-hopping. From the moment I hear "DA-" ring out over the monitor, I can be up, across the landing and in bed cuddling my son before he's even finished the "-DDY". Most nights I don't even remember doing it. I've rediscovered that feeling from childhood that you'd often get while on holiday or staying at a friends' house, when you'd wake up and temporarily be freaked out because you forgot whose bed you were sleeping in (albeit minus the floods of urine that usually followed).

It might not be the smartest decision when it comes to getting to the root of the issue - a child who wakes up and instantly calls my name if someone so much as opens a bag of Walker's Sensations from two towns over - but I console myself with the knowledge that it's a completely unconscious decision. Daytime Ali has legitimate concerns about finding long term sleep solutions for the whole family, but Night-time Ali only wants more sleep, the selfish prick. He's ruining it for the rest of us.

If we're ranking the sleep stations, my infant son's smaller, less good bed is definitely the second most comfortable option of the night, and it's usually the one I'll be stationed in for longest. There are pros and cons. Pro: I get to settle Kid A with a nice long cuddle, which feels nice and scores lots of DadPoints (the official points system of parenthood). Con: Having him pick the dry skin on my elbows in his sleep. Pro: Sleeping on a mattress. Con: Sleeping on a mattress that's three times narrower than my own. Pro: It's not the floor. Con: My son likes to hold extended conversations with me at 4am in the morning.

This is actually quite incredible. If you wake me up at 4am, it'll take me about ten minutes to even be able to formulate a syllable, let alone a recognisable string of words. But the boy? He'll be fast asleep one minute, snoring loudly through his tiny snot-encrusted little nostrils, then the next minute, he'll be bolt upright and telling me - at a normal daytime volume, I might add - about the toy he got on the front of a magazine four months ago, or he'll end a sentence from earlier in the day that he started but never got a chance to finish. His little brain is just bursting with things he's seen for the first time and he can't wait to tell me about them, but honestly mate, it's 4 o'clock in the morning, have a little decorum: I'm half-dressed and semi-covered by a tiny dinosaur duvet, the last thing I want to do is discuss the finer points of Optimus Prime's robot mode.

TOTAL SLEEPING TIME: Approximately four hours, not counting conversation time

LOCATION #5: THE SOFA PART II: RETURN OF THE SOFA

Good morning! This is your early morning wakeup call! 5.25am is a totally reasonable time to start the day, yes? Maybe if you're the type of clean living do-gooder that tortures yourself with early mornings, constant exercise and whatever 'activated almonds' are. Maybe if you're a sailor, or a security guard, or an inoffensive radio DJ who has built a career on a willingness to live like a zombie and has sacrificed any chance of ever having a normal life or a relationship in order to present the thankless pre-breakfast show slot. I am none of those things. I am just a dad. Yet here I am, awake. Good morning. "Good" morning. Good "morning".

Everyone knows that the best feeling in the world is accidentally waking up too early, seeing that you've still got over an hour to go before your alarm goes off, and going back to sleep. Scientists have proved this in labs, although I suppose it is entirely possible a couple of scientists got caught napping on the job and this was their cover story. The adult human body is never more relaxed than in that moment. If I found out the afterlife was basically this feeling on a loop, perennially discovering that I had a bit more time to sleep in, I would die a happy man. They should expand the range of those little 'Experience Day' packages you can buy off the rack in Boots. Some people want to drive a sports car, some people want to skydive, but I would pay upwards of £150 for an entire day of sleeping in a controlled environment that has a specially engineered clock that keeps winding itself back. Get Red Letter Days on the phone.

Kids, however, are not built to experience this feeling. They are incapable of recognising the luxury of more time to sleep. As soon as those eyes open and those neurones start firing up, you're fighting a losing battle if you think you're going back to bed - the war is already over. All you're doing is delaying the inevitable - you're trying to put out a forest fire by wafting a magazine at it. If your kid has decided it is now morning, I have bad news for you re: morning.

Children are actually incredible negotiators because they don't know how to lose properly - they completely cut out the middle-ground of reason or compromise and just go straight to the nuclear option every time. They can't engage in a mutually beneficial discussion designed to leave both parties appeased, but what they can do if challenged is completely lose their shit, raise the volume of their voice by 1000%, kick and scream and wake up the entire street instead. It's quite the effective tactic.

If you're negotiating with a child, you've already lost - the bomb was always going to go off. It's like playing chess with stupid people, or arguing with a Brexit voter: you can't win a competition in which there is an absence of rules and logic. So it turns out there's a 5:25 in the morning now. All you can do is lean into it. But it's okay, because there's an old friend downstairs who might just be able to help you out. Now, I'm not encouraging you to fall asleep on your sofa while your kid is awake. It may look like I am doing that, but you'll notice I'm *not* doing that. I'm being very careful not to do that. Look, I never said I was Dad of the Year, okay?

We have a system. If the hour is too small and my wife and baby are still asleep, I have a window, and as you've learned from this chapter, I'll sleep in a window, fuck it, I'll sleep anywhere. Kid A and I will both trot downstairs, me with pillows once again under my arm like a transient napper, and get set up on the sofa. He sits at one end and puts the telly on with the volume at an acceptable level; I lie down at the other end, under a blanket, with my legs on top of him. He's hardly likely to accidentally stab himself with a bread knife or have a bookcase collapse on him, but knowing that he's effectively contained in a minimum security leg prison is the slimmest justification I can muster to allow myself to drift back off to sleep, leaving no responsible adults conscious.

Everybody wins, in a way. He gets TV. I get to be prone for anywhere between 20-40 additional minutes. It's technically a compromise framed as a victory for him, but you take what you can get when you're on sleep station number five. And in case it wasn't obvious, this is not great quality sleep I'm enjoying here. This is the arse end of sleep. The dregs of sleep. But it still counts.

It's always difficult to get any proper sleep when there's a TV on in the room. My wife physically cannot go to sleep without a DVD playing in the bedroom, so for the last 13 years I've subconsciously ingested every single episode of Frasier ever made during the night. I like to think this is my superhero origin story for how I got my rapier wit. I don't think I've ever watched an episode with my eyes open; every time I hear Kelsey Grammer speak, my eyelids start to droop. It's a decidedly different experience on the morning sofa, however, because weirdly, my young son isn't all that into jokes about Jean-Paul Sartre or delightfully absurd misunderstandings at cocktail parties.

For a while, we let him watch cartoons on Netflix in the morning. Netflix is brilliant for kids because it has approximately one billion programmes for him to choose from, ranging from the popular stuff (Peppa Pig, Transformers, Paw Patrol) to the obscure (Pokémon rip-off Yokai Watch) to the piss poor, bottom-of-the-barrel animations that look like they were made during the fall of the Soviet Union.

Some of them are legitimately great and have genuine educational value (try Storybots, with music by Parry 'Hamster on a Piano' Gripp) but others you need to keep half an eye on. One seemingly harmless show about the courageous adventures of a group of animated vegetables turned out to have overt religious overtones, including blink-and-you'll-miss-them Bible quotes inserted mid-show, when any right-thinking adult had presumably either left the room or long since tuned out. The irony of surreptitiously feeding children something undesirable *via vegetables* was not lost on me.

I don't remember the day we introduced our kids to YouTube, but it's since become one of those ground zero, if-you-could-kill-baby-Hitler-would-you-do-it type events in our lives that I think about often. You can watch YouTube via an app on our living room TV, so we can really enjoy the endless crummy videos shot on mobile phones in portrait mode on our 42" 4K Ultra HD widescreen.

It started with funny cat videos. They got a great response. Then they realised you could watch proper cartoons on YouTube too, albeit framed in an ornate little box with a cosmic background, and with the video flipped so YouTube's piracy department can't auto-detect them - truly as the creators intended them to be seen. Somehow, YouTube's algorithm eventually learned that the primary user of the app wasn't a tired man in his late 30s sporadically looking for video tutorials on how to use a hammer drill, but two extremely impressionable infants who had just mastered the use of the remote control and thus were free to have their tiny minds blown by the sheer volume of recommended toy videos on the internet.

Jesus Christ, there are a lot of toy videos on the internet. Kids playing with toys. Adults playing with toys. Adults filming their kids playing with toys. Adults carefully unboxing toys while their sullen children stand at arm's length. Adults forcing their uninterested children to play with unexciting toys who are clearly being paid by the toy company. Adults who claim to be making high-energy video content for infants but who are clearly getting some sort of weird psycho-sexual thrill out of talking in a baby voice and dressing like a cartoon paedo. Adults who cut toys up with scissors to see what's inside i.e. would-be serial killers.

Some of the personalities on YouTube are tolerable. Some of them are unbearable. Some of them are literally millionaires, and you can tell, because the sounds of their shrill voices bounce off the blank walls of their massive, empty houses. The reason we liked Netflix was because the shows had no ads to brainwash our children, then we inadvertently introduced our kids to a platform that was basically a bottomless advert generator, complete with an infinite number of videos for every toy ever made. You can see why I don't get much sleep down here.

TOTAL SLEEPING TIME: 26 minutes drifting in and out of consciousness

LOCATION #6: MY OWN BED, TO MYSELF, SWEET JESUS HALLELUJAH, WHAT HAVE I DONE TO DESERVE THIS

There are certain audio cues in life that come to take on a greater meaning; sounds that, when you hear them, unlock an emotional response deep inside you. Think back to the incidental noises from your youth that would trigger those seismic sensations: the crunch of a key in the door that signified a parent arriving home; the rattle of the school bell at 3.15pm that freed you up to explore the wider world; that imprintable, unforgettable chime you heard every time you booted up your first ever games console.

These feelings eventually dull over time, like all things from your youth, but you still remain open to them, your body set to receive, just waiting to be triggered again. And now I have a new one: a simple sound that reveals a Pavlovian response, a burst of endorphins that fizz through me like a bath bomb - my wife's first footsteps as she climbs out of bed in the morning.

I can't think of any noise that brings me more pleasure. Vicky waking up is truly the greatest moment of the day, because she's an incredible, beautiful and tireless soul who brings happiness to everyone she meets. Not apropos of nothing, my wife waking up also indicates a reprieve: another shot at sleep, sixth time's the charm! I have already slept in more locations than I have bedrooms in my house, but I'm fixing to squeeze every last ounce of morning out of this damn day. Kid A untangles himself from my legs and jolts himself upright, equally ecstatic that his mother - and, by association, his brother - is awake. He bolts to the bottom of the stairs to greet them with unparalleled zeal, every single morning. It's lovely to watch, which I normally do from a horizontal position, making sure I look as bedraggled as possible so as to inspire sympathy, like a filthy old cat hanging around outside a kebab shop.

Most mornings, my wife and I have an unspoken agreement: if I've had a crappy night's sleep and it's early enough, she'll start getting both boys ready for the day and I get to go back to bed for one final chance at uninterrupted sleep. The unspoken part is essential though: what should really be said, even though it never is, is the additional line: "Even though I've obviously had a much worse night's sleep than you, due to having a small toddler's mouth clamped to a very intimate part of my body for literally the last seven hours."

Make no mistake: even though my night has been all peaks and troughs, ups and downs and ins and outs, hers has been one steady, consistent, uncomfortable experience - breastfeeding a thirsty baby. They care not for your comfort. They only want that milky white gold, and if that means you having to lie in one uncomfortable position for 95% of the night, then so be it. You can't cut a baby off when they've had too much. Babies do not respect last orders. They're always angling for a lock-in. They're basically little piss-heads who don't know when to call it a night.

I am constantly in awe of my wife and her bottomless patience. She is the complete opposite to me, a man who was at the back of the queue tutting loudly when patience was being handed out. Vicky is completely dedicated to motherhood: I often stop and marvel at exactly how selfless she is, completely giving herself over to her family and her children. She fought through weeks of frustration in order to get our babies breastfeeding, then continued breastfeeding them long after it stopped being convenient in order to give our kids the best start in life, even at the expense of her own social life. While I'm at work, she spends her days making sure the boys are stimulated and engaged with fun activities. And at night, she gives her body over to the baby, who understandably clings to her bosom like it's an inflatable life-raft. Sometimes I watch her and the baby sleep together, entwined with one another, one soul sharing the same heartbeat.

Cut to me, having already slept in five different beds. Hi there. Can I have another nap please? Cheers.

I have maybe 30 minutes to turn the night around and end it on a high before I have to get up and go to work. 30 minutes is an unwise amount of time to sleep. Experts say that a 10-minute nap is ideal, because it recharges your battery without letting you fall into a deeper sleep pattern. To the people who conducted that study, let me just say this: SO LONG, SUCKERS. I'm taking the equivalent of THREE perfect naps and I'm going to wake up in 30 minutes' time feeling like a GOLDEN GOD and there's nothing you nerds can do about it.

It's been a long night, but we've finally reached peak sleep. It's all been worth it to get to this moment: the hard floor, the feet in the face, the difficult conversations, the YouTube theme tunes. This is as good as it gets: free reign of the Super King. Sprawled on the huge bed, starfishing even though my arms and legs don't reach the end of the mattress, I feel like the last man on Earth. I fall asleep face down, transform into a lobster, and vanish into the Sunken Place.

TOTAL SLEEPING TIME: 30 heavenly minutes

Location #7: THE GREATER ABELLIO
8.09 TO LIVERPOOL STREET

Except, of course, the experts were right: 30 minutes is a horrible length for a nap. I wake up - correction: I am woken up by members of my family who have more respect for customary working hours than I do - and find that I'm somehow more tired than when I'm started. How does that even work, experts? There's no such thing as minus sleep, is there? It's like an episode of the Twilight Zone. Fuck this to infinity and beyond.

I wake up again, because clearly I just fell straight back to sleep. This isn't over. Not by a long shot. Until I am sat at my desk in front of my computer, with actual human thoughts in my head, there is still sleep to be had. I'll find it. In some ways, I am highly driven in that I will go to great lengths to find a way to do nothing. You're talking to a person who had the quote "Looking for the maximum fun with the minimum effort" on his Facebook page for about ten years. That's the kind of fun-loving, crazy guy I am: if I want everybody to know one thing about me, it's that I'm totally up for a great time unless I have to do something or talk to someone or go somewhere.

You might think that because I am dressed, showered and fed, that qualifies as being awake. False. Technically, you could consider me conscious: my body is upright, all my limbs are moving, I am eating toast without choking and I am engaging other conscious people in what appears to be conversation. Do not be so readily fooled. This is all just for show. I won't reach the state I like to call 'hyper-awake' for a few hours yet, because there's still one more sleep station I've yet to encounter: the train.

I live in Essex but I work in West London, which makes my commute just a smidge under two hours each way. When I tell people this at work it usually elicits a pained reaction, which I enjoy because I get to reap the rewards of the perceived hardship they've imagined I'm suffering. "It's actually not that bad," I'll yawn, bravely, before doddering around pathetically and pretending I'm so exhausted I've forgotten how to make a cup of tea. Great banter.

I'll admit, there are downsides to having approximately four hours of commuting time per day. The biggest, and most obvious, is that it leaves me with much less time with my family than I'd like. By the time I'm home in the evening, both the kids are asleep. So really, during an average week, I'll see my boys for maybe five hours total from Monday to Friday.

It sounds devastating, and it can be, but obviously this does not factor in literally everything I've already talked about in this chapter so far: the early evening wake-ups, the midnight cuddles, the rootless 4am conversations, the important early morning hour of male bonding YouTube time. We get by. I'm no stranger to my kids. It certainly makes you respect the value of a weekend in ways you never could have previously appreciated. Or to put it another way: friends of mine, this is the reason I haven't had a weekend 'free' since 2012.

Another downside of the mega commute is that you cannot avoid becoming a train person. That is, a person who is a professional commuter. Even if you know me from this chapter alone, you'll know that I'm not the type to strike up a friendship with any of my fellow commuters, even the regulars. Sleeping Man With Beanie Hat Pulled Over Eyes. Big Fat Guy Who Dresses Like Sam Neill In Jurassic Park. All-Weather Fur Coat Lady Who Always Speaks Loudly On Phone. Man Who Carries Briefcase With Only Book And Apple In It. Man Inexplicably Eating Chicken Teriyaki At Wasabi In Liverpool Street Station At 8.45am.

Characters to the last, I'm sure, but I've used my many years of the same commute to streamline the process so I avoid as many other people as possible by knowing exactly where on the platform I need to stand to get the cushiest seat on the whole train: the hotly-contested seat that is most conducive to more precious sleep.

Sometimes you spot another train person on your turf so you wind up with two people vying in advance for the same prime seat position, standing inches away from one another on an otherwise empty platform, turning an ordinary commute into a high stakes game of precision engineering. More often than not, a train will sweep in, roll agonisingly past the other guy and stop directly in front of me, where I'll silently mouth "This is my dojo, motherfucker" or "Welcome to the Thunderdome, bitch" or something else I'd never say out loud. I never knew what it was like to have a nemesis until I became a train person. I'm Alan Partridge.

Here comes the upside aka how to turn a negative into a positive. Because yes, two hours' commute each way is wildly excessive and yes, if I could find a way to cut it down then I would. But what this commute does give me, forces upon me, is invaluable decompression time between the different worlds of home and work.

If I have had a tough day at work, then I have two hours to shake off the tension and arrive home stress-free and sofa-ready. Conversely, and crucially, if ever I've had a rough night of it at home (see, um, above, see all of the above) then I have two hours in which to become an actual functioning part of the human race again. Two whole hours of alone time. Two entire hours just for me. Two peaceful, priceless hours in which to learn new skills, to listen to music, to read, to work on becoming a better father and husband. Obviously I use these two hours to sleep, because I am a moron. Sleeping on a train is dangerous at the best of times. I once had a hungover friend who claimed she fell asleep on the Circle Line one morning and woke up 90 minutes later at the exact same stop she got on at. If you travel by National Rail then falling asleep is even more fraught with danger; nod off and you might accidentally find yourself in Diss or Thorpe-Le-Soken or one of those other Oyster-less rural hellholes that people only ever visit by accident.

Luckily, my morning commute consists of two train journeys, both of which end at the stop where I need to get off. Many is the time when I've dropped off one minute and woken up with a start half an hour later to find myself on a static, empty train, cleaners diligently tidying around me. This is slightly less embarrassing than receiving the empathetic 'hand on shoulder' waking technique employed by other commuters who feel the need to make sure you don't end up sleeping through the scheduled stop before hurtling back where you came from at 100mph. Thanks, but I'm actually a train person, this was all part of the plan.

Done right, the train nap can be an invaluable source of rest. If you've done your homework and claimed the best seat for yourself - always go with the solo chair, always strive for a window view - then you're well placed for one last bit of shut-eye before joining the rat race.

A massive screaming locomotive might not sound like an ideal venue in which to nod off, but hey: it's a warm and ventilated area, you're basically being rocked to sleep with white noise like a big adult baby, and hopefully there's no one kicking you in the mouth while you're trying to sleep.

Because I was taught to fear London and all of its vices when I was a visiting teenager, deemed by my parents as highly likely to get mugged, kidnapped or murdered, I fall asleep with my bag strap over my shoulder and my mobile phone clutched tightly in my hand to ward off potential thieves. I am the worst person on the train by some distance, but I am the only one who has slept across multiple beds and counties.

TOTAL SLEEPING TIME: 35 minutes, depending on delays

LOCATION #8: THE WESTBOUND CIRCLE LINE FROM LIVERPOOL STREET TO HAMMERSMITH

There is a joke in Edgar Wright's excellent sitcom Spaced, where Nick Frost's character Mike falls asleep on the Tube and ends up in Sheffield. "The Tube doesn't go to Sheffield, Mike," says Simon Pegg's character. "Yeah I know," says Mike. "I must have changed at King's Cross."

I can confirm that this isn't a joke and is entirely possible.

TOTAL SLEEPING TIME: 45 minutes

***

There you have it. Eight different sleep stations in one sleep cycle, truly a phenomenal achievement if I say so myself. I've never bettered it and I doubt I ever will. To all the new dads out there, stick with it: it took years of practice to get this good, it didn't just happen overnight. Well, technically it did happen overnight, but you know what I mean.

#15

Get Your Baby to Nap! A 'Choose Your Own Adventure' Story

You've been given a simple task: take the baby out in the pram and don't come back until it's asleep. Easy. It couldn't be easier. It requires nothing of you other than the ability to walk, and not spontaneously start yelling at clouds. You can do this, right? Let's begin the adventure. Let's get that baby to sleep!

Option #1

You leave the house to go to the park.

- To turn left, **go to Option #2**.
- To turn right, **go to Option #3**.

Option #2

Sorry, but turning left takes you past the house that has a dog, which obviously starts barking the moment it detects you in the vicinity. Your baby is still awake. **Go to Option #4**.

Option #3

Turning right takes you down the main road. It's usually quiet, but somehow on the 100 metre walk to the park, you are passed by a loud bus, a car playing Heart FM with its windows down, a rag and bone man complete with ringing bell and one of those old-timey recruitment vans with the guy standing out the sunroof shouting political slogans through a megaphone. You didn't think they were still around these days, but here we are. Your baby is still awake. **Go to Option #4.**

Option #4

You are in the park.

- To walk through the park, **go to Option #5**.
- To walk around the outside of the park, **go to Option #6**.

Option #5

You walk through the park, which is a mistake because there are other humans there. Children humans. Which make noise. You attempt to avoid the particularly happy children, laughing their stupid loud laughs, and steer towards the sullen, mumbling teens on the benches. Unfortunately, one of them unwraps a Twix and the scrunchy foil wrapper somehow has the equivalent volume of a dustbin covered in tin foil rolling down a hill. Your baby is still awake. **Go to Option #7.**

Option #6

You take the picturesque route around the park, making sure to enjoy your natural surroundings. Suddenly: wildlife! Squirrels scurry in front of your pram. You're pretty sure there are two pigeons loudly shagging in the bushes. There's a woodpecker - an actual, honest to God woodpecker, like in a cartoon - hammering away at a tree that's been hollowed out to maximise its acoustics. Sylvanian Families are all up in this motherfucker and your baby is still awake. Go to **Option #7.**

Option #7

You have been walking your baby in total silence for 45 minutes and finally, mercifully, they close their heavy little eyes and drift into sleep.

- To take a cute photo, **go to Option #8.**
- Seriously, take a photo, what's wrong with you? **Go to Option #8.**

Option #8

Oh, sorry, that was a bad idea. Even though you delicately slide the phone out of your pocket and are careful to compensate the applied pressure on the pram handles so as not to unbalance it as you hold the camera, you snap the picture before realising that even when on silent, your phone camera still makes that kitschy "SNIPT!" photo sound. Did you get away with it? In the photo, your baby is asleep and peaceful. In actuality, your baby is awake again, rejuvenated at the idea of playing with your phone. Yeah, you shouldn't have done that. **Go to Option #9.**

Option #9

Fuck it, it makes no difference at this point, you've been doing this for over an hour. Do whatever you want.

- To turn left down a back street, **go to Option #10.**
- To walk endlessly and aimlessly, **go to Option #11.**

Option #10

Unbeknown to you, the usually quiet back street is today hosting a parade, complete with marching band of drummers, elephants, a musical interlude from DJ Loud and MC Shouty, and special guest Brian Blessed on the mic, just laughing endlessly, laughing like a mad old bastard while fireworks explode behind him. Your baby is not only awake, but has also done a shit. Keep walking for six hours, and only then, **go to Option #11**.

Option #11

You have achieved an absence of sound. There is no traffic. There are no nearby dogs or children or horny pigeons. You briefly wonder if you are deaf before hearing the world's most perfect sound: the deep breathing of your sleeping baby, in tune with their chest. This is nirvana. All of the waiting, all of the mad people drilling bits of wood at 10am on a Sunday, all of the noise was worth tolerating for this perfect moment, and you never want it to end. Then a gust of wind blows right in your baby's face and it wakes up. **Go back to Option #1**.

#16

Wetting the Baby's Head:
What to Definitely Not Do

Wetting the baby's head is a noble tradition that has roots in Christian baptismal ceremonies but is now basically a time-honoured excuse to go out and get leathered for the first time since the birth of your baby. Thanks, Christians! You guys are alright!

Chances are, unless you are an alcoholic, this will be the first time you've had a proper drinking session since becoming a father (I'm not counting the shots of neat whisky you neck after those particularly apocalyptic bedtimes). The wetting of the baby's head is a fundamental part of being a new dad; it's the first time you get to re-join society, put on human clothes and engage in a variety of conversation with people who haven't recently suffered massive vaginal damage. It's a biggie, so you're going to want to make the most of it.

Listen dads, I can't tell you how to have a good time, I can't prescribe the exact amount of banter needed. Maybe your idea of a great night out differs from mine. Yours almost certainly won't involve heated discussions about which are the superior crisp flavours. What I can do, however, is give you some loose guidelines of what *not* to do while wetting your baby's head, using examples which are random and not at all based on anyone or any evening in particular. Heed these 'do not dos' and you're golden. All totally random.

- **DO NOT** be surprised if over the course of the evening you find you have forgotten the names of one or more of your friends

- **DO NOT** share grisly details of the birth with people who have never previously shown an interest in the state of your wife's perineum

- **DO NOT** be afraid to discuss how precious and fragile and tender life is on the one hand while revealing how desperate you are for a stiff goddamn drink on the other

- **DO NOT** go out for cocktails at a cheap 2-for-1 cocktail bar that smells suspiciously of bleach

- **DO NOT** get so excited to be out of the house you proceed to order two of every cocktail from the menu, which you will then exchange with friends in a sort of modern-day bartering environment, ensuring you will be mixing every type of alcohol, mixer and disgusting sugar syrup under the sun

- **DO NOT** do this multiple times

- **DO NOT**, under any circumstances, try a Dry Manhattan for the first time ever

- **DEFINITELY DO NOT** drink two Dry Manhattans because one of them was free, even though you hated the first one but not as much as you hated the second one, realising far too late that Dry Manhattans aren't just cute Sex and the City cocktails but are actually like drinking a tin of 20-year-old Cuprinol

- **DO NOT** think that downloading the official bar app and taking advantage of the promo to extend Happy Hour by a whole hour constitutes as "beating the system"

- **DO NOT** ignore the voice in your head that says "I should probably make this the last one" and go on to order more drinks, even if just to rid your mouth of the anti-taste of those Dry Manhattans

- **DO NOT** get to 10pm before you realise you haven't eaten anything

- **DO NOT** pretend that cucumber slices or slushed-up ice cubes from your empties count as dinner

- **DO NOT** wait until you slip clumsily in the bathroom and nearly knock yourself out on the urinal before you realise it might be time to call it a night

- **DO NOT** go to McDonald's on the way home

- **DO NOT** take the route to the train station that you know for a fact takes you past a McDonald's

- **SERIOUSLY, DO NOT UNDER ANY CIRCUMSTANCES** go to McDonald's

- While you're in McDonald's, **DO NOT** order a large Big Tasty meal with a vanilla milkshake, and definitely do not order those additional little deep-fried pellets of cheese that are basically scraped from underneath the grill, rolled in breadcrumbs and priced at, like, three quid

- **DO NOT** eat the entire McDonald's immediately, like you're being forced to do so at gunpoint

- **DO NOT** fall asleep on the Tube

- **DO NOT** wake up on the Tube in a frantic rush to do a big dairy-based puke out the closing doors

- **DO NOT** get off the Tube because you think you're going to be sick again, because even though this is true, you clearly don't know where you are

- **DO NOT** get back on the Tube again, then fall asleep from exhaustion, then wake up two stops past your stop, then get off the Tube, then stumble to the opposite platform, then get on the Tube again, then fall asleep *again* and miss your stop by three stops in the wrong direction, taking you halfway back to the bar

- **DO NOT** continue this comically inept process for a good 45 minutes in a sequence of events that, if sped up, would make for a solid Benny Hill sketch

- **DO NOT** emerge from the Tube in the middle of Leicester Square, particularly if you don't live in Leicester Square and Leicester Square isn't even where you need to change

- **DO NOT** make the mistake of thinking just because you have finally boarded the train that takes you home and because you have already been sick once that it will not happen again

- **DO NOT** think that passengers or TfL officials didn't see how you just emptied an entire Tube carriage by spewing Big Tasty all over the floor, then hopped out at the next stop and casually sauntered to the next carriage in an attempt to start your new life as Guy Who Definitely Hasn't Just Vomited

- **DO NOT** close your eyes and make a mental note to open them again in about two stops because you're almost home

- **DO NOT** panic when you are woken up at the last tube stop, eight Tube stops away from where you actually live

- **DO NOT** panic when you realise the Tube is closed now and your phone battery is dead and Uber won't be a thing for a few more years yet and you work out that it'll take you about 90 minutes to walk home, even without factoring in the drunken zigzags you seem to be walking in, which is longer than your entire train journey was supposed to take

- **DO NOT** hold back on cursing at yourself for the entire shameful walk home, you stupid, stupid prick

- **DO NOT** twist your ankle on an uneven paving slab on which you've almost come a cropper while sober many times before, but it had to be tonight, didn't it, the first night in two months you've walked down the street inebriated, your dangerously high blood alcohol levels shattering the already slim chance you could squeeze a settlement out of the local council

- **DO NOT** arrive home, immediately decamp to the toilet to be sick again, fall asleep on the toilet bowl then eventually crawl under a blanket on the sofa for the most uncomfortable night's sleep of your life, your ankle throbbing, your mouth somehow dryer than you ever thought possible, those fucking Dry Manhattans still working their devil magic even after everything you've ingested and regurgitated this evening

- **DO NOT** wake up three and a half hours later, realising that oh shit, oh fucking Jesus Christ no, *it's already morning*, you forgot what time morning is now, the day can't be starting already, this is a bad dream, noooooOOOOO-

- **DO NOT** forget you also have to look after a baby now and the days in which you could sleep off a hangover with a four hour nap and a bacon and egg sandwich and a Friends marathon are long gone, long fucking gone, no chance of that now, because there's a very small baby who's just woken up and who already thinks the world of you and even at an extremely young age you're pretty sure it's still capable of feeling disappointment, so you'd better suck it up, suck it right up and don't dare mention how much your head hurts you pathetic worm

- **DO NOT** expect sympathy for any of this sort of horseshit ever, ever again

- **DO NOT** cry

Follow these simple instructions and I'm sure you'll have a great time like I did!

#17

Rating the 20 Different Types of Poo, From Best to Worst to I MUST LEAVE MY BODY

O h, you're having a baby? Well, I hope you like dealing with lots and lots of shit! This is the subtext of any conversation you'll have with a new father: there are good times, there are bad times, and in between, every single day, there is lots of shitting.

The concept of being on bumhole patrol for another human being takes a lot of getting used to. Yes, not only do you have to feed and clothe this child, but you also have to wipe its arse, again and again and again. And again. Even though it just pooed, like, four minutes ago. The Poo-lar Express runs to an erratic timetable, my friend, and you are now a full-blown, season-ticket-holding commuter who is completely at its mercy.

In time, you will get comfortable with fecal matter, which is just as well because you and fecal matter are going to be spending a lot of time covered in one another. In the early days, a rogue blob of brown escaping the confines of a wipe might make you do a full body gag, but before long you will grow immune to stray sharts and will be able to tolerate the presence of human poo on your person for minutes at a time.

It's funny how quickly picking up another human being and smelling their arsehole feels normal. You'll do this a lot, like a kind of poo-based Poirot, nostrils deep in the arsecrack and protected only by the flimsiest of onesies, detecting for clues.

The most important thing is that you are prepared for the inevitability of the Code Brown. At home, set up a baby changing station where you have a sturdy flat surface, a changing mat (which will quickly become your most germ-filled possession), a big fat stack of nappies and as many baby wipes as you can physically afford. Soon you'll be able to strip and change a baby like a psychopath cleaning a rifle in a Stanley Kubrick movie.

Just beware the ever-changing nature of poo - you don't want to be surprised on the job, so to speak. The following 20 types of turd are the ones you're most likely to encounter, rated from the most amiable plops to the purest iterations of evil.

20. The Phantom

You smelt it and baby dealt it, but to your delight, there is no evidence of any fecal matter in the crime scene whatsoever - it was a victimless crime. The only explanation is that it must have been a fart all along - a horrendously noxious, stomach churning guff, one that is inevitably going to manifest itself as a solid sooner rather than later. The most important thing is that dealing with this fakeout definitely counts as your turn changing the nappy.

19. The War-Paint

So called because you can see it all over their face. A pained expression and a tennis player grunt leads you to believe that you're getting ready to witness an atrocity of war, but in actual fact there's little more than an Adam Ant-style dark smear across the child's otherwise unblemished pamper. Ten out of ten for theatrics, though.

18. The Colman's Special

An inoffensive dash of beige paste, so named because it resembles a light dashing of Colman's mustard atop a, uhh, nappy. Small and wipe clean though it may be, it's still enough to put you off the Dijon for a little while. See also: homemade hummus, Nesquik banana milkshake, porridge.

17. The Playdoh

Not all poops are to be feared - some take the form of a soft and supple plaything (although it's always worth double checking your kid hasn't been eating actual Play-Doh). If you're lucky, this perfectly formed poop will have been molded into the shape of your baby's arsecrack because they've been sitting on it. It's still human faeces, but heck, it's adorable!

16. The Pellet

A distressingly abstract ablution, these tiny poops are alien in appearance and legion in numbers, almost as if they've been jettisoned from a fecal Pez dispenser. There are poops that are way more offensive on the senses and poops that require a tonne more elbow grease, but there's something off-putting about the fact your kid shits like a rabbit.

15. The Chipolata

Not much to complain about here: The Chipolata is your standard, one-and-done baby poop - an average-sized, lumpy log that nestles neatly between the cheeks. Solid enough to make clean-up tolerable, with a detectable odour that you wouldn't exactly describe as pleasant. You will dispose of literally hundreds of these without even batting an eyelid. This is your life now. You are literally a shit shoveller.

14. The Snake

Much like the Chipolata in girth, odour and weight, but weirdly smooth, which is quite unsettling. A bit of texture on your poop is expected, as you would expect from something that's been through an intestine and come out of a bumhole. The Snake, however, could have been pumped directly from an ice cream dispenser, which sounds nicer but is definitely somehow worse.

13. The Turd

It's always odd when you see an adult-sized shit nestled happily in a nappy. It shouldn't be a surprise: you've seen these every day of your life floating at the bottom of the toilet bowl, enjoying their last few seconds of sunlight before The Big Swim. Nonetheless, the first time you witness a small baby pooping a you-sized turd, it's quite something.

12. The Coronation Chicken

So named because it has the look and feel of a particularly haphazard coronation chicken sandwich filling as served by a hungover dinner lady. The texture is compact and sloppy, and the smell is rich and identifiable as food, so much so you could almost appreciate it if only it wasn't horrendous toxic shit that has been recently pumped from an arsetube.

11. The Coke Can

Truly a sight to behold: a turd of such showstopping girth it defies belief - how was this inside a baby? Despite the clean-up required (this is a five wipe minimum situation), you honestly can't stay mad, it's quite the achievement. By your calculations, The Coke Can must have accounted for around 50% of baby's total body weight. That feeling you're feeling? Jealousy.

10. The Mr. Peanut

We're getting into the rough stuff now. Formula-fed babies are most likely to produce the Mr. Peanut, a fluffy brown horror show with the consistency of a half jar of Sun-Pat (crunchy, not smooth). It's the *bits* that get you. This son of a bitch won't go easy into the night: vehemently anti-wipe-clean, it's stubborn and sticky and, shit, look, you've got some on your hand, fuck.

9. The Tony Stark

A rare and unwelcome sight, you will only find the Tony Stark when baby is taking iron, man. You've disposed of fifty shades of brown before, but the green tinge to iron supplement poos will shock you to your core the first time you see it, like it's been ejected from a Ninja Turtle. Imagine someone violently sharting broccoli through a cheese grater and you're halfway there.

8. The Gag Reel

Small and unassuming in appearance but possesses such a toxic whiff that it's liable to get up the nostrils and in the back of the throat, causing anyone within a 3 metre radius to retch. The Gag Reel defies physics, because though it may take the form of concentrated dark matter, it is poo that is transmitted via air, like the killer monkey virus in Outbreak.

7. The Live Poop Show

The kind that only happens when you're down there in the zone and you get to witness it first hand. You can practice with a thousand dolls and nappies and jars of Nutella, but nothing quite prepares the senses for seeing an actual poo get crimped off by a human sphincter in eye-watering HD close-up. Often paired with The Phantom, so don't take your eye off the prize.

6. The Bugs Bunny

What's up doc? My child appears to have full, undigested carrots in his stool. There's no need to consult a medical professional just yet, it's perfectly normal for a baby's body to fail to break down sturdy veg like carrots. Still, it's unsettling to say the least. It's... it's still... orange. And identifiable as the thing that it was... or still is? I'm going to need a minute.

5. The Snot

Oh man. My condolences. There are several horrid things about babies getting ill - their unbearable snuffling, their streaming eyes, the general phlegm-fest - but you should know that the downstairs holes do not go unaffected. The stringy, wet, unholy combination of mucus and faeces is the worst partnership since Mel C did a duet with Bryan Adams.

4. The Black Death

The rule goes thus: the cuter your newborn baby is, the more disgusting its shits. There's no sight quite like a fresh-faced new baby feeling sunlight on its face for the first time, but the inverse effect is already brewing within: a black or dark green-tinged, tar-based dirty protest that looks like something you'd see on a cigarette box warning. A truly foul, radioactive turd: the first is the worst.

3. The Paint Job

When is a poo not a poo? Just one of the existential crises you'll ponder while dealing with The Paint Job, a kind of messy Mafia hit on the nappy area which seemingly has no significant physical substance but doesn't leave a single speck of white. We're talking explosive, wall-to-wall coverage, like one of those dye packs that banks hide in piles of money to foil robbers. Godspeed.

2. The Soup

You've dealt with solids. You've dealt with gas. Welcome to liquid. The Soup is an avant garde, expressionist take on poo, reimagined as a milky broth, different at a molecular level from your traditional faeces. It is, as you might expect, a whole different ball-game when it comes to clean-up. For the first time, changing baby on a flat surface is a requirement, because the nappy is now basically being used as a cup. You are forever changed.

1. The Volcano

You've heard the stories and been told the tales, but nothing quite compares you for The Volcano - the kind of toilet experience you'll one day share with others like a brush with death. The consistency? Runny, like the devil's hot chocolate. The temperature? Hot, somehow? And the coverage? More than total - it's out of containment and there's liquid toilet magma halfway up baby's back. Panic stations, this is DEFCON 1! No training can prepare you, just hold your nose, hope for the best and find out where the nearest Mothercare is because baby is fully soiled from arse to elbow. I will say a prayer for you tonight my brother.

#18

Tits and Teeth:
The Body Horror That Awaits

One thing that pregnancy and parenthood really instils in you is a genuine, long-lasting sense of amazement at the human body and what it is capable of, whether it's small and cute or adult and knackered. Amazement yes, but also horror. The human body is terrifying and spectacular and exhausting and magical and really quite frightening at times, and as a dad you get a front row seat to see absolutely everything it can do.

Think back to the birth. You knew what was coming, you knew what had to happen, you knew who had to be squeezed out of which hole, but all the foreknowledge in the world couldn't really prepare you for those indelible things that you saw. *Down there.* Maybe you'd have been more prepared if you'd paid more attention in biology class instead of drawing hairs on the balls of the illustrated wangs in the textbooks and sniggering at the teacher saying the word "testes". Hurr hurr. *Testes.*

That appreciation of the human body - the female body, let's be honest - does not end with childbirth, but continues well into the raising of children. Birth puts an insane amount of stress on a woman's body, but it's a sprint compared to the enduring marathon of discomfort that woman will undergo during the early years of child-rearing. Take breastfeeding, for example. Childbirth was an incredible physical feat, a real show-stopper, something that's definitely worth mentioning on your family newsletter. But breastfeeding? Breastfeeding is actual, quantifiable magic - it's almost beyond comprehension. And you thought you loved tits before!

Watching your partner breastfeed your child for the first time is an unforgettable moment; mother and baby locked once again in simpatico, still sharing the same body long after the cord was cut. From your perspective, breastfeeding feels incredibly peaceful, where for a few minutes, all is calm, all is quiet and everything is right in the world. Of course, your perspective generally does not involve having a thirsty baby clamped to any tender parts of your anatomy, so it's not exactly the none-more-zen chill-out zone it might seem like from outside the tent.

Let's take this moment to educate ourselves and all of us be better men. Let's move beyond the cheap ogling of breasts and start appreciating them at a chin-stroking academic level. 'Phwooaaarrr!' you'll think, academically. 'Nice rack!' you'll say, before correcting the outraged mother by informing her that, actually, you're appreciating her boobs on a biological level, so actually she's the one with the hang-ups, yeah? Then aggressively high five the nearest man, spilling his coffee.

On second thoughts, please do not do any of this, but do read and memorise these amazing facts about breastfeeding by way of recompense.

AMAZING BREASTFEEDING FACT #1

Breast milk is more than just a meal for baby - it's a living substance. There's a reason breast milk is often referred to as 'white gold'. It contains live cells, including stem cells, that will eventually help form other body cell types like bone tissue, the heart, the kidneys and even the baby's brain. That's a proper mind-blower. In the days following birth, your partner's breasts (yes, I just read that back myself and it does feel a little weird to be talking about your partner's breasts, but I'm not going to stop) will produce colostrum, which is a special sort of full-fat, gold-top, nutrient-rich milk that contains calcium, minerals, proteins and antibodies for baby. So, not only is breast milk breakfast, lunch and dinner, it's also a much-needed vitamin injection and a spoonful of sugar to help the medicine go down. You can have a taste of it yourself if you really want to be That Guy, just know that it tastes like almondy sugary water, and that you are a gigantic adult baby now.

AMAZING BREASTFEEDING FACT #2

Breasts are smart - probably smarter than you. Try and wrap your head around this one: while breastfeeding, the female body automatically changes the biological makeup of the milk to meet the baby's needs, depending on the situation. A bit like when a coffee shop barista sees a customer with blue hair, sleeve tattoos and a beanie and subconsciously picks up the vegan milk. Not only do breasts produce the correct kind of milk for the correct age - i.e. a three-month-old will receive very different milk to a one-year-old - but they're even able to adapt to weather and up the milk's water content on a hot day to aid with hydration. What's more, if baby is sick, the breast milk will contain more white blood cells in order to help combat infection, and your partner's self-aware tits can even detect even a one degree fluctuation in baby's body temperature, cooling them down or heating them up as needed. Take a look at your pathetic, floppy bollocks and ask yourself the last time they did you or anyone else a favour.

AMAZING BREASTFEEDING FACT #3

Breastfeeding is a win for everybody - including you. There's a laundry list of benefits to breastfeeding if you decide that's the way you want to go. It's a win for Mum: mothers who breastfeed are less likely to develop breast cancer and ovarian cancer, not to mention heart disease, diabetes and postpartum depression, and they also have a lower risk of having a stroke in later life. It's a win for baby: regular breast milk protects against respiratory tract infections, meningitis, pneumonia, ear infection, diabetes, high blood pressure, high cholesterol, asthma, eczema, Hodgkin's disease, Leukaemia, and even obesity. I have no idea whatsoever how it's even possible to crunch those kinds of numbers, but I'm inclined to believe scientists who have nothing to gain over the propaganda put out by the for-profit formula companies. Breastfeeding is even a result for Dad: it means no preparing bottle feeds at 2am, or indeed any time of the day or night. Silent fist pump to yourself!

AMAZING BREASTFEEDING FACT #4

Breast milk can be a gourmet feast. There are two periods of your life where you'll eat the same meal every day for six months: as a breast-fed newborn baby, and during your first semester at university when you find out that bumper packs of Aldi Penne only cost 29p. Sucking endlessly on the same teat might sound like a bummer, but in actual fact, the taste and smell of breast milk changes considerably depending on what kind of food your partner eats. So, if she's bang into onion bhajis, baby is going to get a piece of that, while the taste of ginger and other spicy plant roots will flavour breast milk significantly. Exposing your kid to more flavours during the breast-fast buffet will mean they're less likely to be fussy eaters when they get onto solid food, which translates as you spending way less time on your hands and knees scrubbing Ella's Kitchen green smoothies out of the carpet fibres in the living room.

AMAZING BREASTFEEDING FACT #5

Breasts have supernatural, otherworldly powers. I meant it when I said breasts were smart - they are intuitive in all the ways that you are not, almost to the point of being too clever for their own good. For example, the boobs of a breastfeeding mother will often automatically start lactating when they hear the cries of a baby nearby - it doesn't even need to be your baby. In some cases, women who have had trouble with their flow of milk can look at a picture of their baby - or, again, any old baby - in order to aid its release. Final fun boob fact: you can rub breast milk into a baby's cuts or scratches to make them heal quicker. Reminder: men can't lactate automatically, they can't lactate any kind of magical solvent - heck, they can't even lactate at all. The best we can do is produce testosterone, which is like trying to calm a crying baby by strapping it to the bonnet of a flame-decaled monster truck.

There are obviously downsides to breastfeeding, which you'll also do well to learn about - it's not the all-inclusive meal ticket you might think it is. For starters, there's Mastitis, which is when the inflammation of breast tissue caused by breastfeeding leads to infection. This takes many forms, including additional swelling, aching and redness, or to paraphrase my wife when she suffered a nasty bout of Mastitis, 'it feels like your tits are on fire'.

Let's be perfectly honest: breastfeeding is an uncomfortable process at the best of times. Boobs get bigger and heavier, and not in a sexy way - in a 'I'm smuggling two very large and swollen melons under my jumper so don't even fucking think about touching them' kind of way.

It is not especially pleasant for women to think of themselves as a food source - that initial bond felt at the beginning of the breastfeeding process can easily give way to an uncomfortable inconvenience. Boobs can sag and lose their lustre over time as their primary function kicks in and they become both lunchbox and lunch. And that's before we even get into the act of expressing milk i.e. hooking the boobs up to a mechanised pump and siphoning off the excess milk that the breasts are creating (because they need to be emptied regardless of whether baby is hungry, and although boobs are smart, they're not *that* smart). 'Breastfeeding' can feel organic and powerful and beautiful. 'Being milked like a human cow by a small machine' doesn't feel quite so empowering.

All of this can understandably lead to women feeling significantly less comfortable in their own skin - and any existing body issues they might have are likely to be amplified. Make no mistake: breastfeeding can take a huge physical and mental toll on a woman, on both her body and her brain. It is a gigantic responsibility for a mother to bear, and it is not one that can be ignored or switched off at will - it's all or nothing. The benefits are clear from the outset, but what's not clear is how any woman will react to the role. For every convenience there's an untimely inconvenience waiting in the wings; for every penny you save, there's a different cost to be paid elsewhere. Many women try breastfeeding, find it's not for them and turn to the bottle instead, and more power to them for giving it a go.

There are more than enough reasons for a woman to not want to breastfeed, and it is also your job to support that decision if that's where you land. It's a woman's absolute right to choose to bottle-feed: it does not represent a failure or a rejection of responsibility of any kind. The situation has to be right. Breastfeeding might depend on myriad factors, including your partner's age, health, career prospects or social life - all completely justifiable and realistic things that might influence a woman's decision.

You might even find your partner wants to breastfeed but is unable to. It's not necessarily a case of willing it to happen. Often, baby will have trouble latching onto the nipple, or the milk just won't flow. It's a process, a painful and unclear process that might take weeks to work, or not work at all, and it can be a heart-breaker.

Personally, my wife and I saw both sides of this decision. She was intent on breastfeeding from the outset for all of the above reasons and more, but our firstborn didn't latch on easily (not for a lack of trying) so we were forced to bottle feed for the first few weeks of his life. It was an extremely stressful time, because we had not planned for it all - we had none of the kit and even less of the knowhow.

When your first proper attempt at parenting feels like it falls short, you see your life changing in real time; those idealistic images of mother and baby cuddled together get further and further away and it's easy to feel like you've let them down in some small way. It doesn't help that the process of bottle feeding can initially be tedious and costly and wasteful. We got lucky: after three weeks we eventually got a latch. Not everyone will.

For all the benefits that breastfeeding offers, at the end of the day, bottle feeding still gives baby what it needs. You will all adjust to your new reality whatever the outcome, and you will hear few complaints. Babies, it is fair to say, are not especially picky at age zero. Those gullible clowns will try and drink milk from your little finger if you let them, they don't give a shit what they're guzzling or where it's coming from.

Breastfeeding is not a decision that should be taken lightly, so take pains to be careful how vigorously you recommend it as a course of action, bearing in mind you are entirely off the hook and will not suffer any of the consequences or ill effects whatsoever. Well, unless you've been hiding a couple of big milky breasts you've not told anyone about.

When breastfeeding works, it's a win-win for everyone. Baby gets cuddled and fed and goes all milk-drunk and dozy and it's bloody adorable. Mum gets a cuddle and a sit-down and gets to gaze adoringly at her baby. Dad gets a break, in which maybe he can have a luxuriously long poo. Lovely. Peaceful. Almost serene. Just know that, whether you realise it or not, all of you are on the clock, because the days and weeks are ticking down until a radical new wildcard element enters the fray, one which will turn your whole life upside down all over again. I'm talking, of course, about teething.

Ah, teething. How I don't miss you. Nothing good has ever come from adding teeth to anything. The very concept is demented, deranged even. Nature is a cosmic joke. Oh, you like feeding your mewling infant from your soft fleshy bosom, do you? Well, how do you like it now I've introduced one tiny, razor-sharp piece of bone into the equation? Is it still magical? Or is it, in fact, the equivalent of repeatedly dangling your exposed nipples in a spring-loaded bear-trap? Fuck's sake, man. Take me back to the good old days, when baby received all its nutrients via the umbilical cord.

Teething will ruin your life. It will affect every minute of your day, and almost certainly every minute of your night, too. I mean, sure, it sucks for the baby too, but they're babies, they have no idea what the hell is going on, you might as well chuck some painful physical development in the mix. It's not like the introduction of teeth is suddenly going to put a dent in their to-do list.

Baby teeth can start to emerge from as early as four months, or just for yuks it might be as late as 12 months, which gives you a fun eight month window in which to worry about it. Once the fuckers do turn up at the party, they don't stop coming - no sooner does one chopper break the gum, another enamel interloper starts tearing up the joint. All in all, you're looking at approximately two whole years of teething: incisors, molars, canines, the whole gang make an appearance, each taking the time to stagger their introduction and drag out the whole sorry affair like a tiresome and charisma-free dance troupe on Britain's Got Talent.

Let me give you a little bit of a heads-up re: teething - it's not limited to teeth. Granted, teeth are always at the root of the problem - pun intended, you are welcome - but teething is a whole world of physical symptoms unto itself that is only occasionally localised to the mouth.

Even when teething does affect the mouth, for the most part it's still an invisible torture happening out of sight. So yes, a teething baby will start showing symptoms like sore gums, and increased dribbling, but it's also liable to cause less obviously related ailments, like a high temperature, flushed cheeks and sore skin, or even issues relating to diarrhoea. So, from mouth to arse. That's pretty much everything then?

To recap: every possible illness or discomfort a child is likely to suffer from age six months to three years either may or may not be related to teething. I hope you like not being able to figure out why your lovely baby is in constant pain! In summary, it could be, or may just as likely not be, related to something you can't even see. That's crystal clear, thanks. Super helpful. Slots right in with your existing anxieties for your convenience, a mental breakdown package deal. For the longest time, the slightest noise, skin rash or runny shit that emanates from your baby has to be considered a side-effect of teething, like a fun guessing game where there's no right answer. Blaming any sickness or symptoms of illness on teething is the equivalent of those people who blame everything on 'the economy' - it's such a bullshit cop-out answer, but frustratingly, in an annoying, roundabout sort of way, it's probably at least partially true.

There is precisely one [1] upside to teething, which is that it helps bring into focus the Lynchian body horror that your child is living every day of his or her life. As a fully grown and hopefully fully pubic adult, your days of dealing with bodily changes are a distant memory, categorised in the dusty corner of your mind under 'Do Not Revive' along with acne, bumfluff facial hair, and a squeaky voice.

How quickly we forget the pain and stress of existing in a body that is doing its damnedest to outgrow you. Even for babies, think about the sheer unending evolution of a newborn body in those early months and years: the jagged bone jutting slowly through flesh; the bones knitting and fusing and bending; the skull ossifying to protect the exposed brain. Christ, it's the kind of torture you wouldn't wish on your worst enemy.

Babies, unfortunately, are dunked on endlessly by Mother Nature: they can't go ten minutes without living through another godforsaken condition or ailment or fundamental shift in their body chemistry. It all starts around two weeks after they're born, when their umbilical stump turns black and falls off. The birthing process is so traumatic, it's easy to overlook just how unsettling this must be for a baby. One minute, they've got a fleshy little nozzle on their belly; a few weeks later, it turns rancid and rots off. Do they realise? Do they even care? Are we absolutely sure this isn't scarring them permanently? Even from an external perspective, I remember thinking it particularly grim. It's just as well babies don't have much in the way of cognitive function at this age, because remembering a part of your body turning coal black and crusty and falling off like some filthy pirate leper would probably mess you up for life.

It's one thing after another. There's cradle cap, the skin condition whereby patches of baby's head, face or nappy area turn yellow and greasy and crumbly like some sort of dragonscale flapjack. There's Slapped Cheek Syndrome - seriously, who named this, and has anyone checked on the welfare of their kids? - which is a super-literal rash that leaves a light mark on the cheeks, as if your child had been curtly slapped by the stiff leather glove of a prim Nazi gestapo. There's no miracle cure for these agonies, apart from lots of fluids and bed rest. And maybe stop slapping your kids while dressed as a Nazi.

And then there's the Fontanelle. Sweet mother of God, the human body is a beautiful nightmare. In layman's terms, the Fontanelle is a soft spot located above the forehead between the plates of the skull, which stays soft until the connective tissue surrounding it eventually becomes bone tissue. It's bad enough you are aware of this weak spot, a small area of a few centimetres squared covered only by membrane, but at times you can *actually see your baby's brain pulsating through the skin.* It's upsetting, not least because videogames have wired you to think that any creature that has an exposed soft spot that pulsates rhythmically is an end-of-level boss that must be defeated through repeated precision targeting. This is not that. This is arguably the opposite of that.

Once you begin to clock the bodily horrors being inflicted on your offspring, you can only watch helplessly as they slowly grow up, grow out and grow old. They don't stay babies for long, is the thing. As adults we've been conditioned to think that the term 'growing pains' is a shorthand excuse to write-off any uncategorised ache or pain, but that's only because we've put so much distance between ourselves and the torment we once suffered as children.

Growing pains equates to your bones stretching. Your kid will appear to be lying in their comfy bed of an evening and snoozing peacefully, but under the skin they're essentially being elongated on an organic torture rack. Our kid grew three centimetres in two months. That's painful to even think about, let alone endure, and that's before you even get into the mental strain it causes; your own body literally forces you to have a new perspective on life, whether you're ready for it or not.

A quick reminder that all of this grisly development is just your regular healthy bodily activity. God help you when your kids get sick. There is no better way to put a smoking crater in the middle of your week than to throw a sniffly baby grenade at it. Healthy? Sick? Asleep? Awake? It's all the same when you're on poorly baby duty, and their tiny wee bodies start actively sabotaging any plans you might have made.

Babies have tiny lickle cutesy-wutesy respiratory systems that are absolutely not designed to stand up to even the slightest build-up of mucus. If they get a cold, they're fucked and so are you. For you, a functioning adult, a cold is an inconvenience, a downer, an irritant. For a baby, a snotty nose might as well be an ancient witch's curse for all they can do about it.

Kids, I have discovered, are not born with the ability to blow their own nose. I do not ever remember having to learn how to blow my own nose, therefore at some point in my life it became a subconscious process so automated I plum forgot that it's an ability that you have to learn and not just a natural bodily reaction, like scratching an itch. This is one of many sources of frustration with sick children, in that there is a relatively simple way to ease their discomfort if only you could adequately walk them through the process of blowing their own nose. But it's a non-starter. They cannot summon the nasal strength needed to jettison a build-up of mucus from their nostrils into a tissue, and even if they could they wouldn't want to because blowing your nose kind of hurts when you're a kid - another thing you forgot.

Baby colds are particularly horrid to suffer through as a parent, too. To be by their side, listening to them struggling to breathe easily, the wet snot slapping audibly around their ear, nose and throat, and to be unable to help them, is agony. For all the sympathy you have and the cuddles and Calpol you can offer, being a cold bystander makes you feel spectacularly useless.

If you're particularly desperate, you can buy a little rubber doohickey that you put over the kid's nose that you suck on, swiftly transferring the snot from their sinuses to your gob, but a) this is only a temporary solution and does not stop baby's cold from generating more snot in a matter of mere minutes, b) now you have snot in your mouth, and c) you run the risk of misjudging the lung capacity needed and might accidentally snort your baby's brains out through their nose which is definitely a thing that could happen.

Not only can babies not look after themselves in a crisis, they are also terrible at self-diagnosing. When they're babies that's excusable - they don't even know which way up they're supposed to be, so you have to say fair enough. But even when they get a little older, just because they have the ability to talk, it does not mean they have a useful understanding of how to describe pain, or the ability to communicate it properly. They could probably just about tell you if they were on fire, but kids cannot narrow down an injury or rate their pain on any sort of meaningful scale, leaving you to settle somewhere between a dead leg and bone cancer.

And so, because they cannot speak with any degree of accuracy about any of their own ailments, you will fuss and bother and worry and convince yourself that you're living in the worst case scenario, the darkest health timeline, the beginning of the Lifetime movie tragedy about a family torn apart by illness, only for the hypothetical stomach ulcer you invented to turn out to be a stout fart.

For example, I recently had to take Kid A to Accident & Emergency because he did not heed my repeated refrain to stop running in the house and tripped over the vacuum cleaner, landing awkwardly on his arm. There was no break or visible wound but he was in obvious pain and for some reason no amount of me telling him "I told you so" seemed to reduce the discomfort. We phoned 111 like any concerned parent should do, only to be told, true to form, that they recommend we take him to hospital just in case. If ever you need a stranger on the other end of a telephone to give you some medical advice and then tell you that you should probably go to A&E anyway, I cannot recommend 111 enough.

Once we finally got to see a doctor, and I had subconsciously conveyed enough evidence through my tone and behaviour that his injury wasn't the result of child abuse (seriously: *every* hospital trip), I had to watch my son attempt to describe both the location of the pain he felt, and the kind of pain it was. It was, fittingly, painful to watch. I was able to add context, sure, but it wasn't my elbow that was fucked, it was his, and I couldn't tell the doctor what he was feeling on his behalf.

In the end, based on an extremely sketchy self-diagnosis and an inconclusive x-ray, they stuck a plaster cast on his arm, chucked him over the fence to the Fracture Clinic and sent him home with a sticker for his troubles. Two days later, the absolute legends at the Fracture Clinic were able to accurately diagnose it as a mild sprain and the cast came off before I'd even had a chance to draw a wang on it. He's fine now. He got a LEGO magazine and a McDonald's out of it. He's up on the deal.

The point is, for all the physical trauma that your loved ones will go through - from the birth, through breastfeeding, the teething that follows and the subsequent 18 years of growing pains they must endure - the only consistent thread is that you are largely a powerless idiot bystander throughout it all. Although it can take a mental toll on a man to watch his wife and kids suffer through such torment, be real - you and your gonads lucked out on this whole deal.

You need to step up your game and contribute in all other areas, the ones you *can* affect: providing emotional support, making tea, tidying up, cooking meals, buying biscuits, squaring off boring life admin, changing nappies, cutting the grass, dealing with any and all day-to-day bullshit that may arise, giving belly rubs and back rubs and foot rubs and head rubs and all the other rubs. Let your baby gnaw on your fist, chew your fingers, eat your entire fucking hand if that's what it takes.

It is your civic duty as a dad: inactivity is not an option. Make it your life's mission to bring pleasure to offset the discomfort felt by others. Be the pain sponge you were born to be.

#19

Becoming Your Parents

A dult life is a little three-act play. Please take your seat and cease the rustling of Minstrels packets, because the performance is about to begin.

ACT ONE

You are young, maybe a teenager, and you are convinced that your out-of-touch parents don't understand how the world really works. In one of your more petulant moments, you make a promise to yourself: when you grow up, you will be different.

ACT TWO

Life happens. You finish school and get a job. You get on the property ladder. You meet someone. You fall in love. Maybe you get married and have children. This act can drag a bit, but if you're lucky there are some decent sex scenes in it.

ACT THREE

The dramatic reveal: you are the parent now. You were right, you *don't* understand how the world really works. Nonetheless, you press on with parenting the only way you know how: by following the example your own parents set. In other words, you have fulfilled your destiny and become your parents.

Aaaand curtains.

It doesn't matter where or when, but at some point during your first years as a father, the following earth-shattering realisation will come to you: your parents were right. My God. *They were right about everything.* This is where your 'World's Greatest Dad' mug slips from your grasp, falls to the ground and shatters in slow-motion, cinematically.

With any luck, your parents are still alive so you can share this revelation with them - you should, because it will give their entire life meaning. I know this, because I am already looking forward to the exquisite moment my grown-up and stressed-out children come to me with their own children and say 'Papa... parenting is so hard! How can I ever repay you for your servitude?' Seriously, I'm practicing the face I'm going to pull and everything.

Hopefully, your parents will be able to receive this information without exploding from smugness. Dealing with all your bullshit - the full nappies, the sleepless nights, the tantrums, the moaning, the door-slamming, the broccoli-avoiding, the relentless teenagering - it was all worth it. They were right. You were a selfish little asshole, like all children fundamentally are. And you know this because now you are on the flipside of this little familial diorama. All you're doing is trying to do right by your kid, yet without even realising it, you've scanned your sponge-like brain for parenting tips and inadvertently echoed your own childhood experiences. It's like yelling at a wall and taking the advice that bounces back.

The realisation might come when your kid is a little more grown up, old enough to be told off for doing something they know they're not supposed to be doing. Sure enough, from somewhere deep within you, comes a stern tone of voice so startling you may temporarily forget that it's not you who's being told off. It's not a tone of voice you've ever had to use before. It's new... yet familiar and instinctive. Authoritative without being aggressive. Firm but fair. No nonsense and cutting. Dad? Is that you?

If it were just the tone of voice, that could be written off as coincidence, but it's not just the tone of voice, is it? It's the vocabulary you instinctively use during a bollocking; the very particular inflection on certain words and the hand movements that go with it ("Ah ah ah ah!" and a wagging finger is a personal fave); the techniques from times gone by that worked on you and could probably still stop you in your tracks today.

You'll repeat the same mistakes, too; I still remember being appalled at my Dad accidentally calling me by my brother's name ("There's only two of us! How hard can it be to remember which is which?") but lo and behold, here I am with a barely functioning frontal lobe and two kids, known colloquially as 'Thingy' and 'The Other One'. I am guilty of the same crimes as those committed by my father. Arrest me.

In a way, it's comforting: the whole parenting act is a cover version that comes from deep in your DNA. You were literally destined to become your father, as he was with his father before him. It's like some hokey old Star Wars metaphor, only instead you're Luke Skywalker *and* Darth Vader, pointing a leather-clad finger at yourself and revealing "*I* am my father" before bellowing "NOOOOOOOOooo!" and throwing yourself off a ledge.

Look, maybe this is just my experience. It's not necessarily a given that you'll turn into your old man - maybe you didn't have the best upbringing, and you're consciously trying to steer away from exactly that, in which case, more power to you. However, if that doesn't describe you and the concept of this chapter still feels alien to you, then there's every chance that you are becoming your parents and you don't even know it. What a frightening thought! The transformation could have already begun. It's like a horror movie - the call is coming from inside the house!

Right now, your DNA is subtly altering, ageing, getting doughier round the middle, complaining about the enzymes that live in the next cell, becoming noticeably more dad-like. You need to recognise the warning signs of becoming your parents. You need a checklist. Take this quiz and brace yourself for the diagnosis at the end.

Score a point for everything on this list that sounds familiar

☐ You blow your nose routinely in the morning, regardless of whether you've got a cold or not, and always get grim results

☐ You have mild back pain which could legitimately have been caused by, like, three different things

☐ You find quite a lot of hair in a small area of your body that ideally would have no hair whatsoever

☐ You hear yourself complaining that someone has used an Americanisation instead of the proper English word e.g. "tie" instead of "draw" even though it's a common usage and makes no difference whatsoever

☐ You physically cringe when someone adds an extraneous 's' on the end of a name of a supermarket, e.g. "Tescos" and are generally conscious of the fact your pedantry, left unchecked, could become your dominant personality trait

- [ ] There is an unexplained pain in part of your body that you don't bother to remedy and instead just add it to the ever-growing list of personal ailments and bits of you that are falling apart

- [ ] You can no longer discern between gaseous movements that happen inside of your stomach and outside of your arsehole

- [ ] You have to give serious thought to a third pint, like it could be a tipping point

- [ ] The fourth pint is absolutely the tipping point

- [ ] While hosting friends of an evening, you suggest ending the night with a cup of tea and you get a genuinely excited reaction

- [ ] You genuinely need socks at Christmas

- [ ] Slippers, once thought to be extraneous and unnecessary footwear, are seemingly now very much in your wheelhouse

- [ ] Things on your to-do list include any of the following: adding some shelving to the shed or utility room; cleaning the lawnmower; buying some storage boxes; fixing a dripping tap; oiling a squeaky hinge; organising the recycling; sorting your old bank statements and payslips by month, for some reason

- [ ] Going to the dump is genuinely something you look forward to

- [ ] You are suddenly capable of spending upwards of 30 minutes in any branch of Halfords with no specific shopping agenda

- [ ] You come to the dawning realisation that your encyclopaedic knowledge of a particular film series, band or period of history doesn't really have much of a practical application in real life outside of the occasional pub quiz

- [ ] The mismatch between the quantities in which you can buy hot dogs and hot dog rolls legitimately seems crazy, and you briefly consider that it might be something that the good people at Watchdog should take a look into

- [ ] You are physically incapable of speaking to or being comfortable in the company of anyone under 21 years of age and are convinced that doing so makes you look like a sex pest

- [ ] Someone younger than you mentions that they once travelled to Machu Picchu and for the first time, you think, yeah, I'm never, ever going to go there

- [ ] When planning a trip, part of the appeal of any given location might genuinely be to "look at the scenery"

- [ ] You have bought clothes from any of the following shops: Marks & Spencer, Tesco, Matalan, Burton, TK Maxx, any large warehouse of men's clothing found in a local industrial park

- [ ] You own a baseball cap that you bought from a holiday destination which you wear unironically and you're thinking about purchasing and possibly wearing other, bolder hats

- [ ] Leather jackets could potentially happen at some point in the near future

- [ ] You shout at the news

- Yes, you have a favourite newsreader, and yes, she HAPPENS to be female, god, you can't like anything these days can you, here they come, the woke brigade out in force, cuh

- You hear an advert for a thing on commercial radio while driving and think, hmm, I should get that thing

- Talk Radio just has a "better vibe"

- You find yourself using the phrase "real music"

- You can't name more than two acts currently in the Top 40, and the two you do know you only know because you had to Google them because they sung on an advert you liked on TV

- You have listened to any of the following artists in the last seven days: Steely Dan; Fleetwood Mac; The Kinks; Wings; The Traveling Wilburys; ELO; Cream; Rod Stewart; Thin Lizzy; anything that appears on any compilation album that advertises itself as "the best driving music"

- You hear a song you like but don't recognise and so look up who the artist is and, oh shit, oh Jesus Christ, it's Van Morrison, just give up, give up and buy a tweed jacket and start sucking on Werther's Originals you ancient fuck

- You have to stop whatever you're doing and close your eyes in order to fully appreciate a particularly excellent guitar riff

- The last technological innovation you managed to wrap your head around was Bluetooth, and even that took a while before you fully understood it

303

- [ ] You have around 15 minutes of ready-made on demand chat loaded in the chamber about the loss of physical media, how you were part of the last generation who truly appreciated it, and how the youth of today don't know how good they've got it

- [ ] You use the phrase "the youth of today"

- [ ] You have opinions on cyclists

- [ ] You loudly complain that someone has done one of the following things: put a dirty dish in the sink despite the fact it would only take eight seconds to wash; left dirty clothes on the floor next to the washing basket; left milk out of the fridge for longer than five minutes - all despite the fact that you did each of these things yourself, routinely, every day for about twelve years

- [ ] You've given genuine thought as to what form your mid-life crisis might take

- [ ] You refuse to do an activity because you have "just sat down"

- [ ] You hear yourself actually saying the words "kids these days just don't understand" (this one should be worth 20 points by itself because, honestly, it's just too on the nose)

RESULTS

0-13 points: You've got nothing to worry about for now. You have several years of what can generously be described as your youth before you eventually turn into your parents. It's still going to happen, though. You're on the slippery slope already. Don't resist. Just go limp.

14-27 points: You are mid-transformation, stuck in a halfway house between clinging onto your glory days and submitting to the inevitable encroachment of old age. You are quite possibly "middle-aged" but you can't even bring yourself to enjoy the relative comforts it brings.

28-40 points: Woah there, Daddio. You appear to have taken to parenthood hard and have barged headstrong into your twilight years, bypassing your quarter-life crisis and consigning your wild and reckless years to the distant past. You own more than one cardigan. You use phrases like "Daddio". You own multiple albums by Robert Palmer. Beaded seat covers are imminent. You have become your parents.

With the benefit of hindsight, this revelation shouldn't feel particularly shocking. Very few men inherently just *know* how to parent. Unbeknownst to them, young girls are brought up with maternal instincts drilled into them subliminally: play with dolls, change this toy baby's shitty nappy, whip up some treats with your easy-bake oven - society is priming them for motherhood whether they want it or not.

Young boys don't really have that weight forced on their shoulders, they're not really prepared for fatherhood because that's not seen to be their primary role in life. No: you will be a footballer or a fireman or an inept businessman who wears no socks and somehow still gets to the semi-final of The Apprentice. Huge steps have been made in the past 20 years towards reducing needless and harmful gender stereotypes, but the gender bias remains; you only have to look at Piers Morgan having an epileptic fit upon seeing Daniel Craig baby-wearing his child to know that society's ancient and invisible rules about masculinity and fatherhood are still rigid and firm.

So, if you were lucky enough to be brought up in a bog-standard family unit with both parents present, Mum and Dad are the only frame of reference for parenting that you have - *of course* they are going to be your go-to when it comes to adopting the right tone, dishing out discipline or making decisions that affect the family. Either that, or you lean heavily on TV sitcom father figures, who are a mixed bag at best: for every loveable Phil Dunphy or Mr Cunningham there's a Bill Cosby lurking in the shadows. Beware the TV dad: truly they are a minefield of nonces and sex pests.

Long before the slack-jawed Keyser Soze-esque reveal that you have become your parents, the penny actually starts to drop somewhere around the end of Act Two of your life, when you realise that, shit, your parents aren't going to be around to cover your ass for your whole goddamn life. Suddenly you're faced with a deluge of adult responsibilities that cannot be avoided.

For example, if you want to buy somewhere to live, you have to learn how mortgages work. You're going to have to bite the bullet and figure out how to operate a washing machine. You have to figure out how to change your energy supplier or submit to a lifetime of being shafted by British Gas. You have to find a job, ideally become good at that job, then leverage that to get a better job until someone refers to it as a career. It's all bloody hard work.

Sometimes, the forced adulting rubs off on you and you accidentally adult organically, like when you form your own opinions on the EU, or sign up to a new dentist, or create a spreadsheet to track which TV shows you're watching, but otherwise it's all a total bluff.

You have no choice but to get your head down, dive in and get on with it. Throughout your adult life you wait for someone to discover that you're a total fraud and you're not even a real qualified adult, you're actually a child in disguise, maybe even two children, one sat on the other's shoulders inside a big trench coat. But it never comes. No one ever questions your status as an adult. There are no detector vans for this, there's no quality control, no elite fraud squad intent on rooting out ill-equipped and over-confident man babies to stop them from partaking in society. It's a terrifying free-for-all, no qualifications needed and no questions asked, no bouncer on the door, don't even worry about wiping your feet.

The only logical conclusion, then, is that all adults feel like this and always have. Mum, Dad, Uncle Barry, your sexually proficient mechanic, your pissed-up old science teacher, every single man named Jeff, the Prime Minister of the United Kingdom - they're all complete frauds just like you, wearing grown-up clothes and projecting confidence and pretending to have opinions about important things while hoping no one ever actually asks them to explain themselves.

We're all basically getting through life in a knotted mass of nerves, anxiety and malaise, covering our shortcomings in corduroy and hoping that an ironed shirt and a pair of uncomfortable shoes will mask the fact that we'd rather be home playing Pokémon in our pyjamas. Everyone gets old but no one ever really grows up.

If you've already embraced it, then great. If this has come as news to you, at least now you know it's coming, and you can educate yourself on the process. Those instructional sex education videos you watched at school had the right idea, but there's no version of them for adults. Those physical changes that happen to your body as you grow older? They don't stop with pubes, dropped balls and a bumfluff moustache. There's a whole host of 'mature developments' that don't kick in until later life, once the human body has committed itself to the punishment of childcare. Like how? Well... have you seen yourself dance lately?

Dad dancing is real. It's real and it's a curse, and I hate it. It's like contracting a horrible disease, but one that cannot be treated by modern medicine and science, and there's not even the promise of the sweet release of death at the end. No: you are a Dad now, so you are cursed to dance like a prick for evermore.

Granted, there's every chance that you were a terrible dancer before you had kids too. My repertoire consisted of precious few moves, most of which could be categorised under 'Dancing just idiotically enough so that no one could ever accuse you of taking it seriously'. I have friends who visibly clench at the thought of a dancefloor, otherwise confident pals who have all the fluidity and grace of a malfunctioning robot trying to cook an imaginary omelette.

I am an awkward individual at the best of times (hello, hi) but I am proud of the fact that I eventually figured out the way to enjoy dancing, in that it's only when you truly don't give a shit what people think that you can properly lose yourself in it. Bad news for those recently blessed with children: Dad dancing turns that paradigm on its head, meaning you are now psychologically incapable of getting out of your head while on a dancefloor. Everyone is watching you dance like a shit uncle, and nothing you can do will make your perverted dance moves acceptable; in fact, worrying about it only makes your dancing worse. Dad dancing is basically a shame spiral set to music; a panic attack at 120 beats per minute.

When you're young, the source of your dance power is located in your hips and groin; you have, to paraphrase Spinal Tap, an armadillo in your trousers. A sexy weapon in your pants. Add music to testes, shake, and mojo is made. Sadly, one of the first things you sacrifice when you have a kid is your mojo. It ebbs away without you even realising, like a leaky biro full of invisible ink.

Now you're a dad, all the power shifts from the pelvic area into, for some unknown reason, the forearms. Yes, the forearms. On the dancefloors of your youth, your arms would just do what the music told them to do - they were but an extension of the song. Tragically, dancing during parenthood requires a great deal of thought about what your arms are supposed to be doing, what the ideal arm placement is for each move, how do you even dance with your arms anyway, oh god, what are your arms doing now, and so on. It's like your body is a big-ass Humpty Dumpty shell that's been put back together wrong and now for some reason you have a makeshift groin on each forearm and you're swinging them around like bloody great pendulous dicks on the dancefloor, slowly dying inside, acutely aware of every side-eye and pitying glance.

The catch is, even if you recognise this fact, it doesn't change anything - you are forever doomed to dance like a convulsing ape. You can't overcompensate by attempting to channel the energy back through your groin again, because now it just looks pervy and inappropriate and there's a high chance someone will ask you to vacate the premises before you accidentally commit a sex crime. It's just as well you already have kids, because no woman would invite you inside them on this evidence alone.

Dad dancing is your body's way of redistributing your mojo, of offsetting your sexiness to ready you for the vigours of parenthood. It's as close to castration as you can get without going under the knife. Great. Thanks, body. Any more surprises in store? Well, since you asked: yes, lots. The most obvious physiological change is the complete inability to stay awake past 10.30pm. This is especially upsetting if you were formerly a night owl, a clubber, a late night drinker, a shagger, or some sort of prowler or cat burglar, but it's no less distressing even if you used your evenings to play video games or watch endless terrible Bruce Willis movies on Netflix. Parenthood smashes the body clock to shit like Phil Connors waking up on Groundhog Day. Evenings are no longer to be used for enjoyment, but for expressing exhaustion.

Long day? Kids being turds? I sure hope you weren't planning on undertaking any kind of activity tonight outside of sitting or eating or staring at your phone, because you no longer have the battery power, my friend. Welcome to 'The Zonk': the period of the evening in which you are desperate to do anything unrelated to childcare, but are capable only of achieving a vegetative state.

The irony is, of course, that you will never just go to bed if you're tired, perhaps ensuring that you'll feel livelier tomorrow evening. No, you string the tiredness out, wantonly craving any kind of adult validation from the late hours, fruitlessly attempting to stave off the tiredness, desperate to make something, anything of the day. The Chinese have a term for this: "報復性熬夜" translates as "revenge bedtime procrastination", an act committed by people who have little control over the daylight hours who refuse early sleep in order to regain the slightest sense of control.

It's an especially pointless ballet, flirtatiously tip-toeing betwixt the worlds of sleep and wake, unwilling to commit to one state or the other. And yet, come 10.30pm, the universally acceptable adult bedtime watershed, you still can't get to sleep. You collapse onto the bed like one of those old imploding buildings you see in YouTube disaster videos, then proceed to stare at the ceiling for a straight hour. You idiot.

And then there's the toilet. The toilet used to be an unassuming and functional part of your daily routine, used for business and not pleasure. However, during parenthood, the toilet evolves. It becomes more than just a turd receptacle; it becomes a symbol of peace, of sanctuary, of both figurative and literal relief. It is now your safe space, your happy place, your fortress of solitude, by which I mean it is quite literally the only room in the house with a lock on the door, where the tiny claws of responsibility can't scratch at you.

Maybe now you're a dad and a dump is the only excuse you have to stop the day from kicking your arse, your toilet routine takes, oh, I don't know, twice as long. Maybe longer; depends on the day and the dump. What's more, you have a totally legitimate reason for being in there - everybody poops, they literally wrote a book about it - and you'll have left behind evidence if anyone really needs proof.

When I was a kid, I still remember going to my friend Ian's house after school on a hot summer's day and mucking about in the garden chucking bits of wet mud at a wall (it was the early '90s, before children were legally allowed to have fun). Nature called, because we had been drinking gallons of tartrazine, but the toilet was occupied by Ian's dad, who could be heard rustling his newspaper while sitting on the crapper. 15 minutes passed, many little legs were crossed, and yet still Ian's dad had the toilet on lockdown. Half an hour later, and *still* he hadn't finished. In the end, we had to make excuses, knock politely and use the next door neighbour's toilet to save us from making more wet mud in the garden. By the time I was ready to leave and go home, Ian's dad finally vacated the toilet, a quite astonishing *two hours* after he first went in, presumably the time it took him to read The Sun from cover to cover, including all the ads for boner pills and cheap holidays. It must have been a daily routine, like he'd booked it between the hours of 15.30-17.30 like a meeting room and put his out-of-office on.

I specifically remember thinking at that very moment that I did not understand adults at all. The toilet? *Where poo goes?* For two hours? I mean, for all I know he was in there blackout drunk, swilling from a secret bottle of cheap scrumpy stashed in the cistern, or he was off his tits and jacking up with black tar heroin, or just furiously masturbating to a dog-eared copy of Razzle.

Probably though, he was just knackered from the general toll of parenting, and he'd somehow managed to finagle a sweet two hours of bog-based armistice with the other members of his family. I still don't understand adults, but now I have kids and a toilet routine of my own, I feel closer to Ian's Dad now than I ever have. Solidarity, brother. He's probably dead now, stuffed and mounted on the family toilet for posterity.

Dads hiding in toilets is one of those horrendous Purple Ronnie-esque clichés about parenting that is actually more or less accurate (you win this round, Purple Ronnie). It's the kind of cheap and hackneyed gag about fatherhood that you will 100% not be surprised to hear is in all of Judd Apatow's movies about fatherhood. Because it's a universally understood tactic, your excuses will absolutely not fly for very long. Let's be honest, it's a fairly transparent ruse, lads. There's only so many times you can roll out the same few flimsy rationales.

It's not so much that you're hiding, per se, but that you don't want to rush this particular bowel movement. You think you're a little constipated, maybe, after you ate, you know, that thing the other, erm, day? Yes, it's going to take at least another 12 minutes, which is coincidentally exactly how long it will take me to read this Buzzfeed article about 10 Cringe Dads Whose Kids Can't Even Deal With Their TikToks.

Look, hiding in a toilet won't score you any points. It's not an integrity move, it's an occasionally necessary tactic. No one was ever awarded a medal for bravery for hiding in a toilet throughout the First World War, although thinking about it, hiding in a toilet would have undoubtedly been an excellent technique for surviving the First World War, so, you know, let's be reasonable here.

Parenthood changes you in so many ways. It gets inside your head. It exhausts you. It makes you dance like a freak. More than anything else, it ages you: it takes what was once a young and vibrant individual and leaves behind a person who is truly at his happiest when every other single person on the planet just fucks off and leaves them alone.

The ageing can be swift, and will take many forms: bags under your eyes so big that Ryanair will charge you extra; hair so grey you look like you've been recently flour-bombed; music taste so questionable, Paul McCartney's post-Beatles oeuvre suddenly seems credible. You can keep telling yourself you're still hip and cool and 'on fleek' or whatever the kids people your age say these days, and you can choose to thrash against it like a victim of shark attack, but you're only prolonging the inevitable. Don't deny reality. Don't be the dad equivalent of Madonna. Don't be Dadonna. Embrace the myriad undesirable inevitabilities of parenthood and make dad jokes, exactly like that one. Start owning it before it owns you.

You know why? Because if you really think about it, there are way worse people to turn into than your own parents. Sure, it sounds bad, but then so did 'The Frog Chorus' once upon a time. It's time we changed the narrative of becoming your own parents, it's time we restored its reputation. We say it like it's a negative thing, but it shouldn't be: it deserves to be a compliment.

Your parents probably worked their arses off tirelessly for no money and no sleep and enjoyed one measly holiday a year which you probably ruined by being your own shitty childhood self, all with the aim of one thing and one thing only: making you a less shitty adult, so that maybe you too could one day have children of your own who will hopefully be, in turn, even less shitty than you turned out to be. What could be more noble than that?

Don't dance around the issue (badly) any more. Fulfil your destiny, slap on the Give My Regards To Broad Street LP, and become your parents for the sake of your own kids. They'll thank you for it one day. Probably.

#20

Emotions: You Have Them Now!

D id you ever really feel emotions properly before you had children? I mean, really *feel* them? How frequently would you hit the proper highs or sink to the lowest lows? In retrospect, it was all sort of middling, wasn't it? Your brain chemistry never really needed extra bandwidth to deal with any major spikes. High: A pay rise comparable to the cost of living increase - hooray! Low: A tough day at work - boo!

You'd laugh at cat videos on the internet, cry at family funerals, jump like a twat at scary movies and whisper sweet nothings in your lover's ear. Whoop-de-doo. Pre-child, your highs and lows didn't even register on the emotional Richter scale. Looking back on the person you used to be before you had a baby is like looking back at a stranger who is very much can't-be-arsing their way through life.

Well, prepare to be arsed to a whole new level, because now you've had a baby, you're moseying straight into your own personal emotional Wild West, where love is the law but the Sheriff is drunk.

The adult brain can't really cope with parenthood at first, so it goes through a transition period that lasts about as long as the labour does: it shuts down briefly from the shock, leaving you with the emergency tools you need to survive until the brain reboots - basic floundering, hand holding and nervously saying "shit shit shit" under your breath.

When it comes back online, usually about the time your baby is born, all your parental emotions start installing, but you may find you suffer some quite severe system errors in the first few weeks, where it feels like some of the wires have been plugged in the wrong way round. There's no user manual or Google search or brand of coffee that can help you.

For starters, the tiredness that now permeates your entire body and soul amplifies every emotion you feel to a deafening degree. In order to cut through the emotional wall of noise you now experience every day - Happiness! Sadness! Fear! Anger! All of the above, all at once, and also you haven't had a shit for two days! - your exhausted brain and your overclocked heart have to start communicating to you via megaphone. You find yourself getting caught in the feedback loops between them, where you know how you should be feeling, you're just feeling everything louder.

What's worse is that all of your emotions now have to compete with one another in order to be heard, because there's just so much emoting going on - everything is operating at a maximum level. You try to be rational and logical but you're just bursting with a cocktail of terrifying new feelings. Your brain and your heart are basically Mariah Carey and Whitney Houston sing-fighting, both trying to get the final note in a duet that just won't end.

You'll lose count of the number of times a laugh will turn into a cry, or vice versa. Emotions used to be clearly delineated, but not any more: the borders have come down and all of your emotions are mingling with one another in the swingers bar in your brain. You might find that something that used to trigger an emotion now has no effect whatsoever, while seemingly mundane everyday activities can light your blue touchpaper. You are now a loose firework in the back garden - maybe you'll fizzle out harmlessly, or maybe, just maybe, you'll explode into a thousand pieces and take someone's face off.

It can be tough, navigating these newly choppy emotional waters, and it takes a while for them to settle. Take it from me, someone who has at least five active emotions still left in his arsenal: it gets easier. Let me be your guide, the coxman at the end of your emotional canoe, who defuses your emotional touchpaper, defrags your emotional hard drive, mutes your emotional sing-off and restores order to your emotional Wild West. Having a baby also destroys your ability to maintain a consistent metaphor, in case you haven't noticed.

JOY

Men are not good at expressing themselves, which you'll know if you've ever met one. I think my generation had a leg up on my father's generation in that we instantly saw through the wood-panelled macho bullshit of TV dinosaurs like Jeremy Clarkson, who thought that men should only ever talk about cars, wear jeans that cut off the circulation to the testicles and engage in weekly missionary position sexual intercourse with overdone steaks. So many dads fell into the slippery pit of toxic 20th century masculinity and realised too late they lacked the emotional maturity to ask for someone to chuck them a rope.

As someone who, until recently, was still clinging onto their thirties, I was at the tail-end of the laddism conga line and I could tell nobody was really feeling the vibes any more. It's been a relief to help usher in a new enlightened age of masculinity, where men can wear salmon pink polo shirts and slip-on shoes with no socks without fear of falling victim to hate crimes. We're edging ever closer to an age of man where we're as emotionally forthright and open as women. That day will come when modern man learns how to properly express joy. Don't get too excited.

It is nothing less than a tragedy how bad men are at expressing positive opinions. Men cannot let a compliment pass without punctuating it with an insult, good-natured or otherwise. Genuine, extreme joy is primarily expressed in two ways, depending on the company kept. Alone, a sole man learning of some positive news might hiss a "Yessss" under his breath, maybe clenching a fist and adding a "fucking GET IN" for good measure. In the company of other men, joy is typically expressed by loud, obnoxious chanting, and the placing of an upright empty beer glass on one's head, accompanied by a "WEYYYYYYYY". Either way, we keep our emotions bottled up, like a shaken-up share-sized Coke that's bursting with bubbles; as long as you keep the lid on, the pressure fizzes away to nothing.

Parenthood pops that lid right off. When you become a dad, your emotions become too big for the bottle. If not properly regulated, untamed emotions spew everywhere, like champagne jizzing all over a Formula 1 winners' podium. It might sound fun, but someone has to clean that shit up, and it's not going to be Lewis Hamilton.

In my experience, new dads are reluctant to talk about parenthood in an overtly positive way, and not just because most men lack the emotional depth to explain any feelings more complicated than a sneeze. For starters, it's way easier to adopt a cynical stance than it is a heartfelt one. Parenthood is obviously a big strain on your body and mind, so the last thing you want to do is suddenly have to work on improving your interpersonal skills too.

When someone at work innocuously asks you how you're coping, in a split-second you might think 'Do they want the proper answer?' More often than not you'll settle for a cautious, flippant response - it's way easier to steer the conversation into hardship (sleepless nights, possible permanent hearing damage) than it is to put into words the spicy gumbo of new feelings you're currently experiencing.

It's easy to be glib, and in fairness, the chances are your brain can't exactly muster much in the way of poetry right now. In the unlikely event that you could string the required syllables together to tell this person how you were really doing - feeling something akin to a newly untethered kite, drifting aimlessly between impossibly uplifting gusts of happiness - there's every chance the look on their face will tell you that they were just making small talk and you've been blocking the fridge for fifteen minutes now.

It's a lot harder to put into words what makes being a new parent so wonderful, and to be fair, in the maelstrom of the early days, I'll grant that it might be a lot harder to pinpoint exactly why. That clarity might take a little while to pinch into focus, because you're going to be little more than a smudge in the non-stop blur of feeding, bathing, wiping, crying and endless rocking (and then there's the baby, WEYYYYYYYYY). You get a free pass for not immediately launching into a florid Shakespearean sonnet about the sweet breath of your newborn child whenever someone corners you by the coffee machine. So you lean into cynicism, use snark as a crutch. I know because I did this too. And I only know because my wife told me I was doing it and I didn't even realise it. We had just hosted friends for the first time since Kid A was born, and only when they were gone did Vicky inform me that I spent the entire afternoon complaining about exhaustion, making jokes at the expense of the baby (although I maintain telling a crying infant to "stop being such a baby" is still funny) and stopping just short of castrating myself due to the apparent self-professed horrors of parenthood.

I had just assumed it was the done thing; to jocularly play the role of the beleaguered and broken new dad, who's always one teabag away from a breakdown. It turns out that guy comes across like a total prick. I even came up with a name for it: kidnegging.

Perhaps it's because there is still a stigma around parenthood where being seen to be upbeat and effusive about your kids can rub people up the wrong way. Maybe some people don't want to hear you banging on about your little angels, and that's understandable, because offering up endless unsolicited and unrelated parental anecdotes is by far the easiest way to clear a room. You don't want to be THAT person: the guy who physically cannot stop himself from grabbing the wheel of a conversation and steering it towards his own interests.

In fact, the fear of becoming 'that guy' is probably what will drive you towards playing the miser, so terrified you'll be of becoming the insufferable baby bragger. But that attitude can be so damaging. People are actually scared that they'll come across like a wanker because they love their kid, particularly if they're talking to someone who doesn't have kids of their own. The worry of being considered smug and condescending overrides all else; you've no doubt once been the uninterested party in this conversation before, and now here you are on the opposite side, gibbering on about dribble bibs and puréed carrots and Hey Duggee to anyone who'll listen.

Of course you don't think your life is better than anyone else's just because you are the 108,856,120,177th person to experience the miracle of birth... but what if that's what it sounds like? No one wants to be the Peter Andre of the group, endlessly blathering about how much they love their kids like they're angling for some sort of reality show spinoff.

The best way of practically describing this feeling - of wanting to put your own happiness into a context that others won't find offensive - was written by, of all people, a guy on Reddit. I've since lost the exact quote, but I remember being quite taken with it.

Before you have children, your capacity for happiness is 100% and you are free to fill that gauge however you choose. Maybe you're fun-loving and happy all the time, maybe you're not, but everyone more or less has the same capacity with which to experience these emotions. After you have kids, however, you open yourself up to a whole new life-changing event, which can't help but increase your total capacity for emotion - no one can be in any doubt that your life has to get bigger to accommodate all the new responsibilities, routines and complexities that come with raising children.

At first, you might not really know what to do with that extra space, which can throw you off a little, but over time you find new levels of appreciation for the small things in life, discover things about yourself that you never knew (both good and bad) and generally mature as a person, growing into that space.

Crucially though, you can still only max out at 100% happiness. Being a parent does not make you capable of being more happy or more enlightened than anyone who doesn't have kids, but it does mean you're capable of feeling personally more enriched and complete than you did before. That this pseudo-philosophy probably came from a Reddit user called something like 'I_RAPE_CATS' should not diminish its power.

I guess the closest analogy would be finding out that you have a basement in your house. You might put a cool table tennis table in it or you might fill it with wet cardboard, old bits of wood and a broken exercise bike, but it doesn't change the fact your house is still the same height as every other house on the terrace.

Anyway, one other thing you find in parenthood is that the kind of person who'd take genuine offence at an imaginary slight buried deep in an expression of your own happiness is the kind of person that you'll quickly stop giving a single solitary shit about.

Don't bother regulating your own happiness, because it's wasted energy dedicated to an already overwhelming experience. There will be times when you will feel so lucky and overawed you'll feel lighter than air. Every day is a new first: a facial expression, a noise, a weird new consistency of turd. It is, to put it bluntly, a lot. Even accounting for the lost sleep and irregular routines, the joys of parenthood can leave you exhausted and struggling to keep up.

My wife, however, learned of a brilliant way to celebrate the various and ridiculous joys of life with kids: The Happiness Jar. Every time you experience a moment worth remembering - a new gurgle, a perfectly timed baby fart, any micro memory that would otherwise go undocumented in photo albums and video libraries - you write it down on a little bit of paper, date it, fold it up and stick it in The Happiness Jar.

Over the year, the jar fills up, acting as both a diary and a time capsule, forever capturing these moments between moments. Here are a few examples from Happiness Jars past:

- "Kid A woke me up at 4am to tell me something: "Daddy, do you know where my friend Ethan got his water bottle? [whispering as if it were a secret] *Smiths*."

- "Vicky held a cheese grater over my mouth and grated cheese straight into it while yelling 'Let it rain!' and I've never laughed so hard."

- We all went ten-pin bowling and the kids loved it, but mainly because I scored three strikes in my last four balls and the guy in the lane next to me said "Nice shot" and I finally became a man

Then, on New Year's Eve, you crack open the second cheapest bottle of Prosecco you can find, mash an entire slab of Boursin into your cakehole and crack open The Happiness Jar, taking it turns to read back 365 days of happy. The first time we did it was one of the most incredible and overwhelmingly emotional experiences of my life: we were both sobbing like snotty little goblins within minutes.

Even though you've lived through all of these delights before, the daily grind means it's almost impossible as a parent to find the time to look back and take stock of your lot. The Happiness Jar reminds you why you get up in the morning, why you go to work, the kind of stuff you live for now. It's the most perfect distillation of the wonders of being a parent I could possibly recommend.

Oh, and be sure to put non kid-related happiness stuff in the jar too - because nothing says joy like remembering the time you got a few goddamn minutes to yourself six months ago. Whoops, apologies... kidnegging again.

SADNESS

It's fine to cry, obviously. I just wanted to put that out there, right out the gate. The reason doesn't matter: feel free to have a good old cry. Go on. Really lean into it. Let the bottom lip go wobbly. Enjoy it. You've been through a lot. You've earned this cry. Wear the tears proudly on your cheeks like little salty badges of liquid honour. Crying is something you're just going to have to get used to doing, because chances are you're going to be doing a lot of it. I've no idea how anyone could have the emotional and physical strength to both raise a child into the modern world and also maintain their composure at all times. Sometimes, it's all a bit much, and you just want to lock yourself in the bathroom for five minutes and have a really satisfying cry into a big fluffy towel. There's no shame in it. I'm sitting on a toilet and crying into a towel as I write this.

Maybe you are not the crying type. That's fine. There's something to be said for the stern and unflappable brand of dad - the kind of alpha dad that gets shit done with no fuss, like putting up shelves or building walls (literal walls, but also, emotional walls). That's right, stoic dads: cram those emotions deep down into your body, tucked behind the non-essential organs where they can't do any harm, at least until they become MASSIVE WEEPING ULCERS and poison you from the inside out. It's healthy to have a cry when the going gets tough. If you are a man who is having trouble justifying a cry, think of it like expunging your body of impurity. Squeeze out the weakness, tear by tear, sob by sob.

Me, I was already a crier before I had my kids. My tears were usually reserved for movies where mentally impaired people overcome adversity to shine in their own unique and irrepressible way. (If I ever became an actor, my go-to scene for instigating tears would not be the clichéd 'death of a loved one' routine, it'd be the scene in Forrest Gump where Tom Hanks is standing solemnly over the gravestone of his dead girlfriend then blurts out "I love you Jen-nay!" and OH GOD WHY DID I BRING THIS UP).

Also liable to set me off: people that can sing beautifully that don't look like they should be able to sing at all, dogs that go bat-shit crazy when their owners come back from war, other people crying (especially old people), people who fall in love on First

Dates (especially old people), animated animals who are forced to come to terms with their own mortality (I still haven't forgotten you, The Animals Of Farthing Wood) and films about wise-cracking robots that learn to understand human emotions but are denied the chance to really appreciate the joys of life by their own totalitarian programming. It's a rich tapestry, really.

After the birth of your first child, the walls, however fortified they are, come tumbling down. Have you ever tried to build a wall? Neither have I, but I'm guessing it's, like, effort. So you remain in ruins. You'll cry at everything, anything and nothing at all, and unfortunately tiredness only amplifies the teariness. With your floodgates quite literally open, you become susceptible to the vast waves of overwhelming emotions that wash over you.

Your brain, still functioning on an operating system that's clearly in need of an upgrade, cannot properly process the difference between happiness and sadness so it just sort of conflates the two, pushes a bunch of random buttons then sits back as you clean up the fallout. Great, thanks brain. As if it wasn't hard enough being able to express joy properly, now you've fucked up sadness too.

After you have kids you begin to connect with themes of parenthood that you never really picked up on before. And it doesn't matter how cheesy or manipulative or ham-handed the situation is, if there's a father-son moment to be found in it, it resonates in you like a bass drum.

Around the time of the birth of our first kid, Robinsons Squash released an advert in which two brothers played heartily all day, running around, roughhousing and generally enjoying wild adventures until the time came to go to bed. The big brother carries the little brother upstairs and puts him to bed, but just when you're thinking 'Hmm, where are the parents?' it cuts away from the little brother asleep, and the big brother is now his adult dad, standing swooningly in his doorway - because Robinson's sugar-based juice drink keeps you young forever or some shit.

No sooner had the ad ended, Vicky and I looked at each other and instantly burst into tears AND burst out laughing at the exact same time, before instantly swallowing the unholy emotional abomination. What... just happened?

Your first genuine cry-laugh is a most disconcerting development. They're opposites! How can they even exist simultaneously? The cry-laugh is usually accompanied with an equally worrying sound; a sort of rapid-fire "MERR-HERR-HERR", delivered with a limp bottom lip, as if all muscles around your face and throat have given themselves over to madness. It is the tip of the emotional iceberg, friend.

Take the popular motion picture About Time, directed by professional emotion wrangler Richard Curtis. I first saw this film, about a young man who finds he has the ability to travel backwards and forwards in time, in 2011, in a long-forgotten era we will call "pre-child". Star Bill Nighy is the kind of twinkly old actor that you might describe as a "moist-eyed camera hogger". Richard Curtis is also the director of Love, Actually, a bile-duct-tickling romcom which foreshadowed mansplaining in its title alone.

On first viewing, I remember thinking About Time was overly manipulative, saccharine and disgustingly twee, and it made such a conscious and heavy-handed effort to tug on my heartstrings it felt like a bellringer was yanking on my aortic valves. The next time I saw it, however, I was [puffs up chest] A Father Now. I watched it through waterfalls of tears and snot, sobbing wretchedly at tragic scenes between father and son, scenes which were apparently being broadcast on a completely different frequency than before, as if I were responding to a dadwhistle. Since becoming a dad, my critical faculties have been dulled to the approximate sharpness of crayons, leaving me entirely unable to properly assess a movie if any character in it is a father, has a father, or lacks a father. At least I knew where I was with Escape Plan.

It's not just movies and TV. It's everything. A sad-looking pigeon. A single glove left on the pavement, separated from its tiny hand. McDonald's adverts showing families enjoying the great taste of McDonald's family food together, as a family. Stupid stuff like when muscle memory kicks in and you start rocking on your feet like you're settling a tired child when actually you're waiting for a lift.

You are now a walking emotional dirty bomb, primed to explode feelings over a three-mile radius at the slightest trigger. It's especially fun when you can't even identify what the trigger was, and you find yourself rifling through your mental bins to figure out why you're crying, like Inspector Morse with PMT. So there's that to look forward to.

This is all superficial nonsense, of course. Even the manliest men are prone to a bout of the blubs from time to time. But having a child really does open you up to a new world of hurt, the depth of which might catch you unawares.

You will miss your kids when they're not around. It sounds obvious to say, but it's true: the stronger the bond you have with them, the harder it gets to leave the house. If you're a working father, particularly if you're one who works long hours, the lack of children in your daylight hours in your first week after paternity leave is your first real test of fatherhood - dealing with the ache of their absence is perhaps the first time you realise how deeply that connection you've made is entrenched within you.

The cynic in you might joke about "escaping the house" or enjoying some peace and quiet, but the truth is much harder to stomach - there's nothing you'd rather be doing than playing with your kids at home right now, but life doesn't always let you.

Now if you'll excuse me, I'm in desperate need of a towel.

ANGER

Happiness and sadness are a given: it should come as no surprise that bringing a child into your life comes with those ups and downs. Something that is rarely mentioned, however, is how unexpectedly frustrating parenthood can be, and how vital it is that you are prepared to regulate your temper in response.

This is something of a taboo subject, because no one likes to think of an angry parent in the vicinity of a child for obvious reasons. It's crucial to consider, though, because learning how to control and ultimately quash any anger you might feel is one of the most important lessons you'll learn as a new father. You'll quickly realise that one red-faced screaming baby is enough to deal with, and that no one needs an adult-sized one adding to the emotional drama.

Maybe, you are someone who never gets angry; a person of unshakeable faith, made out of 100% good vibes, Matthew Mc-fucking-Conaughey over here, with the patience of a particularly put-upon saint. Maybe you're one of those relentlessly optimistic do-gooders, who has never so much as whispered "OH FOR FUCK'S SAKE" in anger, who says stuff like "It'll work out for the best," or "There's always next year" and actually means it. A person who shrugs and actually says the words "ha ha" in the face of a personal injustice that should make any right-minded and reasonable individual furious. Good for you. Right on, brother. This chapter isn't for you. You're already doing great. I want to read your book. Also I want to see inside your mind to see if it's as Hieronymus Bosch as I suspect it is in there, all hellish and burned and twisted and savage. Fucking do-gooders always have something to hide.

You see what I mean? Anger.

Speaking personally, I am a hothead who is quick to anger, although never in a violent way, only in a useless, hilarious, sort of pointless flapping way. Well, never violence that's been directed at a person, anyway. Inanimate objects, however, feel the full force of my wrath. Know that if you are a brand new printer displaying a cryptic new error message for which there is no known fix, I will shortly be introducing the sharp part of my elbow to your solar plexus should your behaviour persist. If you are a bus that has driven past the stop I am clearly running towards, know that I will loudly curse your back-end with language that would make Malcolm Tucker blush.

Just the other night, I was cooking dinner and added around eight or nine painstakingly prepared ingredients to the blender before adding a "touch" of black pepper, but - in a scene reminiscent of a criminally unfunny sitcom - that "touch" took the lid off the pepper pot and dumped a large fistful of soot all over my formerly delicious meal. As kids were present, I had to be particularly creative with my profanity workarounds. As it turns out, bellowing angrily into a blender full of blackened basil clumps does not help salvage your dinner, but it felt like the only solution at the time.

I love to swear. You've probably already noticed. Swearing is typically thought of as a vulgar act or a substitute for wit from someone with no impulse control, to which I say, fuck off you soppy cunt. Swearing is very big, very clever and very funny: fact. If I couldn't swear I'd probably swell up like a hot water bottle until I eventually exploded and a giant "FFFUUUUUUUUUUCKuck-uck-uck" could be heard echoing from hundreds of miles around as birds fly panicked from their nests.

Unfortunately, swearing around children is deemed unacceptable, so you have to get creative. Rather than substitute profanities for family-friendly alternatives, like the "Yippee-ki-yay, melon farmer" variety, I usually only catch myself after the first syllable of the swear has escaped, which means I have to quickly deviate into song. For example, I might stub my toe and loudly break into an angry rendition of 'Fa-Fa-Fa-Fa-Fa (Sad Song)' by Otis Redding. It's not quite as satisfying.

Such incidents are all clear-cut examples of things that are frustrating for obvious reasons. Toes are designed to be stubbed. Technology is made to decay. Life throws you shitty little sitcom irritants to test you. It's understandable that one would react angrily to these things, because we can mark them under the category 'unfair'.

The situations that you really need to learn how to control, however, are ones that aren't so easily clear cut - and with kids, particularly young ones, it's often impossible to rationalise their behaviour. There is no such thing as 'fair' when dealing with children. They literally do not understand the concept and have no respect for the boundaries of your patience or your sanity. It turns out that babies, for example, are inherently selfish tiny bastards who have little to no regard for routine or schedule. So know that you will be tested, and that you need to have a seemingly boundless capacity for resolve.

A baby crying clouds everything, like the fog of war, or Sambuca. There is a reason that recordings of crying babies have been used by the CIA in torture experiments: the only sane human response to hearing a child crying - and not just crying but *screaming*, for hours on end, at the exact same tone and pitch - is to go insane. Crying babies will take their toll on you psychologically as well as physiologically. Yes, lack of sleep leaves you feeling like a shadow of your former self, but the constant nerve-shredding screams emanating from your offspring is a special kind of mental torture: not only is it excruciating to listen to, but every one of their pained cries feels like a jab at *your* parenting skills or lack thereof. "WHYYYYYYY am I still crying? WHYYYYYYY aren't you doing anything? WHEERRRRRRRE are the proper grown-ups?"

Trying to make logical decisions with a small baby screaming 150 decibels into your earlobes at 2.15am is impossible, so it's only natural that these situations are extremely tense, therefore your emotional reactions to them tend to be heightened. These high pressure scenarios inevitably breed frustrations, which can unfortunately - but understandably - boil over.

When faced with similar situations, of crying babies or kids with insomnia, I have been guilty of getting angry - though crucially, never actually at the children themselves. Because even in the heat of the moment, a hothead like me knows that an upset baby can't stop itself from crying any more than a wound can stop itself from bleeding, and not even adults can will themselves to sleep.

So, you shape and distort your frustrations, until they arc around the children - the obvious source of the problem - and end up focused on something, or someone else. It is highly likely you and your partners will argue often in the early days until you recognise this pattern of behaviour: you can't rant and rave at a baby, but two consenting adults might take a strange sort of comfort from directing anger at someone who can actually answer back.

Communication, or lack of it, is really the source of all of your frustrations in parenthood: until your kid can tell you exactly what the problem is, you're going to have to guess, and when you're all out of guesses, well, it looks like you're just going to have to wolf down a big ol' bowl of tough shit until the problem fixes itself or just sort of goes away.

Parenthood arguments are not fun. For maybe the first time in your life, arguments might actually be about something other than yourself and your own needs. It actually feels like the outcome matters. Arguing about the general well-being of your own kids is always difficult, because it's almost impossible to eloquently argue a point that doesn't have an obvious answer, or might take years to take root.

These flashpoints might be small in nature but who's to say this minor disagreement won't turn into a major issue in later life? If you concede this specific argument right now, without making that all-important one last point, you might be dooming your poor child to a life of misery.

It's important to remember how time can be distorted in these situations - an hour of wailing can feel like a lifetime, but an hour of sleep will pass in the blink of an eye. Often, the cold light of day acts as a cooling salve on any night-time issues - the sun comes up and all is forgotten. It's important to remember that everything passes eventually, and that includes any residual anger you might have expressed in the moment.

Frequently, I'll start a new day and look back on my behaviour in the night - usually some impromptu profanity relating to lack of sleep - and be embarrassed by it in retrospect. That's part of the process: recognising that essentially, anger and frustration, though understandable in the moment, are just pointless expenditures of energy. No one is being their best self at 2.15am.

I can recall two similar train journeys, both of which were laced with frustration, but which were handled in very different ways. The first train journey was to a friend's wedding somewhere far,

far away, in the days before we had a car. We had in our possession: one teething baby, two massive suitcases, and because the venue was a taxi ride away from our hotel, a big, bulky car seat that we had to mount on a little wheeled trolley thing and pull along like a toy dog.

Every 20 feet we walked, the car seat would fall off this fucking trolley thing. It was a nightmare. The train was crowded and we only just managed to get a seat. The baby was screaming super loud, in obvious pain. Vicky and I were exhausted before the train even left the station and argued constantly. I sat and cried for the last 20 minutes of the journey, sobbing loudly with my hands over my eyes, wishing I could disappear.

Still: great wedding. Congrats guys. Please let me know if there's a window between the cutting of the cake and the first dance when I can go and bundle up my suit jacket and use it as a pillow on the toilet cistern.

The other train journey was one on the way back from London, after a punishing day out at an activity centre that was "run by kids, for kids", so you get an idea of exactly how hellish it was for adults. We were all hyper-tired, that sort of zombie state where you aren't really sure if you'll even be able to get home at all, you just have to stumble between one waypoint and the next and hope for the best.

The kids were jacked up on adrenaline but also supremely knackered, which is a deadly combination. It was rush hour, because it always is in this sort of situation. The kids would wriggle, they'd cry, they'd utterly fail to sit still, they'd chuck wet apple chunks at other commuters. Not apropos of nothing, I had also given up alcohol, so there was no promise of a nice warm boozy hug at home after bedtime.

With flashbacks of the earlier train journey in my head, I just decided to lean into the madness and go with it. This was the moment a young Kid H decided to crawl between my legs in a crowded carriage, look up at me with perfect timing, and say - for the first time ever, in a weird, deep voice: "Helllloooooooo".

We all had a good laugh, as indeed did the other travellers - in fact, by the time the journey was over, I'd even had a compliment from one of the passengers regarding our parenting skills. (When I would tell this story back later on, the whole carriage spontaneously applauded and carried me home on their shoulders, chanting my name).

At the risk of sounding like one of those perma-smile happybot freaks, it turns out it takes less energy to laugh than it does to stress out, and the choice to do so is never off the table. Moderation of temper and stress is not an easy thing to learn, and you might find you only do learn when you're pushed to extremes, but there's little doubt it makes you a better, more reliable father, and just generally a nicer person to be around. But god help whatever printer breaks down on you next.

FEAR

Hello there. You join me on day 14 of quarantine of the great coronavirus panic of 2020. As I write this, millions of Brits - and hundreds of millions of people around the world - are on lockdown, stuck at home on government advice while COVID-19 wreaks havoc on the respiratory systems of the elderly and the infirm. The NHS is overwhelmed. The death count defies belief, and rises every day. And the men in charge of the most powerful countries on earth who are charged with the response to the panic, are, to be quite frank, useless cunts. The situation is, shall we say, less than ideal. As I sit here, unable to go outside in case I get coughed on by a rogue phlegmwad, this feels like as good an opportunity as any to reflect on the nature of fear, more specifically the flavour of fear you feel as a parent.

Before I had kids, I was a total scaredy cat. It didn't take much to spook me. I didn't sleep for a month after The Blair Witch Project came out. In fact, on the night I saw it I got stopped by a police car on the way home because I was running as fast as I could - that's right, *running away from the fictional witch* - and they assumed I had just bolted from a crime scene. The only way I could convince them I was not hot-footing it from a nearby mugging was by breaking down and truthfully confessing to them: "I was running because I'm a pussy". I was 18. This genuinely ranks as one of the lowest moments of my life. I have no idea why I'm telling you this. I guess my point is, fear was an emotion I was very familiar with. I couldn't even draw the curtains at night because I was convinced a burglar or monster or zombie or fictional witch would be lurking outside my window.

Naturally, when you first find out you're having a baby, a boatload of exciting new fears get dumped on your doorstep. You're allowed to be scared before the baby is born, that's what the nine months of pregnancy are for: slowly but surely overcoming your crippling anxieties to come to terms with your impending fatherhood. It's nature's buffer zone, the easing-in period. Once the baby is born, however, you open up a whole new box set of fears to binge on. Things were so much easier back when baby was lodging in someone else's womb.

A small amount of fear is healthy, they say. You *should* be terrified of looking after a baby! It's a frightening responsibility! Even so, it can feel quite overwhelming at times. We've already covered the multitude of ways that a baby could theoretically perish while in your care, but crucially, even when they're just sort of *sitting there*, the cogs in your head never stop clicking and whirring, mentally picturing one hundred different horrible

Rube Goldberg-esque methods of death that could hypothetically befall your baby. It's almost enough to paralyse you, which won't help. It's a vicious circle that can run rings around you if you let it.

This feeling really kicks up a notch when baby starts eating solid food at around six months. As an adult, you know that if you eat with sensible bite-sized portions, masticate responsibly and eat at a sensible pace, the risk of you choking is minimal. It's not really something you worry about happening, day to day.

As a father to a six-month-old baby, however, the risk of choking is extremely, heart-palpitatingly likely, every single day. Babies don't know what bite-size portions are because they don't know what bites are and also they don't know what portions are because they don't know what food is. These idiots are out there eating their own fists. They don't know they're not supposed to turn purple.

Therefore, you need to be on watch. It's on you to make sure whatever baby is eating can slide down their gullet, like smushed banana or apple pulp or frappéd carrot. Because you can guarantee the one time you only cut a grape into halves and not into quarters, that solid half a grape is getting wedged in the windpipe of your nearest and dearest. Therefore, dinner time can feel incredibly intense and extremely exhausting. Do babies really even need food to live? They do? Damn.

Even when the food goes down, that's no guarantee the drama is over; there's still a last-act scare lurking in the stomach, a cat-jumping-out-a-cupboard-style shock in the form of lots and lots of vomit.

The first time your beautiful baby does a projectile puke, you will die of fright, or if you're lucky, merely attempt to remove yourself from your skeleton. It's a cliché, but it is honestly like something from The Exorcist: white jets of hot milk spewing from the mouth of a babe, their confused little face betraying no emotion other than, eventually, relief.

After the fact, you can rationalise and break it down. It makes total sense: they have a stomach the size of a golf ball and they've been clamped on a tit making the most of the all-you-can-eat buffet - it figures there's going to be some blowback. Over time, when it happens more often, your reaction mellows; it becomes less like white-knuckle fear and more like 'well *that* cushion is ruined'. But in that moment, those horrifying, drag-me-to-hell, spontaneous first few slow-motion seconds of volcanic chunder, as you futilely point the wet end of the baby anywhere but towards you in a mad panic, it feels like it takes a year off your life.

You will need to get comfortable living on the edge. You will exist permanently on the precipice of sanity. You should go ahead and update your Amazon delivery details to the brink of madness. Babies need 110% of your attention, which really isn't fair, because it's impossible to give more than 100% of your attention to anything, yet that is a cast-iron fact about babies, so what are you going to do? Take it up with the police? 'Hello Officer, if at all possible I would like to spend *less* time worrying about the physical well-being of my baby,' you'll say, as you're led straight to a jail cell with the murderers and the rapists.

Sorry, it's the law: no matter how much you worry, you are somehow still not worrying nearly enough. The complete and total lack of logic in all baby-related situations frazzles your central nervous system like crispy American bacon, until you're a quivering wreck who's second guessing everything you have done.

You live in fear of forgetting simple safety measures that could prove to be fatal, which, due to your current Cro-Magnon state,

337

is not outside the realms of possibility. Like leaving a stair gate open, for example. You know you closed it. You *always* close it. You even took a specific mental picture of you closing it less than 30 minutes ago. You heard the little click when the latch clipped into the housing. You rattled it to make sure, like you always do, every single day. Case closed, case literally closed.

Except... Was it definitely closed? Are you sure that wasn't yesterday? Or some other stair gate? Did you imagine it? Or could it have been a false memory implanted by the CIA? How sure are you, exactly? Would you stand up in court with your hand on a Bible and admit to being of sound body and mind? Yeah? Are you sure?

The defendant says he is fit to look after his child, Your Honour, but please look at Exhibit A, a photograph of the defendant with both his t-shirt AND his pyjama bottoms on back-to-front. I ask you, ladies and gentlemen of the jury: does this look like a man who can be trusted to close a stair gate?

Think again. There's reasonable doubt. You almost certainly, maybe, possibly, definitely forgot to close it. Okay, fair's fair: so maybe it's 0.1% plausible that you left the stair gate open. Are you willing to take that chance? Even things that are 0.1% likely to happen happen sometimes. Remember when Leicester City won the Premier League? If you'd have trusted the form guide and the statistics, you'd never have said Leicester City could win the Premier League. You'd have sworn blind. The odds were 5000/1. And yet, in 2016, we were all having a Vardy party. What if, in this situation, 'Leicester City' is you and 'winning the Premier league' is accidentally killing your child because you thought you closed the stairgate? Sigh. Better go up and check just to be sure.

Yep. It was closed. Goddamn it. But was it though? Repeat ad infinitum until insanity.

The fact is, even though your brain may have the stability and neurological capabilities of a plate of cheap jelly, you have to trust your instincts, because you have no other choice. Instinct is one of those wishy-washy, unquantifiable traits that you may have previously called on from time to time to navigate low-stakes situations like taking a shortcut or choosing a pub, but instinct now acts as your sole shining beacon of hope to guide you through the dark times. Instinct won't stop the What Ifs, but nothing can. They never go away. What if baby's high temperature was actually meningitis and you don't take them to the doctor right away and instead go to Nando's? My god, the consequences could be horrendous: you'd never be able to eat at Nando's ever again.

As long as you listen to your instinct, act sensibly and responsibly, consult with your partner and reach an understanding on how to move forward in case of crisis, no fear is so big it can't be dissolved or decayed via positive actions, or even the mere passing of time.

Allow me to deploy another overused but accurate cliché: you're better off safe than sorry. If you're scared about a baby-related illness or injury and you're unsure of how to proceed, don't internalise that shit: do something, like phone NHS 111, or the second emergency service, your parents. Book an emergency doctor's appointment, or if you would really rather see off the issue, take the kid to the emergency room. If nothing else, Sod's Law is likely to kick in the moment you start to treat the ailment seriously; you can guarantee the patient will start to feel, act and look healthier the instant they step inside a healthcare facility manned by trained medical staff, all of whom have actual sick people to care for.

I can't tell you how many times my wife and I have had this exact same conundrum, and every single time we've laid down the gauntlet and made the trip to A&E, the issue has all but evaporated under that harsh NHS lighting. A few years back, Kid H bashed his head awkwardly on a metal kitchen drawer handle, and fearing a possible concussion, we took him to the hospital to have him inspected. Obviously the moment we entered the doctor's surgery, he started dancing around the room wearing his sick bowl as a hat. It's an odd emotional cocktail that swirls through your brain in that moment; a mixture of relief, amusement and irritation. Mostly exhaustion.

There is so much going on in the world that can cause anxiety, from the universal to the personal to the microscopic stuff you can't see and therefore might not even exist, but to worry about all of it, all of the time, would only serve to put you six feet under. Like politics, for example. If you actually put aside some time to sit down and invest in the current state of affairs of world politics, you might never stand up again. The news - the fucking news! - is a major source of worry, beamed via multiple channels of communication directly to every flat surface in your pocket, home and workstation. How about the looming threat of climate change? Nuclear war, anyone? Or, oh, I don't know, just for example, some sort of once-in-a-lifetime global pandemic?

If you want to cast your net real wide, how about the nature of mortality itself? One day you, and everyone you love, including your children, are going to die. Try that one on for size for a laugh. The world at large is a continuously frightening place, but whereas before you were maybe able to shake off such distant concerns, now, with a baby in your arms, you are newly invested in the world your child will grow up in - one that you will one day leave behind.

My preferred analogy that I call upon in times of trouble is, unsurprisingly, food-based. Picture a pizza. You've just ordered a pizza. You're staring at a gigantic takeaway pizza. Looks big, doesn't it? It's big and round and meaty and contains four kinds of cheese. It almost, *almost*, looks too big to be consumed by a single human being, doesn't it? But how do you break down this overwhelming situation into a more manageable affair?

You eat it piece by piece, slice by slice, until eventually it's all gone and you hate yourself. That's the key to dealing with scary problems that feel too big to even comprehend: you deal with them one slice at a time. Start small, don't get ahead of yourself, resist the temptation to look at the bigger picture, just stay focused.

When you're ready to move on to the next stage, then do so, at the same pace and with the same attitude: one thing at a time. A second slice of pizza may not be needed. Maybe you shouldn't have even ordered a whole pizza. Maybe you already had pizza for lunch? I'm losing track of my pizza metaphor. I think the cheese represented... mortality? Never mind, I think you've got it. Consequently, I don't feel like much of a scaredy cat these days. It's weird how having children prioritises even your most irrational and subconscious fears. I have actual, real-life worries to keep me occupied, like putting money in the bank, keeping the kids healthy and putting food on the table, so I don't really have the brain capacity to be scared about fictional witches any more.

I just recently watched the remake of Stephen King's It, a movie about a killer clown who eats children, which ordinarily would have had to be viewed from behind a blanket with the DVD subsequently locked in a steel case and buried in wet cement. But, because we are still in the grip of coronavirus lockdown - a very real concern for the well-being of my family that could literally be lurking outside my window - such cheap thrills almost felt like a fun distraction.

Yes, the world is terrifying right now. Life is terrifying. Babies are terrifying. Responsibility is terrifying. *It's all terrifying.* But the good news is, if you're feeling the fear, then you must be doing something right: it means you're paying attention.

As long as you don't let it define you and you learn how to portion it out, fear will ultimately make you a stronger, more confident father - and, hopefully like it did with me, it'll make you less of a pussy.

DISGUST

Contrary to what the popular Pixar motion picture Inside Out may have you believe, 'Disgust' is not actually an emotion, because 'not liking broccoli' doesn't really register on the full spectrum of human emotion - it's just a correct opinion.

Nonetheless, for symmetry's sake, let's dive headfirst into the world of disgust without protective clothing on, because friend, you are going to be more disgusted than you ever have in your entire life. Not only will you be disgust*ed*, you will be disgust*ing*. You will lower your standards. You will wallow in filth. You will, for all intents and purposes, put Oscar the Grouch to shame.

We've already covered off the poo. There will be lots of poo. For a short while, your life will seemingly revolve around baby poo: the fact that a poo hasn't happened for a while, the facial expressions that suggest a poo is in progress, the immediate clean-up of a poo, the wafty aftermath of a poo, the fact another poo is coming down the pipe so soon after the last poo, and so on. And yes, it is remarkable how quickly you become au fait with the presence of poo. You will become numb to poo. You will become immune to poo. You will become one with poo.

Before you start thinking you've cracked it - pun very much intended, WEYYYYYYYYY - just know this: wiping arses is only the beginning. Eventually, when baby graduates from nappies, comes potty training. Maybe your exposure to potty training has been limited thus far, restricted only to adverts of kids contently pooing in a plastic bucket, high-fiving mummy and daddy who can't believe how unbelievably grown-up and photogenic the child actor is.

Well, let's get real for a second: potty training essentially equates to a tiny person pissing and shitting all over your house for weeks, nay, months on end. While the kid attempts to learn the fine art of precision pooing, there are going to be a lot of misfires, brown misfires, smushed into surfaces both wipe clean and not, that are unwittingly transferred to socks and the soles of bare feet. Living in a potty training house is like setting up camp in a minefield: tread carefully or suffer the consequences. There's no finer way of re-evaluating your home decor and furnishings than by assessing which fabrics will stand up to an impromptu flood of urine. Carpets, sofas, beds: all will know the wrath of a tiny and indiscriminate bladder.

Your new-found affinity with turds might come in handy in other ways. I still think about a story a friend told me about a friend of a friend - and the sheer distance between subject and storyteller should clue you in about how much disgust is contained therein. Settle in: this is going to get gross.

Picture a young married couple, who have just been blessed with child. Aww. Baby, however, came out swinging his elbows, which meant Mummy's lady parts were left pretty raw after the birth. This caused Mummy a great deal of pain and discomfort, which was particularly apparent when she was sitting on the toilet. When the urge to do a poo came calling, that urge was ignored, put off, quashed; women are capable of a great many feats after giving birth, increased control over their colon being just one of them. Entire days passed without poo, then weeks, with Mummy and Daddy rightfully focused on other issues, like having a baby to look after. Eventually, the build-up became intolerable, and as with any blockage, the dam had to burst - it just happened at the worst possible time.

Mummy was visiting the in-laws with Daddy when the urge became intolerable and a poo decided to crash the family dinner, clenching be damned. Mummy rushed up to the bathroom, but found that sitting on the toilet was too painful a position to adopt, so - and this is where the story really devolves, in case you were wondering - she found herself on her hands and knees in the bath, basically ready to give birth for the second time in a matter of weeks.

This delivery was considerably quicker but a whole lot messier, and unlike in hospital, there was no one to swaddle this thing in a pristine white blanket and rush it away. There's no way of sugar-coating it: she did a massive shit in someone else's bathtub. Enter Daddy, who, after a quick and panicked phone call - the kind you can imagine was etched in his mind for evermore - was summoned upstairs to take responsibility for clean-up.

In the end, Daddy had to go and get a fork from his parents' kitchen to break up the turd into manageable chunks so they could finally mash it down the plughole. Now that... *that* is love. If you aren't prepared to take a potato masher to dispose of your loved one's fecal discharge in a toilet emergency, you might as well start serving up the divorce papers now.

The key to enduring this disgusting period of your life is to lower your standards to hitherto unthinkable depths. This is nothing less than essential for your survival. With your baby making outrageous demands of you every minute of every hour, you cannot hope to manage your day-to-day life on the same level that you used to. This means that, for a short while at least, you must let yourself go. *Really* let yourself go. No, it's okay! It's allowed! This is the only officially sanctioned time in your life when it's expected, or even encouraged that you let yourself go! Own it!

Paternity leave is a golden ticket for the slovenly man. It's a green light to be as disgusting as your mother-in-law always suspected you were. If you want to attempt to grow a beard, you bloody well attempt to grow a beard! It's not like anyone has to see you try! There are no co-workers to smirk at your pathetic four-days-growth bumfluff in this house: the only people you'll be interacting with are either a) cohabiting with you and therefore preoccupied with keeping a small baby alive, or b) a small baby who has no context for what a successful beard should actually look like. Your face is an open goal just waiting to be kicked in! Be beardless no longer!

Remember way back in Chapter #4, when I advised you to get all your exercise and healthy living done early so you can concentrate on being a slob once the baby arrives? Time flies, because it's slobbering time!

Gaining weight during the first few months of parenting is unavoidable and legally enforceable. Bellies will form. Moobs may happen. You will know your Deliveroo guy by name. You will find a meal between breakfast and brunch. All because society demands you sacrifice your figure on the chunky and robust altar of fatherhood.

You 1) are a Dad, and 2) have a body, therefore you have a Dadbod, whether you like it or not. Cram your marshmallow arse into that pigeonhole and hibernate in there until your kid goes to college, safe in the knowledge that you have full diplomatic immunity. Once one domino starts falling, they all fall eventually. Is ironing clothes really the best use of your time right now? No, of course not. Is it even really necessary to change out of your pyjamas today? No, of course not. What's the point of folding clothes and putting them away when having them in a big heap on the bedroom floor makes them so much more accessible in a crisis? Does this make me a monster? No, of course not. Does this hoodie, which hasn't been washed in 14 days despite the fact it has takeaway bhuna and baby puke down the front of it, really smell so bad? No, of course not. Is it really so wrong to get another day's use out of these boxer shorts by turning them inside out? Actually, yes, it is - congrats, you found the line.

Your home - your precious disgustatorium - is your safe space, where Misters Clean and Muscle are no longer welcome. There literally aren't enough hours in the day to raise a child, continue being a functioning human being and do the washing up - you're not gunning for Father of the Year here. Let your cup of tea go half-drunk. Leave the odd biscuit crumb here and there. Wear that same slightly undersized t-shirt for two days running. Your hair basically washes itself after a while anyway. Change the kitchen bin tomorrow. Oh, you said that yesterday? Move the goalposts mate, it's all above board. Nobody is policing you, no crime has been committed. You've got nothing on me, copper.

You see, it's all in the job description, check the small print. Lowering your own standards is an integral part of caring for another human being. It's a form of self-care, in a roundabout sort of way - relaxing your own rules on healthy living and cleanliness can be liberating at a time when it's more important than ever that your focus lies elsewhere. Becoming immune to disgust is a slippery slope for sure, but seize the opportunity to sled down that slope like a kid at Christmas - you just have to be willing to trudge your way back up to the peak again at some point.

Hmm, maybe take a shower first.

#21

Toys, More Specifically the Tidying of Toys

T hey say you have to make room in your heart for children, but what that platitude conveniently neglects to mention is that you also have to make room in your *house* for children, and that is way harder because it's a real thing you actually have to do.

Babies are small, this we know: they can essentially be tucked away in a drawer or bunged in a cupboard with a couple of cheesestrings and you're golden for a few hours. The space you really need to create is to accommodate the mountains and mountains of tat that comes with the kid as part of the parenthood package deal.

At the beginning, the tat is manageable, and baby will have a crib where his or her stuff can be stashed away neatly. We're talking minimal lift: a play mat here, a bouncer there, a job lot of rattles under the cot and maybe a Sophie la Girafe roaming around the living room savannah for the kid to wrap their gums around. If it came to it and you had to go on the lam, you could probably pack the baby and all of its worldly possessions into one of those blue heavy duty Ikea bags and hit the road pronto.

But be warned. When the baby gets older and develops likes and dislikes and its every whim absolutely must be catered for or else it'll throw a world-ending wobbly, then the toy pile multiplies. Tat begat tat begat tat. Plastic tat, wooden tat, rubber tat, rattan tat, cardboard tat, cloth tat, paper tat, cuddly tat. Tat on every surface, tat in every direction, tat as far as the eye can see. You are basically now Stig of the Dump. Your home, which you worked on every spare weekend for years and years in order to make it feel truly yours, is now full of things that aren't for you.

Do yourself a favour: extract and isolate that thought, that bit where you briefly felt sorrow that you don't get to spend as much time with your possessions as you used to, then stamp on it with both feet until it's completely fucking atomised, because if having to tidy away your Star Wars action figures in order to make room for your kids' toys makes you sad, then I have bad news about the rest of being a father.

I think the single thing that surprised me most about parenthood was how much tidying was required. I will not surprise you to learn that the amount of tidying involved in parenthood is 'a lot', but it's not so much the volume of the tidying required as it is the frequency. It's hard to overstate how relentless the tidying becomes. It is never-ending, like being stuck in a Groundhog Day-esque infinity loop. It becomes second nature; if you let it, tidying may become one of your dominant personality traits.

Cleaning up kids' toys is like some sort of Twilight Zone-esque curse that you're doomed to repeat at the end of each and every day, safe in the knowledge that you'll be right back here in 24 hours performing the same menial tasks, with absolutely nothing staying tidy. It's possible to spend half of your day cleaning up and somehow your place will still look like shit at the end of the day. I'm realising as I write this that I spent a year working at Toys 'R' Us as a young man where it was my job to clean up toys, so maybe I'm just a sucker for punishment.

After a while, you begin to question your own logic, like you've just discovered the secrets of The Matrix. What's the point of tidying up if everything is just going to get messy again anyway? Woah there. Stand down, Neo. Determining a state of 'acceptable mess' is the parental equivalent of letting your hair 'wash itself' - this is a dangerous and extremist way of thinking. 'Actually, there are actually several net benefits to a race of AI squid robots using the human race as a battery source'. Can it. This is just the way things are done, the established order of things. Put those big ideas of yours back in the box and keep tidying. Here, you've worked hard today, take this blue pill with your glass of sauvignon blanc.

Unfortunately, it's not just a case of squaring things away until you can see carpet. Kids being kids, they like to take their toys on a whistle-stop tour of the house, and because they have memories like particularly grubby goldfish, they tend to leave toys in places where they do not belong, spreading component parts to the four corners of the Earth, to the point where it'd take a charismatic adventurer and his ragtag group of friends an entire four-part mystical quest to reunite the separate pieces.

Logic takes a leave of absence, so when the inevitable happens and a toy gets lost, all bets are off as to where you might find it. This isn't like you misplacing your keys, because there are probably only three or four places your keys are likely to be: table by the door, kitchen worksurface, coat pocket, windowsill. When kids lose their toys, no room is off limits, and no nook or cranny can be ruled out; there is every chance the missing piece is going to be wedged into a rotten apple core, zipped inside a pencil case and stuffed in the shoe cupboard.

As an example, I did a quick inventory check in my house this morning, and here's just a small sample of the number of randomly misplaced items I found: pencil sharpener in sink;

magic wand in kitchen cutlery drawer; LEGO Spider-Man toy hanging from leaf of cheese plant in downstairs loo; paper 'fingermouse' sitting on top of ring holder in bedroom; Jack-Jack Incredibles doll lying face down on garden patio; small toy crossbow on my bedroom pillow, as if placed there by a tiny and vengeful Mafia don; toy miniature bag of M&S Petis Pois on the bathroom floor; entire legion of Transformers organised in battle formation in vegetable drawer of toy kitchen in kids' bedroom. I could go on.

And don't get me started on puzzle pieces. Missing puzzle pieces have aged me by approximately eight years. I would estimate that at least three quarters of the puzzles in my house are missing one or more pieces. If you can successfully keep all pieces of a single puzzle together in one cardboard puzzle box for longer than three months without i) the box being trodden on, flattened or destroyed, or ii) one of the pieces vaporising from this plane of human existence, then congratulations, you will soon be bathed in a golden light as you ascend to Heaven because you have completed parenting on Hard level. It's just you and Marie Kondo up there.

I don't want to be too down on kids' toys, because obviously they bring your beautiful children no end of joy, but let's face it, they usually do so at the cost of your own. There are some toys that I can really get behind, because they have either an aesthetic or an educational value. You can't go wrong with an abacus, said the 80-year-old man. I can't stay mad at LEGO, because its inherent blocky crappiness forces kids to develop their imagination to compensate. And sure, I will give you cuddly toys. Cuddlies I will allow, for reasons that I will soon elaborate on. Everything else? Shit. Shit to the nth power. Expensive, flimsy, pointless and shit. The worst culprits are the single-use plastic toys that perform exactly one function, which the child must - and will - repeat until the space-time continuum eventually atrophies and turns in on itself, and if even one tiny part of the toy breaks or comes loose or gets lost then it essentially becomes a gaudy paperweight.

Sadly, the crappiness of a toy is proportionally inverse to how much your kid will love it. Last Christmas, I caved and bought my boys a toy they wanted from the new Grinch movie. It's not an action figure or a cuddly toy or a playset, but a blue plastic house with a snow-covered roof, with the Grinch hiding in the chimney and his dog in a little plastic removable sled. You pop the Grinch into the chimney, put a present on his head (?) then pull a drawstring, and the dog's sled circles the chimney and the Grinch pops out.

...That's it, is it? Brilliant. The lifespan of the toy is about six seconds. It cost me twenty five quid. It has no other use. We lost the dog and the present after about two weeks. From memory, there is no scene in the movie where the Grinch hides in a chimney with a present on his head. To my kids' credit, they got their money's worth in that first fortnight, pulling that string again and again and again. Did I mention that it makes an ear-splitting mechanised screech every time you use it? Imagine Janice from Friends at 2x speed being forced to do an impression of a TIE Fighter at gunpoint after having seen Star Wars once. Eeeeeeehgrrhhh. Eeeeeeeerrrhhhhh. EEEERRGHNNNHHNN. Honestly, you just don't get this sort of aggro with an abacus.

There is a special circle of hell reserved for people who buy horrendous toys for the benefit of other peoples' children, specifically musical instruments (slogan: "The perfect gift for someone you hate!"). We've played host to an orchestra's worth of musical instruments over the years, including but not limited to: a Peppa Pig keyboard, a wooden xylophone, some electric bath bongos, one of those weird washboard things that old guys play in taverns in the American deep south, a miniature guitar that's now tuned so far below the musical register the strings slap the fretboard like wet spaghetti, and about eight fucking plastic recorders, all of which have only ever been used to inflict pain on other human beings, all of which were snuck into the house under the guise of cover gifts from kids' magazines. I would love to say my children are musically gifted. I would love to say that. I really would.

Often in the course of your day, you will find yourself absent-mindedly humming along to an unspecified tune before realising that it's a jingle from one of your kids' musical toys, and that the repetitive electronica resulting from so many frenzied button pushes has permanently etched itself into your brain. I am sorry to inform you that you can no longer enjoy music for adults; you now only have the capacity to enjoy three-note bleeps and bloops that tell the story of how sleepy Bedtime Bear is. To be fair, some of these little ditties are insanely catchy. You think the real talented songwriters are your Fiona Apples or your Cardi Bs or to a lesser extent your Gary Barlows, but no: the real home-grown talent is coming straight out of Fisher Price. Put a donk on Bedtime Bear and you'd have BTS beating your door down.

At some point, perhaps in order to fulfil your end of a bargain that you were assuming would go unfulfilled, you will take your kids to a toy shop. More toys is rarely the path to enlightenment, but it can occasionally be used as a shortcut to happiness on an otherwise underwhelming payday weekend. I will admit the first time we took our boys to the local toy megastore, I did feel a frisson of excitement myself. Endless shelves that stretch to the sky! Rows and rows of things that you never played with as a child but can totally afford as an adult! A whole bit with trampolines and garden slides and ride-on remote-controlled trucks that seem like death-traps!

As a kid, maybe you fantasised about the day you could one day stride into Toys Toys Toys with your chequebook out, Pretty Woman style, to buy up the entire stock of Beanie Babies. As an adult, reality bites a little harder and there are altogether too many bills to pay, but it's still a kick to finally be in that position of power, even if Toys Toys Toys haven't accepted cheques as payment since 2003.

Take a moment to look at the face of your kid as you enter this toy shop. They are like Mecca for kids. This is the promised land, tantamount to a religious experience. With my Toys 'R' Us work experience I know what really goes on behind the scenes (there's certainly way more people smoking dope and giving handjobs in the warehouse than you might expect) but the facade is convincing enough to bewitch the little ones: toy shops are child nirvana. Your kid would kill you dead in an instant if it meant they could take home one of those ride-on remote-controlled trucks, as long as your corpse didn't slump face down onto the pocket containing your wallet. Toy shops are quite cruel really, because kids know no limits and care little about moderation - they want all of it, right now, and as far as they're concerned, the only thing preventing that from happening is you and your insufficient monthly wage. They don't need to worry about storage space or bank balances or having spoiled children. They just want you to do whatever it is that adults do with that little card with the numbers on it that makes the big things be in your car, and every second you delay is agony.

If you think I am exaggerating for effect, then wait until you first ask your kid to choose between two toys in a toy shop, and

353

take note of the emotional fallout that results. A lot more thrashing and pounding of the floor than you expected, no? To kids, having to choose which toy to take home is exactly as traumatic as Sophie's Choice, and may I remind you that you are the Nazi commandant in this analogy.

Hopefully, out of such trauma comes acceptance, and maybe even love. If you are lucky, your kid will eventually find a toy that they love more than anything, maybe even more than they love you. It might take a lot of failed relationships to get to that stage - the bedroom littered with fallen soldiers, played with once on a wet Wednesday and abandoned ever since, cue the *in memoriam* reel - but they will soon find a toy they form a meaningful relationship with.

It's at this point where you develop a begrudging affection with the toys, because you can see how much they mean to the kid, and only an inhuman monster - say, one who still mentally ranks toys by their price tag at the point of purchase - could fail to be moved by that.

A true toy for life gets invited into the inner circle, and will be present at breakfast, lunch, dinner and all daily toilet trips. The toy *du jour* may change over time, because kids do not feel it necessary to wrangle with the concept of loyalty, but the only constant is how hot these relationships run. It's very much an 'all or nothing' scenario: woe betide you if Bedtime Bear goes AWOL at bedtime, because nothing else will do. You will turn the house upside down before your kid settles for a bear that clearly has no business deputising at bedtime. The clue's in the name, Daddy. *Jesus.*

Usually, but not always, it'll be a cuddly toy that occupies this space in your little one's heart. My kids had very different but equally valid relationships with different types of toys. Kid H, bless his heart, was inexplicably into toy tractors, and it got to the point where, because it was widely apparent that he loved tractors, visiting relatives would bring him more tractors, until we reached critical tractor mass and we had to have a tractor intervention.

Kid A got super into this bizarre Netflix series called Dinosaur King, so we bought him a little cuddly yellow Triceratops called Chomp, and we left him in the hall and pretended we had no idea how he got there. It was love at first sight. It helps that kids are gullible and don't bother questioning stuff like this. Which brings me onto the subject of Peepee.

Peepee was the first toy that was more than just a toy - she was part of the family. I can't even remember how we came to acquire this small beanie toy penguin, but by god, she made her presence felt soon enough.

When he was around three years old, Kid A carried Peepee absolutely everywhere; around the house, on the move, and clutched tightly to his chest every bedtime. Peepee's absence would be greeted with sheer sweating panic if she was ever out of his sightline for more than six seconds. They were inseparable. Soulmates. Best buds for life. Lads on tour. You know where this is going.

One fateful afternoon, Kid A and Peepee were left in the care of Nanny who was babysitting while myself and Vicky enjoyed a blessed four hours of not being responsible for a child's welfare. Nanny took Kid A and Peepee into Canary Wharf to experience the delights of a £7 coffee, but at some point in the day, Peepee was liberated. She must have fallen off the buggy. She did not make the return journey home.

Nanny was devastated and couldn't apologise enough, but we knew that telling Kid A the straight truth - that Peepee was more than likely lost forever, left homeless in an East London back street, getting smacked off her beak on cheap speed with a bunch of off-brand Tamagotchis and defective Furbies - would be too harsh a lesson in the perils of attachment. So we improvised.

Peepee, we decided, very much on the hoof, didn't get lost: Peepee had gone on holiday. Yeah, that sounds about right. While we waited the two-week delivery period to have a back-up Peepee shipped out, we concocted a story: Peepee had grown tired of suburban life and decided she'd pop off to the Caribbean for a couple of weeks. Yes son, technically I guess it *does* make more sense that a penguin would probably be more likely to visit the Antarctic or a location with a similar cold climate [mumbles] *you smartass*, but look, I have the postcard to prove it!

We photoshopped the postcard and laid out an elaborate story and everything, adding an almost suspicious level of detail. And he bought it! We'd turned a potentially catastrophic event into a fun one by using child logic instead of adult logic. One day, approximately 14 working days after Peepee first went on holiday, we all came home from the shops and she was sat in the hall, facing the door, looking quite satisfied with her trip. The postcard is still on my son's wall, and Peepee II is sitting staring at me on my desk as I write this, although she is now housebound and cannot afford any more exotic holidays.

About a year later, I was on my way home from work one day when I saw a boy on the Jubilee Line carrying the same Peepee toy. I was momentarily overwhelmed with feeling and said "PEEPEE!" out loud to some very puzzled commuters, who backed up a few feet on the assumption I was about to piss myself. I decided to myself that it was definitely *our* Peepee, and that she had been found later on that fateful day and was adopted by a nice family, and that she was bringing another boy as much love as she had brought to our son. It was a whole minute later that I realised that there was no reason to invent this story at all, given the flawless cover-up we'd already carried out, and that this sugar-coated version of events was all purely for my benefit. Just one of the many, many ways your brain will become broken.

Kids make you malleable, but toys like Peepee truly make you go soft. You will spend so long telling your kids to treat their toys with respect to no avail, so *you* have to afford them that respect. Frequently, I've found myself propping up toys that were haphazardly discarded so they're upright or not facing the wall - you know, just on the off chance toys are real and alive and suffering from discomfort and because you don't want them to hate you. What's more, you'll find you can't bring yourself to throw the special toys away, even long after that special connection has dissipated, because of what they once meant to your kids. Toy Story really does have a lot to answer for in this respect. Even toys like Peepee fall out of favour and go into rotation - it's only a matter of time before cuddlier, cuter or cooler toys take their place, regardless of what their holiday plans may entail. Once loved companions will go from the heady heights of the all-inclusive guest pass to the second-class citizen treatment, hoiked behind the sofa without so much as a smell you later. These toys, of the 'pre-loved' variety - meaning they've been cuddled and clutched closely for so long the very fabric of their being is worn to tatters - start to take on greater meaning. They become symbols. When they are cuddled and loved, you feel that warmth. Later, when they are discarded and downtrodden, you feel that too.

I still have a treasured toy from my childhood in my possession, although to be fair, he is a totally rad dude with attitude to spare, so of course I'm going to keep a massive legend like him around. His name is Ian and he's a cuddly lion, who is wearing what I now recognise to be a Game of Death-style yellow tracksuit complete with trainers and a hoodie with 'The King' emblazoned on it. It's not weird, I don't play with him - I mean 'it', I don't play with *it* - but if you try to take him away from me, I will go full John Wick on you and will fucking slaughter your extended family in a heartbeat. See? I told you it wasn't weird.

If I interrogate these hypothetical feelings of murderous rage, it becomes clear that Ian is obviously more than a stuffed toy with an inflated sense of self - he's an emblem of what my life used to be, back when it was much less complicated. These special toys, the ones lucky enough to be granted that vaunted VIP status, the ones that have been through good times and bad, the ones that just *understand*, well they absorb all of that feeling and innocence with every cuddle, they soak in every tear they helped wipe up, and they retain it all like a sponge, waiting patiently on your shelf or face down on the floor, ready to share that love back with you whenever you need it, whether you've since grown up or not.

Eventually, your kids will start to venture into more mature territory - iPads, video games, heroin needles, etc. It seems like only yesterday the house was ankle-deep in tractors and toy dinosaurs, but these days my kids seem to predominantly be into more complex pursuits, most of which involve hitting, shooting and/or capturing things with miniature plastic crossbows. And that's fine, I am respectful of the things my kids are into, as should you be with yours. You can't force that special relationship between a kid and their toys; they either feel it or they don't. But the sad fact is, the less they need their toys, the less they need you. So, maybe a trip to the toy shop this weekend wouldn't be quite such a bad idea after all.

#22

The First Birthday

Remember calendars? Those weird paper spreadsheets that you would use to plan your life before you had kids? January, February, March and so on? You know, you would use them to track the passage of time and make note of the many social engagements you used to keep. Not ringing any bells? Well, you'd best start remembering, because a truly noteworthy day is almost upon you, and this one is worth celebrating: it's baby's first birthday. One year since The Event.

I *know*, right? One whole year of two being three. 52 of the most intense weeks of your life. 365 days of arse-wiping and vom-cleaning and belly booping and being constantly on the verge of tears. Chances are that, by now, you don't really chart the passing of time like you used to: days of the week are interchangeable, weeks and months pass you by, seasons come and go and the only thing that ever changes is how thick your jumpers get.

But a year? That's a biggie. That's a proper milestone. None of this 'I am 15 weeks old today' prompt card bullshit. Your child has sampled an entire calendar year of life, and as best you can tell, they seem to quite enjoy it.

Baby's first birthday is celebrated on two levels. On the surface, it is a celebration of your beloved child and the anniversary of their birth, a celebration of which they have no understanding whatsoever. It's quite liberating, to be honest, to organise an event for an infant who doesn't even know what day it is. They're not big on notes at this age, nor are they especially vocal on their likes or dislikes. You've got carte blanche, so feel free to go to town on an ornate birthday cake that they will smash into pulp with their tiny fists; drape the house in birthday banners despite the fact they can't read; assemble the nans and commence the cooing.

Operation Pointless Party is underway, and your input is strictly limited to clearing up the wrapping paper the moment it is shed and thinking that gathering it all in a bin bag constitutes a constructive solution and that, actually, *actually*, you can't recycle this shiny kind of wrapping paper, actually, nans, because they just reject it at the recycling plant and they have to throw the whole shipment away. Happy birthday!

The real reason you want to celebrate baby's first birthday is because you want to celebrate yourself, because by Christ, somebody's got to. Baby isn't going to blank you or start getting curt with you for not adequately celebrating its birthday - I mean, Jesus, it's been sat there squatting on a mudpie for the warmest part of an hour, it's not exactly sitting on a high horse, is it? It's about you and your partner, not just a celebration of the fact you created this small individual 12 lunar cycles ago, but that you kept it alive for that whole time, against all odds. Okay, against *some* odds. Okay, you performed the absolute basic requirement of parenthood, which is to say you managed to survive the year without being criminally negligent in your duties. Crack open that champagne!

Once in a while, you will quickly realise, parenthood requires you to put on a bit of a show. Ordinarily, you and your family are happy to exist within the four walls of your home: your business is your business, you raise the kids on your own terms, and external influences are fairly minimal, give or take the odd invasive mother-in-law. But the first birthday is often the first in a series of family 'productions' you will create for the benefit of others - because you have to keep the kid's shareholders happy.

In these productions, you are essentially trying to communicate two things. The first, which is easy, is to show how much you love your kid. Check. Done. Nailed it. Could do it with your eyes closed, and do, as often as they'll allow it. The second point you need to get across, which is less easy, is making a show of how absolutely *fine* you both are with parenthood; it's a staged PR event in which the intention is to illustrate *how well you are coping with all of this.*

This means drawing back the curtains temporarily and showing other people how you live by letting them in and answering their questions. It may start to feel less like a celebration and more like a parenting evaluation.

Throughout the birthday bash, you will smile like a maniac and reel off scripted small-talk like an automated chatbot made flesh; the day before, you'll tidy your place harder than you have ever tidied, and there will be one room which is absolutely off-limits to guests into which every filthy piece of random crap you own will be crammed. It's all needed to present the perfect picture of how *great* you're all doing and that you *are basically smashing it* and that you *no longer cry every day.* We're fine! Everything's fine!! The extra exclamation marks are practically visible when I'm talking!!! Take them as an indicator on how *totally fine* everything is!!!!

If I grope backwards blindly into the mists of time, I am reminded of my eldest son's first birthday. That man on wrapping paper patrol, executing the clean-up with military precision, he was me. That man with the perma-grin, schmoozing the nans to within an inch of their lives, he was me.

Shocking I know, that these weren't completely invented scenarios. Anyway, Kid A's first birthday was the day I decided I was going to write this book, a book which, somehow, appears to be winding down before I've even really dispensed any worthwhile advice or said anything of note. My bad! Hopefully you enjoyed the poo jokes? Some of them at least?

As you enjoy your end of year evaluation, maybe I too will sign off with a period of reflection. I will summon all my experience and collected knowledge and leave you with the five most important things I have learned during my many years as a parent; the five indispensable nuggets of wisdom that you will one day come to hold very dear and close to your heart.

Yeah, that'll do, sounds like that'll eat up some word count.

***

INDISPENSABLE NUGGET OF WISDOM #1
Babies were easy. Now the real work starts.

Yeah. Sorry about that. I've been meaning to bring this up but I never really had the chance until now. You've been busy! I hereby regret to inform you that the act of bringing up a baby, formerly considered a heroic and life-changing undertaking, has been reassessed in light of new developments, and is now actually considered to be a massive piece of piss.

This is your classic last act twist, the twist being it's actually only the end of the first act. Surprise! The hard work isn't even close to being over; in fact, it's barely even begun. There's a reason I'm delivering this news to you now, while your home is full of family members, because otherwise it may have prompted you to do a very loud swear.

Babies are easy. They just are. They're basically a doss. You've been bowling with the bumpers up, cycling with stabilisers, playing Mario Kart with the steering aids on. I've been treating you with kid gloves for the last 12 months because that's exactly what you needed to hear to get through it - that you're a bloody champ and a trooper and you have achieved something truly incredible by helping raise a baby. I'm afraid to say that is not really true. I mean, Christ man, they sleep for most of the day. For the first few months they can barely even move. They are basically sentient bags of flour. If we're being completely honest with ourselves here, at most, you have suffered a slight hardship. A series of mild grievances. What could rightfully be described as 'a rough couple of months'. It's not like you've worked down a mine or fought in a war or anything. Soldiers don't get sent home from the frontlines of Afghanistan because they're tired.

Don't get me wrong: compared to *not* having a baby, having a baby is extremely challenging. But now you're one year into parenthood and you've passed your probation, you can't really keep comparing your current situation to your old child-free life. It's time to face up to the fact that baby is here to stay, and that your child-full life is going to get considerably more difficult the older the bloody thing gets.

For starters, it's not really even a 'baby' any more. You need to upgrade your terminology. Try the word 'toddler' on for size. Say it, say "I am father to a toddler." Feels... kind of uncomfortable, doesn't it? Good. *Good.* It should be uncomfortable, because that means you are out of your comfort zone. 'Toddler' suggests the act of 'toddling', and 'toddling' sounds completely bloody exhausting. Toddling is just the beginning. Now you've entered Year Two, you have walking and talking to look forward to, among other things. You may want to wrap them up in cotton wool and tell them what to wear and eat and say every day, but there comes a point where they need to stand up on their own two feet, literally.

The child, the infant, the toddler formerly known as bag of flour, whatever you want to call it, it'll go through more physical and mental developments over the next 12 months than it will over the rest of its lifetime. Probably, I dunno, that sounds about right. My point is that only now does parenthood really kick up a notch: you will have to radically shift from your position as doting baby cuddler to your new role as full-time damage limitation coordinator. You go from wanting to protect them from the world to protecting the world from them. The chaos is unending, the trail of destruction they leave behind is total. Being a dad to a toddler feels a little like what I imagine being Shaun Ryder's tour manager was like in the nineties.

Some parents say that they'd love another baby, if only they could keep it as a baby forever and it never grew up, like some awful on-the-nose Peter Pan allegory. I totally understand that and I completely see the appeal of a part-exchange rent-a-baby business model; you coo over it and love it and raise it from birth, right up until the point it starts to think for itself, or talks back to you, or discovers YouTube, at which point you take it back to the shop and trade it in for a younger, stupider, more helpless baby. I won't bother costing out a full business plan because it's the kind of thing that's liable to get you arrested or chased out of town with pitchforks, but I totally understand the desire to want to keep your kid from growing up - because them growing up makes your job exponentially more difficult.

Think about it. The older they get, the more life throws at them. Before you know it, they're slowly becoming actual people, with feelings and emotions and likes and dislikes and haircuts. It used to be that they'd be thirsty so they'd drink milk and that'd be the end of it, but now they want a specific kind of squash and only from a very specific cup which may or may not be in the dishwasher and they spill half of it on their shirt and half on the sofa and then five minutes later they're thirsty again and OH GOD JUST BE A BABY AGAIN ALREADY.

Life as a parent is nightmarishly relentless in this regard. It's just one bloody life-altering thing after the other. *Walking! Talking! Reading! Writing! Making friends! Being social! Being cool!* Eventually, the never-ending conveyor belt of major life incidents stops at *Nursery!* and eventually *School!* and to some extent, you get to hand off a lot of this childhood developmental work to a third party. You might think that this is a moment of respite of sorts, a much-needed pit-stop in the parenthood grand prix. Really though it's just a different kind of exhaustion and anxiety, because at least when it was you who was holding your kid by the hand and guiding them through the big bad world, you had complete control over the environment they were in.

School is really the first time you subject your kid to external influences and you're powerless to do anything about it. Not in a kind of 'Amish parent desperate to hide the existence of the Nintendo Gameboy from their child' sort of way, but there's definitely a loss of innocence around this period that will make you feel utterly helpless. The comedian Louis CK used to do a bit where he joked he wanted to kill himself when he no longer had to wipe his daughter's arse because they didn't need him anymore, and although I can't being myself to completely align with a sexually aggressive public masturbator, I do see what he was getting at. Yes, when they get older there's less physical exhaustion, less manual clean-up, less hands-on maintenance and more sleep, but you never stop worrying about them or looking out for them, never more so than when they're expected to figure it all out for themselves.

There will come a time when you look back fondly on those early days of bringing up baby, where it'd sleep for sixteen hours a day and burble quietly to itself, amused by no more than the fingers on their own hand, capable of being shushed by half a banana and a silly face. You didn't have to worry about baby's education or baby's friends or baby's social status or baby's literacy level or baby's attention span. There were no other babies in your baby's sphere of influence. Baby was a perfectly formed, self-contained little bundle of joy.

And yet, think back to those times, go deeper, try to separate those rose-tinted picture postcard moments from the actual experience as you lived it and remember how you really felt throughout that period: half-dead, teetering on the emotional brink and praying you would survive until the next life-changing developmental step. Here you are, yearning for those days like a motherfucker.

You know the phrase 'the grass is always greener on the other side'? Fatherhood is a new spin on an old classic: you will exist in a permanent state of looking back fondly to the past and looking forward to the promise of the future while just sort of surviving in the present, never really feeling like you have ever experienced the greenest grass. Is it ever possible to reach a parental equilibrium, even momentarily, where you're completely satisfied and happy and content with everything? I'll let you know if it ever happens to me, but until then, go ahead and assume it's a straight no, chief. The struggle is real.

Fatherhood doesn't stop being hard. Whatever age your kid is, you will always carry that baked-in emotional turmoil with you, that inescapable worry, that dread of the unknown. Sometimes it might be front of mind in big bold type, sometimes it's humming away silently in the background, but it's always there, that asterisk hovering above everything you say and do.

I guess this never really changes until you're, like, 70, and your kid is, like, 40, and the pendulum finally swings the other way and suddenly it's them who are looking after and worrying about you because you've finally begun the long and steady decline into senility. Man, I can't wait for those sweet, sweet good times.

***

INDISPENSABLE NUGGET OF WISDOM #2
It's not about you anymore.

You've probably already got here on your own, but if not, this big revelation is incoming very shortly. Let me be the first to say it: Congratulations! Your life is essentially meaningless!

Contrary to the title and subject matter of this entire book, you are no longer the most important thing in your life. It's just not about you. You had a good run at #1 but it's time to cede the throne to another: think Bryan Adams' seminal Robin Hood theme tune, 'Everything I Do, I Do It For You', in terms of both its staying power and its subject matter. (Fittingly, Adams was eventually knocked off the top of the UK charts by U2, which sounds a bit like "You 2", which sort of sounds like how you might describe your offspring. I couldn't quite stick the landing here but I'm 75% of the way towards making this joke work, so I'm leaving it in).

As you will have no doubt realised over the last year, having a child and making them your new first priority is a huge paradigm shift in your life that does not come easy. For inherently selfish people like me - think back to that Facebook motto, "Looking for the maximum fun with the minimum effort" - this is a big deal. Selfishness comes in many forms; you can be selfish without being outwardly nasty or mean. Maybe you just put your own needs above others, which almost sounds reasonable. Maybe you've lived your entire life convinced you were the centre of your universe. In a sense, maybe you were.

But not anymore. With the introduction of children, that axis was turned on its arse. This realisation is not unique to parenthood, but babies are often the best way to facilitate it, the tangible little bastards.

So, no more being selfish. Never again can you make a big life decision based solely on what you and you alone want. There are myriad factors to all aspects of life now, endless considerations to consider endlessly. Often - usually, even - the thing that is best for you will end up being the polar opposite of the thing you actually do. Imagine that!

Once upon a time you may have called this an act of self-sabotage; now, it's merely the right thing to do. No grumbling, no complaining, no hesitation. Those are the new rules. Know your place and act accordingly. Are there things you would rather be doing, right now, other than listening to Grandad tunelessly murder 'Happy Birthday' and sing the wrong grandchild's name for the third time today? Yes. Would you ever be caught dead doing any of them instead? Not a chance.

This rash of involuntary selflessness spreads like a virus throughout every aspect of your existence, for decisions large and small: deciding what to have for dinner, booking a holiday, going to the pub, buying a car, nipping to the shops, putting on music, buying an ice cream, taking five minutes out of your goddamn day to get some peace and quiet - all events must be run through the committee and receive a majority vote. There's now an extra head to consider in all matters, and unluckily for you that extra head looks up to you and loves you and needs you to be considerate of them at all times, for fuck's sake. In having a child you basically knocked yourself down a peg on the league table, forever loitering in mid-table of the unspoken familial hierarchy, like a human Southampton Football Club.

What's more, it's not enough to not be selfish - you have to make life interesting for everyone, too. So, you've come to terms with the fact you are no longer making decisions for just one or two people, but did you ever stop to think how much extra mental bandwidth you'll need to expend on making life un-boring for all of you? The tried and tested 'coast through life doing whatever' technique that has served you thus far does not really have the votes. You'll have to broaden your thinking considerably in all aspects, which you might rightfully surmise sounds like an absolute arseache.

You need to constantly think of things to do, fun games to play, exotic places to go, weekends to fill, nutritious meals to make, interesting people to meet. Obviously you won't have to do this alone, but you need to be involved; being passive in these pursuits is simply not an option unless you want your role in this family described as 'absent financier'.

Being the architect of your kid's existence starts off a noble aim, but you quickly find the natural boundaries of your life can rein in your ambitions, so you push and you push and you push some more. Trying to keep life exciting and interesting and un-boring is a constant source of exhaustion, and is, in a roundabout sort of way, in itself incredibly tedious. Stop pushing and the end result is an extremely dull and uncreative child who will one day perform administrative work in a solicitor's office and express an interest in the music of Nickelback. So the stakes are massive.

There are upsides to the whole selflessness deal, it must be said. Being more selfless is a weird sort of relief, in that you can now focus your energies externally and on other people and not let them fog up your own stupid, useless brain. Having kids necessitates getting out of your own head and dealing with the daily physical tasks that are required of you: feed this, clothe that, burp here, wipe there etc. Kids are many things but complicated they are not. If you must devote a significant quantity of your brainpower towards their continuing survival, be thankful that they contain no deeper levels and do not need to be second-guessed or over-analysed. If they need a poo, they'll tell you (unless, of course, the poo was faster than you).

No one goes into parenthood thinking 'What's in it for me?' so in essence raising a child is a selfless act, but as you will be well on the way to finding out by now, kids are very much their own reward. So there is a *little* in it for you. In side-lining your own needs and putting your own existence on hold, you get to see life from a perspective other than your own, which is essential in your continuing evolution into a fully-functional human being.

Your child's achievements are your achievements, their highs are your highs, their happiness is your happiness. You get to tap into all that good stuff and siphon it off at will like an emotional vampire. As I've said before, if you chose to do nothing else with your own life other than be a parent to your child, this approach wouldn't just be tolerated but actively encouraged.

Once you start living for your kid, you start to realise how insignificant and small your old life concerns used to be in comparison. Kids are absolutely the making of you; they are the reason you get up in the morning, the reason you go to work, the reason you start puke-inducing conversations with office colleagues at after-work drinks. Every improvement you make to their life is an improvement to your life, and vice versa. This symbiotic relationship is the only true thing in your life that matters, and keeping that bond strong at all costs is worth any hardship you might have to suffer as a result. And yes, that includes this birthday party, which has now seemingly entered into its third hour.

***

INDISPENSABLE NUGGET OF WISDOM #3
Time is now your enemy.

You will make many enemies as a parent. The neighbour with the subwoofer who just got into hardcore Belgian trance. The psychic postman who always knocks at nap-time. The tanned couple in the big detached house on the corner whose Egg stroller cost more than your car. The family member who just gifted your kid a drum kit. But there's no one you'll grow to hate more than Old Father Time, the wrinkly old geezer who is stealing the best years of your life out from under your nose. Have a coronary and die already, you Prince Phillip-looking old fuck-stick.

It's only natural to start feeling nostalgic on this, the first birthday of your first born. You're more aware of the passing of time these days, even as it slips helplessly through your fingers - it's something you are prone to watching pass you by. So, although today is a celebration, as you cycle through the four acceptable birthday-themed songs on your 'Happy Birthday!' Spotify playlist, it also represents a period of mourning for the things you have lost over the last year.

(If you're wondering, the four acceptable birthday-themed songs on Spotify are as follows: 'Happy Birthday' by Stevie Wonder; 'Celebration' by Kool and the Gang; 'Happy Birthday' by Altered Images; and 'Birthday' by The Beatles. This book does not accept requests.)

It's extremely difficult to enjoy a new milestone without feeling nostalgic for the last one. That feeling never really goes away. Parenthood's sense of escalation is so rapid it can honestly feel like you can't keep up with how fast the kid is growing. You'll pull your wallet out and huff jokily about them growing out of their new clothes in a matter of months, but each time you do it's undercut with genuine sadness at the sense of gradual loss that represents.

Myself and my wife, for example, really struggle to dispose of old keepsakes because we are rife with soppiness, so the cupboard under our stairs now doubles as the final resting place for dozens of barely-worn baby shoes in varying sizes. Seriously, it's like an off-brand Shoe Zone under there; the volume of tiny trainers is so alarming I have to make it very clear to any visiting electricians reading the meter that I have children and do not live alone in case he thinks I'm a serial killer.

You notice this feeling more in the early years, because the milestones fall so quickly in sequence. All of the firsts fly by so fast it's liable to make your head spin off your neck. I cannot overstate the magnitude of difference one calendar year makes with young kids: compare a newborn to a one-year-old and a one-year-old to two-year-old and you might as well be looking at three different kids, like when soap operas recast their child actors and expect you not to notice.

Once you realise they'll never be babies again, it's a harsh tide to swim against so you'll find going with the flow is the only option available. You rarely have the time to get comfortable before more developmental changes are upon you: sleep, speech, movement, learning, comprehension. No patterns have time to bed in, routines are routinely hdisrupted, the winds of change are cold and bitter and relentless.

As a child of the eighties who naturally looks to movie characters for tried-and-tested wisdom, I tried to channel the mantra of Ferris Bueller: "Life moves pretty fast. If you don't stop and look around once in a while, you could miss it." But once you realise that Ferris Bueller had zero children and displayed the kind of carefree attitude that suggests he would have found parenthood a burden, you resign yourself to the fact that this one fictional Chicago teenager maybe didn't have all the answers, and would have probably been a shit dad to boot.

I'm sure you've casually tossed off phrases like "there aren't enough hours in the day" before, but the early years of parenthood is the first time this actually feels true. Whether it's hours in the day, days in the week or weeks in the month, you genuinely want to slow time down, or at least pause it, Clarissa-style, while you take a moment to get your shit together.

Eventually, you realise an important truth: your only weapon in the war against time is memory. It's absolutely fine if you can't carve out time to stop and appreciate the finer things - because the finer things tend to spend quite a lot of time shitting and puking everywhere - but you should try and soak everything in at all times. Be porous. Be SpongeBob SquareDad. Mop up every last memory - the good, the bad, the average stuff in between. It's so vital that you attempt to retain these experiences, because one day in the not-too-distant future, you will honestly look back on them as the good old days, believe it or not.

Memory sometimes needs a helping hand. Having, or more specifically, raising kids does tend to turn a man's brain to wet Weetabix. Be prepared to add 'doddering' and 'staring vacantly at an open cupboard' to your list of pastimes. Thankfully, help is at hand in the form of technology. I simply cannot fathom how parents of the 20th century even remembered what their kids looked like before the advent of digital photography.

Whether you want to or not, parenthood will turn you into a 'photo person': no activity can be enjoyed without being captured in JPG form; no notable event or occasion will be remembered until it is digitally catalogued and Facebooked; you will frequently find that you've taken photos of stuff without even realising, so strong is the muscle memory. If fun is had but no parent was around to photograph it, did it even happen? The answer, unfortunately, is no.

I am not exaggerating when I say my wife has, at the time of writing, over 10,000 photographs of our children on her phone, and that only spans the lifespan of that particular device; if I had to hazard a guess, I'd say we have at least 100,000 pictures littered across various phones, laptops and external hard drives. It's far too many photos to efficiently organise or enjoy, but the important thing is they exist. There will be plenty of time to finally look at them when our adult children leave for university or jet off to establish a man-made colony on Mars in 2042.

This new instinct to capture every memory made me recall my own childhood, specifically how my Dad would constantly be cooking up new ways to capture family life for posterity. In the late eighties he spent a small fortune on a 'compact' camcorder that was roughly the size of a small international aircraft carrier and came with its own back brace, and not a Sunday roast would pass without my brother and I being vox-popped over our peas and potatoes. Before that, he'd set up an old cassette tape recorder that would hum in the background throughout the meal, capturing every awkward conversation of a family eating as if through a police investigation. At the time I thought it was intrusive and annoying, because I was not a 'camera ready' child, but looking back I realise now it was never for my benefit - it was my Dad using the best tools he had at his disposal to supplement his own memories, to capture something, anything, that would hopefully one day be worth remembering. I would give anything to watch those videos back with my Dad today. He's not dead, he just taped over them with Walker: Texas Ranger.

Cameras, phones, professional recording equipment, it all helps but they won't provide the full picture. You're going to find yourself keeping as much sentimental bric-a-brac as possible, including but not limited to: drawings, paintings and scribbles, toys and cuddlies, old clothes and shoes, particularly round pebbles they picked up somewhere that could simply not exist anywhere other than your kitchen windowsill, interesting twigs for the stick collection, a litany of single-used plastic toys from a variety of gift shops, fridge magnets, promotional cinema cups from long-forgotten terrible family movies, 'special crystals' discovered on beaches (i.e. more pebbles) and everything in between, an assortment of odd individual items that collectively accumulate a significant degree of emotional resonance. Without even realising it, you'll slowly turn your house into a childhood museum, or even a mausoleum of sorts, memorialising all the children they used to be.

I found a tweet that sums up this eternal struggle perfectly:

"I've realised it's a constant voyage of discovering the people they're becoming while losing the people they once were. But that I'm the guardian of all they have ever lost, if they should ever want to find it again. If only in a story." - @TwistedDoodles

This made me cry when I read it, probably the twenty-third thing that set me off that day, but it struck me as particularly profound because it allowed me to reframe my entire existence as a parent, from permanently exasperated tidier-upper to mysterious and twinkly-eyed museum curator. So much of being a father is about playing that role of gatekeeper, of storing away all those treasures, hoarding them and keeping them safe. Knowing them better than they know themselves and having the goods to prove it.

You can pretend you're performing a public service, the wizened old librarian keeping your ancient artefacts under lockdown for the benefit of history, but it's ultimately a selfish act. Because, really, your kid is your greatest achievement, by far the best thing you have ever been associated with, and you're going to want to surround yourself with the detritus of their lives, like Gollum sitting in his cave, stroking all his preciouses.

So snap away today, whip out the cameraphone and fill your Facebook with new birthday photos, jam your hard drives with picture after picture of candles being blown out, presents being unwrapped, cake being crammed into gobs. It's a privilege to have known a person for literally their entire life, and to have memories of every single minute they have been on this planet. Every day they get more independent and they need you less, and there's nothing you can do about it, other than fill your Aladdin's cave with gold and helplessly watch the clocks tick on.

Even though the number on top of the cake is small, you are still conscious it won't stay this way forever. One day, they'll have left home. There'll be no call for cake, no Spotify playlist, no wrapping paper to clean up. All you'll have left is an empty chair, an empty house, and your photos. Your millions and millions of photos.

**

INDISPENSABLE NUGGET OF WISDOM #4
Kids are, and always will be, unpredictable, and you will probably never truly get the hang of this.

I cannot tell you how many times I've fallen for this one. Infinity times. Maybe I'll never stop falling for it. It happens roughly every few weeks. I'll have a nice afternoon doing excellent parenting with calm and well-behaved children, and I'll think to myself: "Maybe you've finally cracked it". Yes, I've finally reached an agreement with the kids: I understand their needs, and they understand mine. Maybe this is what happiness is. Maybe, just maybe, everything's going to be just fine from here on out.

Then, roughly 48 hours later when I'm dealing with whatever hellish surprise was lurking around the corner, I'll look back at the idiot I was and despise my own naivety.

Inconsistency is part and parcel of parenthood: just when you think you have a measure of your kids, they change again. It's tempting to think they're doing it just to keep you on your toes. That's not true, of course; kids are just a mess of ideas and characteristics and personalities that evolve and change depending on about a billion different things, and it's sheer coincidence that they change course the moment you get comfortable. Really the only way to avoid this is to never be comfortable again. That should be one of your guiding principles. The moment you feel yourself start to relax, go limp and get ready for impact.

There's no anticipating the constant change, as there's no real logic to any of it. So how do you navigate this maze? Child psychology might be worth a go if you're willing to hand over fistfuls of cash, but there's always a chance that they'll take your money and tell you in fancy boffo words that kids cannot be controlled, which you already know.

If I could be arsed, maybe I'd read up on chaos theory in an attempt to see patterns in their behaviour, to make sense of the madness. Inevitably though I'd get no further than the foreword before one of my kids choked on a muffin or fell out a window or got humped by a dog or something. The essence of chaos!

The thing I find difficult about the constant shifting sands of parenthood is how hard it is to get a sense of what the kids are into or how enthusiastic they're going to be in any given situation. Reactions will always vary to a wild degree, and it's extremely hard to get a read on what will spark joy and what will be met with scorn.

The other day the kids and I were playing in the garden and I saw an old war plane flying overhead. "Look boys!" I said excitedly, "Look at the plane!" Silence and eye-rolls all round, the sight of a Spitfire was clearly not as interesting as the rocks they were playing with. Then, no less than one minute later: "Daddy, Daddy, come quickly!" I ran over to see what they were so animated about. It was an ant. Literally one ant. I feel like we've seen ants before, guys. I'd file this away if I thought the information had any kind of value, but you can guarantee that next week I'll find myself being eaten alive by giant ants and the kids will ignore my screams because they're so engrossed in the latest issue of Big Jets magazine.

It's exhausting trying to keep up with what they think is cool, and the more effort you expend trying to appease them, the more out of touch you feel. Grandpa's speech to young Homer in The Simpsons lives in my head rent-free: "I used to be with 'it', but then they changed what 'it' was. Now what I'm with isn't 'it' anymore and what's 'it' seems weird and scary." Never a more sensible word has been spoken.

Even the basic building blocks of life are subject to change. You'll grow weary of second-guessing what your kids do and don't like to eat. There are no sure things in life any more, least of all favourite foods.

Using first-hand anecdotal evidence, you might think you're fairly sure that your kids like potatoes. They've eaten potatoes maybe a hundred times before without complaint. That kind of dataset is the basis for a pretty reasonable assumption re: potatoes. Yet today, out of nowhere, potatoes are on the shit list, and you weren't consulted. It would have been great if you could have been given a heads up before dinner was served, but nah. Potatoes are out, old man, haven't you heard? Maybe this dislike of potatoes will last for the duration of this particular meal, or maybe it'll last for the next ten years. Hahaha, terrific. Just add 'Potatoes???' into your random oversized Bing Bong brain dump where it'll sit with all your other unverified assumptions and fester for the rest of your life.

The unpredictable nature of children is in their DNA. They can't help being so chaotic, it's just their chemistry. Every child is an unstable bomb of emotions that's liable to explode if you attempt to defuse it, and woe betide any parent caught in the blast radius. If I may attempt some child psychology of my own, the way I see it, there's a lot going on in there - and you can have that advice free of charge.

I think about this often, every night in fact, when bedtime comes around and the kids need to be peeled off the ceiling. The reason they are so energetic at the time they most need to be calm is allegedly because they are 'over-tired'. This does not make sense.

This does not happen with any other feelings. Kids cannot be 'over-hungry', so starved of food that they go full circle and start turning down biscuits. When one is 'over-cautious' one doesn't suddenly start jumping in front of cars. It's just a universally understood facet of being a small child, one of many insane anti-logics you just accept as part of parenthood. Add it to the pile.

Rather than try to predict these changes, I found it easier to try and analyse them after the fact, or at least better understand the conditions that led to them. I came to a very simple conclusion: the reason kids are so unpredictable is because they don't know how to be predictable because they don't know what normal is. They have no frame of reference or context for anything, because their worlds are so small and contained.

As adults, with our years of existential experience, we can make assessments as to what behaviour is considered appropriate or inappropriate in any given situation, about what course of action is expected and what should be avoided. There are a million different things that factor into even the smallest decisions we make. But kids do not have that luxury of experience. They are creatures of impulse who live moment to moment without having to worry about consequences - this is one of the joys of being a child.

So, maybe they did enjoy potatoes in the past, but this potato, right here right now, on this fork, looks gross. They don't have the mental capacity to understand that if they ate the potato they'd probably enjoy the potato, and other potatoes like it. They acted on their impulse, and they've already moved past the potato. Why do you keep going on about potatoes? It's just making them hate potatoes more.

This inability to find a frame of reference can be frustrating, but it's fascinating in its own way. The other night before bed, Kid A wanted to put some water in a cup for him to drink if he woke up. Now, you or I would perform this action without a second thought. It would be a simple task for us, but he'd never done it before, and he just couldn't get it right. There are four notable volumes of water you could put in that cup:

1. Clearly not enough water, a pointless amount of water.
2. Enough water.

3. Slightly too much water, a little over-full, an unnecessary amount of water to keep by your bedside.

4. Clearly too much water, a ridiculous amount of water.

Try as he might, he just couldn't get between amounts 1 and 3, because he wasn't able to take into consideration the numerous variables that us adults have long since internalised: the hypothetical frustration of being half-asleep, thirsty and having an empty cup; the all-too-real risk of knocking a too-full cup over in the middle of the night; the high chance of drinking too much water and needing to get up to go for a wee. This isn't me holding him to an impossibly high standard, it's just an observation that kids often lack the reference points that adults might take for granted. Parenthood in a nutshell is having to unpick the subconscious and make it conscious; relearn what you already know so you can teach it yourself.

In some ways, the unpredictable nature of kids is part of the fun. They need you to help them make sense of life, and that's a huge and daunting responsibility, but it's an essential one. When they get older and they develop their own critical faculties to assess information and see trends and patterns and interpret social situations and process everything properly, life does become more orderly and predictable. That's also around the same sort of time they discover stress and peer pressure and then puberty kicks in and it all goes off the rails again. Life as a little kid, living a random and consequence-free existence, seems like the more preferable option by far.

Being a father to a young child may be difficult and stressful and tiring, but it is never boring. You will long for a more boring life, but in their own unpredictable way, your kids are helping you out by doing their very best to deny you one.

INDISPENSABLE NUGGET OF WISDOM #5
You will continue to make mistakes, and that's okay.

So many mistakes. Small mistakes. Big mistakes. Mistakes every day. If parenthood was marked like a driving test, with minor and major faults applied to all errors, well, you'd never get hold of your licence. Most of these mistakes won't matter in the long run, they are theoretically absorbed by the difficulty of parenthood and written off as collateral damage, acceptable wear-and-tear. But as hard as you might try, as careful and thoughtful and considerate as you may be, you will never really stop making mistakes as a parent.

No one is born with the skill to do this well, you have to learn on the job and pick it up as you go along. The old joke is that "kids don't come with a manual", but that never felt right for me, because not having a manual is generally not the cause of frustration when attempting to create something. The issue is usually that there *is* a manual, but that manual is shitty and overly simplistic and leaves too much open to interpretation. So, even when you think you're doing things right, it later turns out you're actually doing them wrong. And sometimes vice versa. I'm telling you: mistakes err' damn day up in this house.

Take me, for example. I have made multiple mistakes today already. They're ranked on a sliding scale. There are clear and obvious errors that I regret, like watching an episode of TV on the iPad while I was doing the washing up this morning and one of my kids walked in the room at the exact moment a character yelled out "BASTARD, BASTARD, FAT BASTARD! FUCK OFF! FUCK OOOFFFF!"

There are micro mistakes, almost imperceptible mistakes that don't amount to much on their own but probably gain mass with frequency and time, like me sitting and having my morning toast alone for a moment's peace instead of sitting with the kids and feigning interest in whatever cartoon they were watching like a proper dad would. I haven't made any major mistakes today, but there's still time. It's entirely possible I'll sneak one in under the wire before bedtime.

If you're lucky - or, more likely, if you're attentive and caring - you will hopefully avoid the epic, extinction-level, "David Cameron leaving his daughter in a pub" style mistakes, but they happen to the best of us. These are the mistakes that stick with you, the ones that you'll ruminate on for the rest of your life - and if your kids are old enough, they'll remind you for the rest of your life too. It's all relative, of course, because most mistakes are unintentional and are borne out of drama that's not of your own making, so unless you're a crazed Michael Jackson dangling your infant child off a fourth-floor balcony for yuks, there will almost always be a path back to redemption. The point is, it just isn't possible to get through a single 24-hour period without some kind of fuck-up.

It's important to recognise when evaluating one's own parenting that there is no such thing as the perfect father. Peter Andre came pretty close, but then he named his daughter 'Princess Tiaamii' and all his goodwill went up in flames.

It's worth examining what you consider the benchmark to be when assessing your own parental skills. What are you comparing your experience to? Is it a real person, who exists in the real world? Or is it, in fact, just a bunch of unrealistic ideals that you've personified into existence, based on a series of assumptions and unreasonable expectations?

Not to sound like a decrepit old granddad, but I cannot overstate how poisonous the representation of masculinity in modern media is. Social Media Dads whose blogs have a 'Shop' button. Celebrity Dads, who make a career out of getting Celebrity Mums pregnant and holding a Hello! Magazine photoshoot every year. Sitcom Dads who have six sassy kids of ascending ages and who live in a massive house yet never seem to go to work. Just like young women are rightfully warned of the toxic nature of fake plastic celebrities and lifestyle magazines when growing up, young men should be cautioned not to fall into the alluring orbit of the 'Professional Dad', who makes six figures a year by monetising his offspring. These twats never made a mistake they couldn't make an Instagram Story out of.

Sometimes you won't even know if the mistakes are actually mistakes or if they are necessary evils. Parenthood unfortunately requires you to occasionally be a bit of a bastard to keep the ship running smoothly. No one enjoys it but it's a sad fact of life: often you have to be cruel in order to be kind and start enforcing some tough love.

There will be many a time when you will be called upon to make decisions that are unpopular with your kids, because the way you see it, inaction may be more damaging in the long run. The hypothetical alternative is being the sadsack walkover with shitty screaming kids who have no manners, respect or job prospects. Raising your voice and putting your foot down is a small price to pay to avoid this fate, or at least that's how you analyse it in the moment.

The problem is, you're never quite sure which of these occasions warrant this kind of approach. Is this a prime opportunity to teach a lesson? If I raise the volume of my parenting voice to ALL CAPS is that actually going to achieve anything? Or is bringing the thunder at this moment in time just an extension of the frustrations that *I'm* feeling, and am I actually just exacerbating the issue? It's inevitable you won't get it right every time.

Fatherhood - specifically the frustrations inherent in fatherhood - will reveal some things about yourself that you may not like. It's truly a journey, and not in the X Factor, 'I was already quite a good singer but now I'm quite a good singer *on TV*' kind of way, more like a 'dawning realisation that you might actually be a flawed person who honestly needs to work on themselves' kind of way.

Even if you're not one for self-reflection or soul-searching, the real you gets laid out on the line for all to see. How you handle extreme pressure. What your breaking point is. How you react when you're permanently evicted from your comfort zone. You will be tested like you have never been tested before. You will be broken down and rebuilt, over and over, never quite sure if you're stronger or more brittle for the experience. And, in the process, you make mistakes. All you can do is pray to Saint Andre of Insania for forgiveness.

If this doesn't sound like you, and you are coasting through parenthood without a care in the world and you think being a father is easy peasy lemon squeezy, then I regret to announce to you that you are Tory MP and Beano toff Jacob Rees-Mogg and you have clearly hired a nanny who you are almost certainly not paying enough to do all your grunt work. Stop reading this book immediately if so, you wanker.

It's hard being a good dad. It's really fucking hard, and it never stops being really hard. It's not enough that you have kept them alive for the first year of their life - you have to do it *every* year. And what's more, you have to shape them, inspire them, motivate them, raise them up and make them more than they would be without you. On no sleep and for no remuneration and there's not even a medal ceremony at the end. How the fucking fuckedy fuck are you supposed to do all that with a flawless service record?

You have to draw deep, and you have to be realistic: despite what your mug might say, it is physically impossible to be the World's Greatest Dad every day of the year. Even on your best days, there's probably some guy in Miami who hired his kid a bouncy castle for their birthday. You can't compete with that.

You'll have numerous down days, rough patches, tense weekends of fraught arguments, weeks where nothing works, periods where you genuinely can't see the light at the end of the tunnel and start to worry that, somehow, somewhere along the way, you did a thing wrong, maybe multiple things wrong, and you messed up beyond repair, and maybe you ruined your kid's life without even realising it, and there's no way to ever really know. You will fail. You will snap. You will do things wrong. You will do stupid things. You will make mistakes.

But hopefully, you learn each time you do. Every major mistake is another line etched permanently in your forehead; a reminder of the roads you've already been down. Don't ignore them, don't try and forget them. Think about them often. Have them litter your mind like a minefield. Use them to teach *yourself* a lesson, and in doing so, raise your tolerance levels, your capacity for foolishness, your resolve. Fatherhood is work, hard work, but it can yield great results if you're willing to work on yourself as hard as you work on your child.

Above all else, go easy on yourself. No one is asking you to self-flagellate with stiff birch branches or throw yourself on your sword or hold a Fathers 4 Justice-style pity party where you drape a sad-looking homemade banner off a well-known landmark, instantly ensuring that your mortified child will only retreat further from your desperate clutches. Remember: you're only human and you're not trying to win any awards. You cannot compete with back-to-back Premier Inn Dad Of The Year winner Peter Andre (2010, 2011) so don't even try.

Oh look, there's some wrapping paper someone left on the floor. Ah, fuck it, just chuck it in the bin. Then eat the last sausage roll. Go on, one more delicious mistake won't hurt.

***

Well, that's it. That is the sum of my amassed knowledge of parenthood to date. Hopefully you found some of my advice useful. I take no responsibility at all if any of it was actively damaging, please don't make me call my lawyer (because I do not have one).

Once you understand the five fundamentals I've laid out above, there's honestly very little I can teach you. Some might argue that was also the case at the beginning of the book. Anyway, I'm spent. Anything else I say from this point on is just going to be a regurgitation of an earlier point, with a slightly altered punchline, perhaps paraphrasing a different popular television programme.

I'm dead proud of you, honestly. Not just because you bought this book, but also because it sounds like you're well on the way to becoming a great dad (because you bought this book). How will you continue without any more of my invaluable insight, I think I heard someone say at the back? It's really a case of looking inside yourself and building on what's already there while I frantically raid the dregs of my drafts for a follow-up.

Just focus on getting through to the next birthday, and the next birthday, and the next birthday after that. And, just in case it wasn't clear, all of the subsequent birthdays after that too, up until, I don't know, age 23? That's my rough estimate for when you can actively stop worrying about having to sort elaborate birthdays for your child. Technically I think you could take your foot off the pedal for the 22nd, but you don't want it to look like you've been waiting for the first excuse to stop.

The birthday party looks like it's winding down. All the best nans have left, the last sausage roll has mysteriously disappeared and everyone is up to their kneecaps in discarded wrapping paper while you've been reading this. Now the mayhem has died down, make sure you take the time to think about how much you've changed over the last 12 months. A year is an arbitrary measure of time but it's as good a milestone as any to judge your progress as a father, and as a human being. Many of the same issues you faced right back during the early days are still present and correct - lack of sleep, child-related anxiety, a heightened sense that the world is becoming an actual hellhole - but you've come on leaps and bounds in other ways since then. Might I even say it: you wear being a dad quite well.

It wasn't through choice, but through your experience you have adopted many of the tell-tale traits of Dadhood: the choice of comfortable clothing and footwear, the noises you make when you sit down *and* when you get back up, the bags under the eyes, the terrible jokes.

As physical transformations go it's not exactly An American Werewolf in London, but if you stare at yourself in the mirror, you might be shocked by the older, wiser, more knackered version of yourself staring right back. This guy is running the show now. The younger you, the pre-birth you, the infant-fearer, the guy who would have a panic attack if someone so much as said the words "baby gem lettuce", he no longer exists. He has been recast with an older model. And it feels kind of right.

And really, if you think about it, the level of stress you're dealing with nowadays doesn't feel quite so apocalyptic as it used to. With each passing day your kid learns a hundred new lessons, about their body, about their abilities, about their surroundings, about what and what not to eat and do and touch.

With every new sunset, they are less likely to climb into the washing machine or choke on a cat turd or fall foul of some sort of elaborate Tom and Jerry-style slapstick injury. Yes, there are still several things they can climb into or accidentally swallow or be electrocuted by, but it's all relative; after spending a full year on red alert, downgrading to amber feels like sweet, blessed relief. They're still in mortal danger and you continue to be essential to their survival, but at least they're not actively trying to end themselves any more. Take five with a paragraph break!

Look at you, taking five! There's a good chance that you may even be able to take another five later today! The one year mark is the perfect time to start making plans on how to recapture some of what made you *you*. At the beginning of this book, we talked about how parenthood is essentially a giant pause button on the story of your development: as much as it may have hurt at the time, you had to sacrifice certain elements of your life because the all-consuming baby just didn't leave any room.

Well, here you are, one year later, and slowly but surely you'll start to find there's a little more room. Not much, just enough to keep your interests alive for another season. But that's enough. Your life is the fragile little green stalk blooming from the old boot at the end of WALL-E, formerly considered a lost cause but still alive and still growing despite being situated in an otherwise arid wasteland.

One question that I used to get asked by non-parent friends is "Do you ever miss your old life?" It might take a minute to compute, but the honest answer is 'no'. I can barely remember my life before children and what I can remember seems mostly unimportant and dull. It's mostly a blur of playing video games, drinking and spending lots of money on things I didn't really need or use: they were hardly halcyon years.

Maybe it's different for some, I don't know. Maybe you used to be high-flying banker on £300k who suddenly found themselves shovelling shit for a change. Maybe you used to be a massive shagger and parenthood has blunted your pencil. My theory, though, is that most ordinary people don't embark on the parenthood adventure if they're not already yearning to fill some sort of empty space in their life, some kind of hole that needs to be filled. Hopefully, being a dad was always part of the plan, and fatherhood has scratched that itch. If it didn't, then, shit, sorry.

God, you don't have a chance to miss your old life. The introduction of children essentially renders it null and void: fun not found. Parenthood, the hurricane that it is, picks you up and flings you around and shakes you down, but it forces you to grow up, to mature and eventually become the man that maybe you thought you already were. Kids are occasionally maddening but otherwise wonderful creatures that change your life with their pure innocence and inherent goodness. Once you're fully onboarded after a bumpy start, you don't spend any time pining for the life you used to lead. You think: 'How did we ever live without them?'

And look, I fully respect anyone's decision if they don't want to have kids, because it's not an equation that works the same way for everyone, but having had them and enjoyed (almost) every minute of them, I dread to think how dull my life would have been without them.

I know, deep down in my heart, that without the love of a good woman and the responsibility of fatherhood running through me, the best thing I could have aimed for as a single childless adult man was 'journeyman eSports day player with a mediocre

Twitch stream'. No disrespect meant to the pro gamers out there, I'm sure you all make more money than me.

Anyway, like I said, it's not really about us guys, it's about the little ones. Look at the little champ, birthday hat at a jaunty angle, going back in for another fistful of Colin the Caterpillar, stuffing it in their literal cakehole like they were born to do it. Like father, like child. Staring at them is something you do more of now, just simpering in silence at their little ways - they scrub your brain of all impurities like grubby-fingered palate cleansers.

You feel free to stare. You can get lost in a stare for minutes on end, because there's much to look for. You're only one year in but already you see so much potential in your child, even if they have somehow got cake in orifices which aren't even on their head. Even at this early stage you start to get a sense of their appetite for learning and their thirst for adventure, that insatiable curiosity for life that's just beginning, literally in its infancy. You start to see glimpses of yourself in them, sudden perceptible flashes of you and your partner hidden deep in their DNA, an indescribable feeling that warms the core of you. You see a part of you that will outlive your physical being but keep your memory alive long after you're gone; a part of you that represents your only true lasting contribution to the human race. You see someone who could potentially cure cancer, or explore the furthest reaches of space, or save a thousand lives with their bravery. Or, like, design some really cool trainers. A blank canvas is a beautiful thing to lose yourself in.

The very best thing about parenthood is that it opens you up to this kind of love, a swoon-worthy, heart-eyes-emoji, everything else blurs into the background love, and when you let it flow through you, swell up with it like a balloon, are open with it and acknowledge it and share it, it makes you feel super-powered, unstoppable, like you've figured out the meaning of life. Every crappy movie or TV episode that preaches the power of love as a deus ex machina that solves everything or motivates men and women to do extraordinary things suddenly rings true. There is only one thing that matters now, one rule that overrules the rest, one and only one credo to live by: you would do anything for them. Extraordinary things you never thought possible. You are bigger than yourself because you have this new love in your life.

Although this feeling of being emboldened by love may be fleeting, and though it will doubtlessly be dulled through stress and complications and life's cruel habit of getting in the way, just know this: this love is inexhaustible, it can and will save your life and it is always there to be called on when you need it. It costs nothing but it means everything, and you are one of the luckiest people in the world because you have it at your disposal. Please, do me a favour and never, ever, ever forget it.

The bad news is, your partner almost certainly wants another kid, and that is when the shit *really* hits the fan.

Acknowledgements

Thanks to my wonderful wife Vicky, who is blessed with infinite patience and wisdom and resolve to a truly chilling degree. I could not, and will not, ask for a better Mum for our kids. Cheers for keeping them entertained every other weekend for about five years while I wrote this bloody thing. Thanks to Luke, Matt, Ed and Neil for the continuous support, encouragement and feedback. Sorry I never abided by the proper writing days. Thanks to my Mum and Dad for being way better parents than I probably deserved and for always, annoyingly, being right in the end. Thanks to the other parents and kids of the extended family for the inspiration and apologies if I've dropped any of you in it. Thanks to anyone else I've mentioned in this book for letting me steal your valuable life experiences and allowing me to make fun of them/you. Most of all, thanks to my lovely, ridiculous, hilarious, exhausting children for making everything else worth tolerating. I sincerely hope you never read this.

Printed in Great Britain
by Amazon

33236203R00223